T. S. ELIOT

MODERN MASTERS

EDITED BY frank kermode

t. s. eliot

stephen spender

NEW YORK | THE VIKING PRESS

Copyright © 1975 by Stephen Spender
All rights reserved
Published in 1976 by The Viking Press
625 Madison Avenue, New York, N.Y. 10022
LIBRARY OF CONGRESS CATALOGING IN PUBLICATION DATA
Spender, Stephen, 1909-
  T. S. Eliot
  (Modern masters)
  Bibliography: p.
  Includes index.
  1. Eliot, Thomas Stearns, 1888-1965.
PS3509.L43Z8694   821'.9'12   72-78997
ISBN 0-670-29184-6
Printed in U.S.A.

Acknowledgment is made to the following for permission to use material:
Faber and Faber Limited and Mrs. Valerie Eliot: Extracts from letters from T. S. Eliot to Conrad Aiken, Herbert Read, Bonamy Dobree and Stephen Spender. Reprinted by permission.
Farrar, Straus & Giroux, Inc.: From T. S. Eliot: *The Elder Statesman*, Copyright © 1959 by Thomas Stearns Eliot; *Knowledge and Experience*, Copyright © 1964 by T. S. Eliot; *On Poetry and Poets*, Copyright © 1943, 1945, 1951, 1954, 1956, 1957 by T. S. Eliot; and *To Criticize the Critic*, Copyright © 1965 by Valerie Eliot.
Harcourt Brace Jovanovich, Inc.: Excerpts from the following books by T. S. Eliot: *Collected Poems—1909-1962*, *The Waste Land: A Facsimile and Transcript of the Original Drafts*, *Selected Essays*, *The Family Reunion*, *Murder in the Cathedral*, *The Cocktail Party*, *The Idea of a Christian Society*, *After Strange Gods*; Copyright 1932, 1935, 1936, 1950, by Harcourt Brace Jovanovich, Inc.; Copyright 1939, 1940, 1943, 1949, 1950, 1960, 1963, 1964, by T. S. Eliot; Copyright 1967, 1968, 1971, by Esme Valerie Eliot. Reprinted by permission.
Harvard University Press: From *Use of Poetry and Use of Criticism* by T. S. Eliot.
Macmillan Publishing Co., Inc.: From *Collected Poems* by William Butler Yeats. Copyright 1924 by Macmillan Publishing Co., Inc., renewed 1952 by Bertha Georgie Yeats. Reprinted by permission.
The Bertrand Russell Estate: Extract from Lord Russell's letter to Lady Ottoline Morrell (1914).

Second printing October 1976

TO STUART HAMPSHIRE

ACKNOWLEDGMENTS

I must gratefully acknowledge comment and assistance in writing sections of this book from the following: Richard Wollheim, who most generously provided me with the notes on Bradley's philosophy which I have here incorporated; Professor John Bayley and Mrs. Bayley (Iris Murdoch) who read the first and the last two chapters and suggested improvements; to Richard Todd; to the General Editor, Professor Frank Kermode, for his patience and criticism; and to my wife.

Finally, I must thank Valerie Eliot for finding the time to read through the final manuscript and for pointing out several factual errors. With her kind permission I have incorporated these corrections into the text.

For permission to quote from the poetry and prose of T. S. Eliot grateful acknowledgment is due to Harcourt Brace Jovanovich and Valerie Eliot.

CONTENTS

ix

Contents | *x*

BIOGRAPHICAL NOTE

1670   Eliot's American ancestor Andrew Eliot leaves East Coker, Somerset, to settle in Boston, Mass.

1834   Reverend William Greenleaf Eliot, the poet's grandfather, settles in St. Louis.

1888   September 26, Thomas Stearns Eliot is born, seventh and youngest child of Henry Ware Eliot (in business in St. Louis) and Charlotte Eliot (née Stearns).

1897   Eliot's father builds a house near the sea at Gloucester, Mass., and the family spends its summers there.

1906   Enters Harvard College.

1908   Reads Arthur Symons' *The Symbolist Movement in Literature* (1899).

1909–10   Studies at Harvard as a graduate student. "Nocturne," "Humoresque," and "Spleen" published in *Harvard Advocate*.

1910–11   Studies at the Sorbonne in Paris, October–July. In 1910 writes first two "Preludes," "Portrait of a Lady," first part of "Prufrock" (completed 1911),

"Rhapsody on a Windy Night," and "La Figlia che Piange." August 1911, visits Munich; begins reading F. H. Bradley.

1914   September 22, calls on Ezra Pound in Kensington.

1915   At Merton College, Oxford, studies Aristotle under supervision of Harold Joachim and works at thesis on Bradley's *Appearance and Reality.*

1915–16   Leaves Oxford and Harvard, teaches at schools in London, lectures, reviews, etc. July 1915 marries Vivien Haigh-Wood. Writes "Mr. Apollinax" and several other satiric poems. Thanks to Ezra Pound, "Prufrock" appears in *Poetry.* Finishes Bradley thesis.

1917   Becomes an employee of Lloyds Bank. *Prufrock and Other Observations* published by *The Egoist* in June. Poems in French written, and also the "Sweeney" poems, influenced in style by Gautier.

1919   Essay "Tradition and the Individual Talent" published. "Gerontion" written.

1920   *Poems* published. Goes on tour of Brittany with Wyndham Lewis. They visit James Joyce in Paris.

1922   Edits *The Criterion. The Waste Land* published.

1924   *Four Elizabethan Dramatists* published.

1925   *The Hollow Men* and *Poems 1909–1925* published. Joins Faber and Gwyer.

1926   *Fragment of a Prologue* published. Essay on Lancelot Andrewes published.

1927   *Fragment of an Agony, Essay on Seneca* published. Received into the Church of England.

1929   "Dante" essay published.

1930   *Ash Wednesday* published.

1932   Delivers Charles Eliot Norton Lectures at Harvard (*The Use of Poetry and the Use of Criticism*, published 1933) and Page-Barber Lectures at University of Virginia (*After Strange Gods—A Primer of Modern Heresy*, published 1934 but not reprinted). Decides to leave his wife.

1934   *The Rock* first performed.

1935   *Murder in the Cathedral* performed at Canterbury Festival. "Burnt Norton" published.

1939   *The Family Reunion* performed at the West-
        minster Theatre on March 21. *The Criterion*
        ceases publication. In Paris, delivers the Cam-
        bridge lectures (*The Idea of a Christian Society*,
        published 1939).

1940–44 Published the last three of the *Four Quartets*. In
        1940–41, is a part-time fire-watcher on the roof
        of Faber and Faber, and is a Church Warden and
        later a fire-watcher in Kensington.

1945   Lectures in Washington: visits his old friend
        Ezra Pound at St. Elizabeths Hospital.

1948   Awarded the Nobel Prize. (Vivien Eliot dies).
        Publication of *Notes Towards the Definition of
        Culture*.

1949   *The Cocktail Party* performed at the Edinburgh
        Festival.

1953   *The Confidential Clerk* performed at Edinburgh
        Festival.

1954   Awarded the Hanseatic Goethe Prize. Delivers
        lecture on Goethe in Hamburg.

1957   January 10 marries Valerie Fletcher, previously
        secretary at Faber and Faber.

1958   *The Elder Statesman* performed at the Edinburgh
        Festival.

1963   Eliot and his wife visit New York for the last time.

1965   January 4 Eliot dies.

A Ritualist Sensibility

1

It would be absurd to attempt to guess who, if any, of the three great poets in the English language of the first third of the present century— W. B. Yeats, Ezra Pound, and T. S. Eliot—will be considered the greatest a hundred years from now. If asked this question, Eliot would undoubtedly have answered "Yeats," on account of the poems Yeats wrote at the end of his life. And it may well be that Yeats will triumph through having been the last great poet to write in the high romantic style, so much against the current of the time and so impossible for any later poet to follow. Pound, despite the long stretches of contemporary jargon in his poetry, will be seen as nearer to "the proud stones of Greece" of Yeats on his Mediterranean shore than to the shored-up ruins of Eliot's London.

Eliot was different from either in being a poet who brought into consciousness, and into confrontation with one another, two opposite things: the spiritually negative character of the contemporary world and the spiritually positive character of past tradition. He was obsessed with time. The past and the modern coexist in his poetry as an imagined present of conflicting symbols to which are attached values of spiritual life or death. Although he had in his mind very vivid pictures of the past, he never saw that past as a nostalgic world into which he could escape from the present. He always saw it as a force still surviving within the present which could be brought into life and action. And he derived from Dante, and placed at the center of his picture of the contemporary world, the idea of a life not bound either by its pastness or its presentness: but the same always in being outside any particular time (though very consciously placed within it), and related to what he called "final facts" and the supernatural.

To achieve what he did required intense powers of critical analysis of the contemporary situation, and of those pasts which were not just historic and picturesque —the rhetorical dwelling places of great spirits like those of Yeats and Pound who could not abide the modern world—but forces still active, and capable of being further activated, within the present. Eliot required not only to be a poet but also to be a penetrating analytic critic both of the past and of the present; a critic who, while guarding the integrity of literature, saw literature as still living past values operating within contemporary life.

Eliot had, then, to be a critic. But in writing poetry he had to avoid being a critic writing poetry about the values he maintained in his criticism. He had to avoid being a twentieth-century version of a writer with whom he had affinities, namely Matthew Arnold. In a word, he had to be in his poetry nothing but a poet, while bringing to bear all his critical perspicacity.

Eliot was a visionary but he was very realistic. His poetry retains the sense of the mystery which is poetry itself, but, although he sometimes employs rhetoric, it is totally unrhetorical. His beliefs, even when they are in things that many people would regard as incredible, are always based on reason; they are developed in his prose with close reasoning and, in his poetry, with the logic of the imagination. He is, then, a very different kind of poet from his great rhetorical contemporaries. One cannot discuss him without treating him as a unique case. It is his complete intellectual grasp of his situation in the history of his time and in relation to the past, combined with his grasp of the fact that intellect and poetic imagination, poetry and criticism, though capable of the utmost cooperation, were separate spheres of mental activity, which made him the poet who best understood the problems of writing poetry in English at the beginning of the present century—which was also the end of the last one—and of solving those problems in his own way in a unique body of poetry and criticism.

What is immediately striking about the poetry of T. S. Eliot is the difference between the work of the early, middle, and late periods. It is not just that Eliot never repeated himself and that he wrote a new poem only when he had something new to say and a new way of saying it, but that, at successive stages of his development, the poetry seems to proceed from a different consciousness.

For purposes of simplification, I shall indicate three stages in his development. First, there is the early poetry in which the consciousness is that of an individual (Prufrock, and the young man in "Portrait of a Lady") situated within the circumstances of a very limited society whose values are those of the drawing room or salon. This individual feels himself to be spiritually outside the social world of which he is nevertheless a part. Although playing an inferior role in it, he has values that are superior. These values are essentially aesthetic. They enable him to see through the false and shallow opinions of those among whom he lives. They offer the vision of a grail which is vouchsafed by art.

Second, there is the *The Waste Land*—a poem of many voices—in which consciousness is completely conditioned by the circumstances of the civilization, and unable to escape them. The civilization is fragmented. To be fully conscious is to be aware that consciousness itself is an object created by the historic conditions within which it exists.

Third, in *Ash Wednesday* and *Four Quartets*, there is the individual alone with God, exploring experiences that point to the possibility of a life where eternity intersects with time.

These different stages of Eliot's poetry are not connected by the confessions or expression of an autobiographical personality, the "egotistical sublime," from which the reader is able to deduce a picture of the author; a unity in which all the different phases of his development meet, as happens, for example, with Wordsworth. Eliot deliberately and programmatically cultivated impersonality in his poetry. He believed that the aim of the poet should be to make an object out of words, a poem which was itself part of a larger whole: the tradition of poetry in the language. He drew on his personal experiences only as material which he could turn into poetry.

Some critics have argued that while abjuring the aim of "self-expression" in his poetry, Eliot nevertheless is a very "personal" poet. They point out that his poetry is immediately recognizable in reflecting his unique sensibility. The rhythm, the imagery, and the tone of his poetry are intensely personal to him. And they quote lines such as these from "Preludes":

> *I am moved by fancies that are curled*
> *Around these images, and cling:*
> *The notion of some infinitely gentle*
> *Infinitely suffering thing.*

However, there is no contradiction between a poet writing in rhythms and using images that are unique to his sensibility and his writing poetry that does not express his personality.

In Eliot's critical writings, too, there is a very wide difference between the early, the middle, and the late periods. In his early criticism he writes as the poet-critic and critic-poet who is concerned with defending poetry against any standards for judging it except those which derive from the study of literature. He is the young poet writing polemical essays that clarify his aims as an artist, relating these to the scrupulously examined and analyzed works of the past tradition, and recommending the creative and critical activities of himself and those contemporaries, like Ezra Pound, of whose work he approves. These early essays have the interest and passion of Keats' writing in his letters about poetry, although Eliot's style is nearer to the prose of Samuel Johnson than to that of Keats.

In his criticisms of the late 1920s and early 1930s, when Eliot became part of the English literary scene, his essays and lectures seem less those of the poet who considers criticism an extension of his own creativity and more those of the professional critic and lecturer. The critic now becomes the man of letters whose values derive from analysis of the works of the tradition and of all the facts relevant to them.

This near-academic Eliot is succeeded in the mid-

1930s by the poet who, in *After Strange Gods*, relates the works of his contemporaries (Thomas Hardy, Rudyard Kipling, Ezra Pound, and D. H. Lawrence) to standards of Christian orthodoxy. At a still later stage Eliot becomes primarily concerned with the Church, theology, culture, and society, though, while frequently referring to theology in his essays, he rarely enters into theological exposition or argument. He still continues to write literary criticism of great interest, but he places it on a par with discussion of general problems of culture, education, sociology, and politics.

One aim which runs through Eliot's criticism as well as his poetry is that of escaping from the subjective self into a world of objective values. In all his work there is the search for the merging of individual consciousness within some wider objective truth—at first the tradition, next the idea of the supernatural, and finally the dogmas of the Catholic church (Eliot considered the Church of England to be Catholic). His search for an authority first found within the tradition and, later, in the dogmas of the church provides the connection between different stages of his development. The connection is objective not subjective.

Even before he became a Christian, Eliot assumed that critical standards of art must derive their validity from the hypothesis of there being supernatural values. To say that he assumed this is perhaps another way of saying that he was always religious. In a sense this was true. The word "religious" might indeed have sufficed to describe his attitude if he had been living in the Europe of the thirteenth century when Christianity meant a certain body of doctrines dogmatically taught by a church which represented God on earth. But in the twentieth century "religious" is more likely to be used to describe an attitude or emotion than the acceptance of a set of doctrines. That this is so may help to explain why for many years after his adolescence Eliot remained irreligious. His family was Unitarian. For Eliot, religion meant the submission of the individual to the idea of the absolute imposed as dogma.

"Ritualistic" is, it seems to me, the word that best describes his attitude to life. He had a vision of the relationship of the living with the dead through the pattern of rituals that extend into the modern world the pieties which remain unaltered from the past. He thought that when these rituals were disrupted—and when, indeed, the observance of them was not the foremost aim of living—there would be no connection of the living with the dead, of the present with the past.

In his poetry up to *Ash Wednesday*, Eliot saw the destruction of past rituals and their replacement by ones which were mockeries of them as the most characteristic feature of modern life. Prufrock portrays a society in which lives are "measured out" not by the sacraments but "with coffee spoons."

The background to Eliot's early poetry is a secular, temporal world in which religious belief has become impossible. All that remains is the tradition: the life and values of a society in which there was true ritual crystallized in certain monuments of art and to which it was possible for the modern artist, by incessant study of these works, to relate, creating his truly new art. In the new, the really new, work he could criticize the decline of values in the world in which he lived. One great masterpiece of the past provided Eliot with a system of metaphors for the hell that was the secular modern world. This was Dante's *The Divine Comedy*.

The poet who in Eliot's view was intermediary between the modern spiritual emptiness and Dante was Baudelaire: though, as Eliot pointed out, Baudelaire, living in the nineteenth century, could only study his

own suffering. He was "in this limitation . . . wholly unlike Dante, not even like any character in Dante's Hell."
(*Selected Essays*, p. 423).* However, the fact that
Baudelaire had a vision of the modern negative conditions of boredom and horror suggested the possibility
of a positive condition, if not of beatitude, at least of
inferno and purgatory.

Before his religious conversion, Eliot used in his
poetry parts of the *Inferno* and *Purgatorio* as metaphors
for the condition of man in the modern world, but he
could not use the *Paradiso*. It is possible to imagine a
secular society containing degrees of hell and purgatory
but not of beatitude. Paradise can only occur in eternity,
and outside the limitations imposed by time. There is
no idea of beatitude in his poetry until *Ash Wednesday*,
in which Eliot characteristically strikes the note of
Dante's *Vita Nuova* negatively by renouncing the vision
(just as Prufrock renounces the possibility of hearing
the mermaids sing to him):

> *I renounce the blessèd face*
> *And renounce the voice*

After his conversion Eliot found it possible to write
about the life outside time in which beatitude was
capable of being imagined: he did this in the *Four
Quartets*. Eliot had at last fulfilled in this poetry what
might be described as the consistent aim of his life on
the level of his imagination: the discovery of the true
ritual of the sacraments and prayer.

I must now qualify the impression which I may have
given here that Eliot's poetry is the spiritual record of a
poet who progressed from an ironically viewed individualist attitude of aestheticism, through the des-

---

* All page references to books cited in the Short Bibliography are to the British editions.

pair of realizing that modern man is totally conditioned by the breakdown of value in the society in which he lived, to the idea of the city which is not of this world but of God: an idea for which he found confirmation in the *Confessions* of Saint Augustine and in *The Divine Comedy*. Supposing even that one were to trace a journey of this kind as the theme which gives the different phases of his poetry their unity, nevertheless the poetry itself does not consist of poeticization of that search. It is important to emphasize that for Eliot the subject of a poem—whatever it might be—was the starting point of another journey whose goal was that of turning the material into the poetry itself, "language rich and strange."

As a result of Eliot's insistence on poetry as an end in itself, it is sometimes argued that he was a "symbolist" poet, like those French *symbolistes* by whom, as we shall see, he was greatly influenced as a young man. But if this were true, his development would have been toward an ever-greater density of texture in his work, form and language which had, as it were, broken off connections of meaning common with the subject from which they derived. But this did not happen in *Four Quartets*.

On the contrary, in his later poetry the subject matter becomes increasingly important. However, Eliot never lost the sense that whatever the poem "said," it was its being poetry and not the saying that mattered. The conflict between the meaning of a poem, as belief, philosophy, report on an emotion experienced, and the poem as being nothing but itself—the poetry—was one which preoccupied him all his life. If it remained something of an unresolved problem, the fact that he left it unresolved is important. For the relationship between the work of art as art, and its being "about" something, is a dialectical one of fruitful conflict. The energy of the struggle between "saying" and "being" within the work may indeed be the most significant energy communicated.

For some readers the idea of Eliot as a poet is overlaid by that of him as a political reactionary who, in some of his early poetry, gave vent to some strikingly anti-Semitic remarks. I shall discuss Eliot's politics in my last chapter. Here I am only concerned with them as an extension of his ritualistic attitude.

At first sight it may appear strange that a writer whose view of poetry and criticism was so purist should be concerned with politics at all. However, in this Eliot was very much of a generation which derived from the end of the last century. Matthew Arnold, John Ruskin, Oscar Wilde, Yeats, Ezra Pound, E. M. Forster, D. H. Lawrence, and Eliot himself, while opposing all idea of ideological art nevertheless, in their different ways and at their different times, thought that art depended on civilization and that civilization had to be defended by the artist. The artist had a responsibility, outside his art, to defend the values of civilization, and doing this might involve him in politics. Politics were an outer wall of defense protecting the freedom of the inner citadel of art. This was pretty much the attitude of Eliot when he was a young man and became enthusiastic about the French royalists of the Action Française who called themselves *"les camelots du roi."* He saw them as the defenders of the old France against the disintegrating and demoralizing forces of democracy and progress, and in defending the French tradition they were defenders of the soul of Europe.

Eliot's conservative politics were based on the wish to recover a past ritualistic civilization. Translated into action this often meant supporting movements whose catchwords were "discipline" and "authority," "aristocracy" and "order." The young Eliot seemed to visualize politics as the war of the traditional forces in the society against the liberal and progressive, cosmopolitan ones. His anti-Semitism was based on the same habit of pictorializing the issues of the time as his antiliberalism and antihumanism. Jews had names like Bleistein and caricature Jewish faces.

Metaphorical thinking about traditionalism and the classics may help to provide models for relating the forces of the past to those of the present in works of art, but it becomes dangerous if the world of actuality is treated as if it consisted of symbols to be arranged like those in a poem, in an order which is significant within the interior life of the artistically minded individual. With Ezra Pound, the results of trying to project his creative-critical theories into the world of politics were tragic. With Eliot they were not so, because although he was attracted by the idea of regarding social forces as symbols called "progress," "cosmopolitan Jews," "liberals," etc., which were opposed by other forces called "royalism," "order," "church," "dogma," etc., he was kept in check by realizing that politics was not just a battleground of symbols and abstract principles; he saw that real people were involved.

For Eliot, the past of the tradition meant Europe, the old civilization which reached to parts of America (where, nevertheless, it was impossible, in Pound's and Eliot's youthful view, to write poetry). The rituals of living which he yearned for come within the medieval Catholic tradition, though they have roots in ancient Rome and classical Greece. Unlike Pound, Lawrence, and Forster, Eliot had no nostalgia for pagan ritual. To him, the value of Greek and Latin was chiefly as sources of mythology and as the roots of English and other European literature. He thought Greek a more beautiful language than Latin, but preferred Virgil to Homer. In a late essay he recalls that when he was a schoolboy, he instinctively preferred the *world* of Virgil to the *world* of Homer—"because it was a more civilized world of dignity, reason and order." The whole passage —especially since it is written in the spirit of the poet summing up, late in life, views he had held since childhood—is revealing:

> The Romans were less gifted than the Athenians for the arts, philosophy and pure science; and their language was more obdurate to the expression of either poetry or abstract thought. Virgil made of Roman civilization in his poetry something better than it really was. His sensibility is more nearly Christian than that of any other Roman or Greek poet: not like that of an early Christian perhaps, but like that of Christianity from the time at which we can say that a Christian civilization had come into being. We cannot compare Homer and Virgil; but we can compare the civilization which Homer accepted with the civilization of Rome as refined by the sensibility of Virgil.[1]

Part of the interest of this passage is that it expresses the point of view of a writer who has formed his idea of civilization in America, who has decided that there is no civilization in his own country, and who has gone to Europe in search of it. This is an attitude common to Henry James and Ezra Pound, as well as to Eliot. These expatriates looked to Europe for civilization. They had based their idea of Europe on a past which seemed more real to them than to most Europeans. What they saw was decadence.

[1] "Virgil and the Christian World," in *On Poetry and Poets*, pp. 124–25.

For Eliot, as we have seen, civilization meant the Europe of Dante with its roots in the Rome—better than Rome—of Virgil. Beyond this there was an outer darkness of the African blackness. When Greek antiquity emerges in his poetry from the shadows of myth into the palpable, it is as the Eumenides, the Furies, or as the "stiff dishonoured shroud" of the murder of Agamemnon or the rape of "Philomel, by the barbarous king / So rudely forced."

Eliot's poetry has been written about so extensively that the symbols of darkness and horror which he employs tend to seem almost abstract concepts. Here I want to emphasize that Eliot was a man with feelings about places, persons, and smells which affected him as powerfully as allergies affect others. Toward the end of his life, when his health required it, he had to spend winters in North Africa or Barbados. He dreaded this. He loved London, he hated desert wastes, stretches of sand, cacti. He seems to have had that horror of places associated with murder or violence of a kind which one supposes Edgar Allan Poe to have had. Lady Ottoline Morrell (who appears under various disguises in novels by D. H. Lawrence, Graham Greene, and Aldous Huxley) wrote to me in the 1930s:

> I saw T. S. E. again . . . he was ever so Nice—but—I think he is very queer. . . . I showed him photographs of Greek IVth and Vth Century Statues and he said they gave him the Creeps. They were so akin to "Snake Worship." Now of all Art. Phidias/The Time of . . . seems to me to be Sublime—and—Not Corrupt. Don't you think it odd of him—I feel he has Demons —on the Brain—

Eliot would certainly have been amused at this, and perhaps at her tea party he was pulling Lady Ottoline's leg. All the same he had a haunted imagination—

haunted by real fears and fantasies, the starkness of which has become fogged over in the mass of exegesis gathered round his work.

The Africa of "cactus land," impenetrably black nights, suffocating heat, scrub deserts, ticking insects, and throbbing tom-toms means in his poetry the horror that will finally engulf the Dantesque light *"lume"* of the European civilization. Celia Coplestone, the heroine of his play *The Cocktail Party*, is crucified "very near an ant-hill" at an African village of Kinkanja. (The account of the sacrifice, Robert Speaight tells me, was so frightening in the original version, performed at the Edinburgh Festival in 1949, that Eliot had to be persuaded by the producer, Martin Browne, to alter it.) If Eliot was obsessed by the idea of civilization, the horror of barbarism haunted his imagination also.

If Dante's cosmography provided him in imagination with a map of civilization, then on it an area which represented tradition was marked Glory, one which represented the modern world, Boredom, and one which represented Africa as seen through the eyes of Joseph Conrad—"The horror! The horror!"

Education, Harvard Style

● ●

11

Eliot left instructions that his biography should not be written. This was not only because there were things in his private life which he did not wish made public: for instance, his unhappy first marriage that ended with his wife going insane. The poet who viewed poetry not as "an expression of" but as "an escape from personality" felt that his private life, which he had taken such pains to keep out of his work, was irrelevant to his poetry. His relationship with his public should be through his poetry, not through his biography.

Yet Eliot did not take the line advanced by W. H. Auden late in life, that (except for writers like Byron, Shelley, and Oscar Wilde who were concealed autobiographers) an artist's biography, like his correspondence, was an illegitimate object of inquiry. He had indeed admitted, in "The Function of Criticism," that the critic should be

a master of fact, and facts include biographical information about the writer.

In a circumspect way, Eliot let out biographical information about himself which indicates the kind of
fact which he thought might throw light on his poetry.
For instance, this in a letter to Herbert Read (April 23,
1928):

> Some day I want to write an essay about the point of
> view of an American who wasn't an American, be-
> cause he was born in the South and went to school
> in New England as a small boy with a nigger drawl,
> but who wasn't a southerner in the South because his
> people were northerners in a border state and looked
> down on all southerners and Virginians, and who so
> was never anything anywhere and who therefore felt
> himself to be more a Frenchman than an American
> and more an Englishman than a Frenchman and yet
> felt that the USA up to a hundred years ago was a
> family extension.[1]

Perhaps the confusion about his origins explains why,
after only ten years' residence in England, Eliot began
to state opinions from an English point of view—as
though, indeed, he were an Englishman. In 1926, in an
essay on William Blake, he reminded his "fellow"
English readers: "we are not really so remote from the
Continent, or from our own past, as to be deprived of
the advantages of culture if we wish them." In 1917 he
wrote poems almost exclusively in French, as though
he really did feel himself to be more French than either
American or English. Introducing himself to his audience at the University of Virginia in 1933, he remarks,
"I speak as a New Englander." This international Amer-

[1] Quoted in Allen Tate, ed., *T. S. Eliot: The Man and His
Work*, p. 15.

ican "felt that the USA up to a hundred years ago was a family extension. . . ." Eliot's friend Professor Theodore Spencer, who also had extremely remote New England ancestry, once remarked to me, in his precise English: "You have no idea how lonely one feels in this country if one's ancestors arrived here in the seventeenth century." Eliot felt this kind of loneliness, coupled with positive dislike of what America had become since Andrew Jackson's Presidency. He would probably have felt still more isolated had his family remained in Massachusetts, to which his ancestor Andrew Eliot came from England in 1670.

But his family went to St. Louis, where his grandfather, the Reverend William Greenleaf Eliot, a Unitarian minister, had traveled in 1834, and founded the first Unitarian Church and Washington University. As a child, Eliot must have had the virtues of this grandfather drummed into him. William Greenleaf Eliot was a New Testament Christian of a saintly kind. During the 1849 cholera epidemic in St. Louis, for weeks on end he visited the sick and dying and slept only three hours each night. His right hand was paralyzed as a consequence of the exhaustion he experienced then. In his *Notes on Some Figures Behind T. S. Eliot*, to which I am here much indebted, Herbert Howarth records that William Greenleaf Eliot "constantly and passionately thought how it is to the holy throng of apostles and martyrs, God's saints on earth, that all progress in wisdom and goodness, and all triumphs over evil, are due. . . ."[2]

Henry Ware Eliot, the poet's father, reacted against the family tradition of the sons going into the ministry. To the consternation of his father he became a business-

[2] Herbert Howarth, *Notes on Some Figures Behind T. S. Eliot*, p. 5.

man, giving as his reason for his choice: "Too much pudding choked the dog."[3] Eventually he became President of the St. Louis Hydraulic-Press Brick Company. Nevertheless, he remained a devout churchgoer and supporter of charitable and cultural enterprises.

The Eliot family was literate, cultivated, institutional: but their attitude can hardly be described as aesthetic. Eliot's mother (before marriage Charlotte Champe Stearns) came from the same kind of background of good works, refinement, and business as her husband's family. Like the Eliots, the Stearnses had a President of Harvard University in the family. His mother was intellectual and ambitious but, being a woman, received no university education. Lacking academic qualifications, she became a schoolteacher. After her marriage she bore seven children, of whom the last was Thomas Stearns Eliot, born September 26, 1888. But she regarded her life as a failure. She became an embittered feminist. During Eliot's childhood she started a career as a social worker, supporting feminist organizations.

Some of her verse contained the germs of ideas which later became transformed in her son's poetry. It is interesting to note that one poem, called "A Musical Reverie," was divided into three movements: *Andante*, *Presto Agitato*, and *Poco Tranquillo*. Her most ambitious effort was a play entitled *Savonarola*. Herbert Howarth writes that in this play "Savonarola turns aside from the early temptations of human life and love, then from the temptations of the Cardinal's hat:

> *All earthly honours I would feign resign.*
> *Is this the hat I wish, a hat of red?*
> *If so then let it be*
> *The crown of martyrdom upon my head.*[4]

[3] *Ibid*, p. 19.
[4] *Ibid*, p. 32.

The shadow of this hat seems to fall across *Murder in the Cathedral.* Thomas Becket, likewise, rejects the Tempters' offers of worldly power and glory and chooses martyrdom. Fantasies about martyrdom seemed to be in Eliot's blood, on both sides of the family.

Poetic influences on the poet in his childhood are Keats, Shelley, Byron, Tennyson, Browning, and Fitzgerald's Omar Khayyám. The earliest of his *Poems Written in Early Youth* show this romantic influence. Toward the end of that volume it is broken abruptly by that of Jules Laforgue. But even in middle life, in the seemingly automatic writing of "Five-finger exercises," he falls back on Tennyson tinged with Edward Lear:

> *The long light shakes across the lake,*
> *The forces of the morning quake,*
> *The dawn is slant across the lawn . . .*

Henry Ware Eliot, at the turn of the century, built a country house in the neighborhood of Gloucester, Massachusetts, where the family went every summer. Here the boy gazed into rock pools and saw sea anemones, small fish, and crabs, heard the conversation of sailors, later learned to sail.

After his schooling at Smith Academy in Latin and Greek classics, English and history, French and German, Eliot went to Harvard University in 1906 and remained under its aegis until 1914, when he was trapped in England by World War I. At Harvard he not only laid the foundations of his extensive education but also covered the ground of almost all the spiritual and intellectual material which was to preoccupy him for most of his life. A university student is always at one remove from real life, and this prolonged period of educational incubation had the effect of dividing Eliot's life before his middle age into two halves: the Harvard period of study, supported by his parents and university, and the London period of real economic hardship, in the early stages, and prolonged personal unhappiness.

At Harvard he first studied the Greek and Latin classics, the history of ancient art, the history of ancient philosophy, French and German, and some Dante. Later he attended George Santayana's course on the "History of Modern Philosophy" and also his course on "Ideals of Society, Religion, Art and Science in Their Historical Development." When, in early 1914, Bertrand Russell went to Harvard and gave a seminar on symbolic logic, he was much impressed by Eliot, one of his best students. In a letter to Lady Ottoline Morrell he referred to him as "ultra-civilized" and "with manners of the finest Etonian type." He "knows his classics very well, is familiar with all French literature from Villon to Vildrach, and is altogether impeccable in his taste but has no vigour or life—or enthusiasm. He is going to Oxford where I expect he will be very happy."[5]

Eliot also attended Josiah Royce's course, "Study of Various Types of Method," and became particularly interested in primitive religion and ritual. After his return from Paris in 1911, he joined C. R. Lanman's Indic philology course and studied Sanskrit and Indian philosophy for two years. He became rather mystical, though distrusting this tendency in himself. But Buddhism remained a lifelong influence in his work and at the time when he was writing *The Waste Land*, he almost became a Buddhist—or so I once heard him tell the Chilean poet Gabriele Mistral, who was herself a Buddhist. The Buddhist and Christian mysticisms in the *Four Quartets* seem very close.

Eliot went to Paris in September 1910 and stayed there for a year (ending with a visit the following summer in Munich) studying French literature at the Sor-

[5] Bernard Bergonzi, *T. S. Eliot*, p. 27.

bonne. He attended lectures by Henri Bergson at the Collège de France and took French conversation lessons with Alain-Fournier, author of *Le Grand Meaulnes*, that novel which more than any other creates a dreamlike, idyllic vision of legendary France. Paris was a city of enormous intellectual vitality. Eliot remembered of this year his impression of the *fourmillante cité* of Baudelaire's Paris, the sight of a friend coming into the Luxembourg Gardens waving a branch of lilac, and doubtless the idea of a Quartier Latin of sex and sin.

For Eliot, France and Paris meant, first, Baudelaire, then perhaps Charles-Louis Philippe's *Bubu de Montparnasse* (1901), a novel about a French prostitute for the English edition of which, many years later, he wrote an introduction. More intimately than either of these it must have meant Jules Laforgue, a poet with whose poetry and life Eliot in his youth almost identified. He first heard of him from reading at Harvard, in 1908, Arthur Symons' book *The Symbolist Movement in Literature* (1899). Laforgue was one of the symbolists, but perhaps it was not this which attracted Eliot to him and his work. Laforgue wrote dramatic monologues in which the narrator, though speaking in the first person, was viewed objectively and ironically as if by an outsider. There was an elaborate disguise, a mask, which was the form of this inner dramatic monologue or soliloquy written in the first person, but in which the poetry seemed to have a separate consciousness projected looking ironically at the first-person "I" as a third-person "he."

In his actual life Laforgue played a muted and subdued role and was dressed for such a part. There was no meretriciousness. He simply acted not being a poet, retaining an air of ironic detachment from himself. He wore a dark suit, carried an umbrella, and conversed in tones of inflexible politeness. Eliot wrote later that

Laforgue seemed to him an elder brother. He taught Eliot how to speak in his own voice, to write idiomatic poetry subtly turned against its own idiom. He provided him with examples of dramatic monologue that were not deliberate with the moral lesson to be drawn like those of Browning (and Eliot admired Browning).

Laforgue also exemplified for Eliot the role the poet should adopt in modern life. It had seemed to the poets of the end of the last century that a poet, as such, had come to be regarded by his contemporaries as an oddity. He must resist this by creating a role—variously called mask or persona—for himself. Most poets adopted, as Oscar Wilde had done, and as Yeats and Ezra Pound later did, aggressive and flamboyant poses. But Eliot was too profoundly ironic to do this. His pose was that of a poet who has nothing of the poet about his appearance and behavior and who is very deliberately, but a bit discomfitingly, an ordinary man—even a bit more ordinary perhaps than others. Laforgue provided him with a wonderful model, for in his poetry the poet's role of ironic correctness blends into a moonlit, somnambulist one—Harlequin, Scaramouche, correct but faintly sinister, shadow among the shadows of the city street.

There was one teacher at Harvard some of whose ideas Eliot accepted with enthusiasm, others of which he rejected with something like revulsion. The two reactions helped him to define his own attitudes. This teacher was Irving Babbitt. Babbitt was one of those professors who are antibodies upon the carcasses of academic institutions. Howarth records that in his youth Babbitt had been a cowboy. He was reputed to have "pulled a rattlesnake out of a hole by its tail." He had fought with an eagle, the scars of whose talons marked his hands.[6]

6 Howarth, *op. cit.*, p. 127.

It must have been rather awkward for this Oedipus-like figure to be pursued (as he was throughout his life) by a young poet with impeccable manners—and what Wyndham Lewis was to call later a Gioconda smile— with one half of his nature admiring Babbitt, and the other, perhaps the more telling half, being his most remorseless adversary.

Babbitt attacked what he described as the slovenly attitudes of Harvard and "the democratic inclusiveness of our sympathies," whilst he found great merit in "the aristocratic aloofness of the ancient humanist." The young Eliot welcomed Babbitt's classicism, his conservatism, his advocacy of aristocratic values, his contempt for originality as a prime aim among modern artists. He admired the aristocratic goals of Babbitt's humanism. However, with his penetrating irony he saw through one defect in this system. Humanism was based on Babbitt's admiration for the qualities which were those of individual humanists, men of "aristocratic aloofness." However, as Babbitt himself admitted, these men of ancient virtue had derived their qualities not just from their humanity but from religious values based on their belief in the supernatural. Babbitt maintained that in the modern world, where such beliefs had been made untenable by science, the outstanding individual himself could, through his own imitation of the virtues of those exceptional men of antiquity, establish a new humanist philosophy. Eliot saw that to do this would be to abstract from the antique models the metaphysical faith which had made their almost superhuman achievements possible.

A modern humanism without religious belief would be, in Eliot's view, one of two things: either a club for like-minded exceptional academics and intellectuals, worshipers of antiquity but whose aims, admirable though they might be, would have no reverberation beyond themselves; or else a substitute religion setting up belief in the virtue of certain exceptional individuals in the place of the worship of God.

Babbitt's idea of humanism as a modern philosophy with religious overtones by which modern men, deprived of religion, might live, was totally alien to Eliot's way of thinking. Babbitt's humanism provided the pattern in his mind of a modern tendency to attempt to fill the void left by the death of God with some substitute religion. He objected to this tendency in Matthew Arnold's discussion of poetry as taking the place of religion in modern life, and equally in I. A. Richards, whom he attacked for recommending readers to prepare themselves for a poem by practicing "something like a technique or ritual for heightening sincerity." As Babbitt's humanism was the first example of this tendency to come to Eliot's attention it remained a kind of red flag to a bull or even a King Charles's head for him to which, as readers of *The Criterion* will recall, he frequently reverted in his "Commentaries."

Although Eliot had written some of what were to become his most famous poems (including "Prufrock," "Portrait of a Lady," and "Preludes") while he was at Harvard, it was still uncertain whether he would become a poet or a philosopher. The seriousness of his philosophic studies cannot be exaggerated. After 1912 he was a teaching assistant in the philosophy department at Harvard for two years, and in 1913–14 president of the university philosophical society. He had already read, among his anthropological studies, some of Frazer's *The Golden Bough* and Jessie Weston's *From Ritual to Romance*.

He chose, as the subject of his dissertation, the philosophy of F. H. Bradley. He wrote his thesis in England between 1914 and 1916 but, owing to the war, never traveled to Harvard for his oral examinations and for this reason never obtained his doctorate. (The thesis was published in 1964, when it appeared under the title *Knowledge and Experience*. The Introduction contains a characteristic disclaimer by the author: "Forty-six years after my academic philosophizing came to an end, I find myself unable to think in the terminology of this essay. Indeed, I do not pretend to understand it.") Bradley's philosophy attracted Eliot because it is concerned with the relationship of the subjective consciousness with the objective world. The idea that the human mind was the only center of awareness in the universe filled him with terror akin to that of Pascal on gazing at the infinite spaces of the universe.

It is necessary now to try to summarize those points in Bradley's philosophy which particularly concerned Eliot in his poetry. In order to do this I have consulted with my friend Richard Wollheim, who was so kind as to supply me with the following notes:

> Bradley's philosophy may—at any rate from one point of view—be seen as centrally concerned with the relation of consciousness to reality. As such it tries to answer such questions as: Is my consciousness a consciousness of the external world, or is it simply confined to private internal sensation? Is there in the universe any consciousness other than mine, or do all experiences belong to me? If there are other consciousnesses than mine, how are these related or are they the centres of quite independent realities?
>
> In his thesis Eliot dealt with Bradley's attempt to answer all three of these questions. And Eliot clearly felt, like Bradley, the need to reject a negative or solipsistic answer to them. My consciousness is not self-enclosed: my consciousness is not unique. But it is very easy to see that it was really the last of these

questions, and Bradley's answer to it, that meant most to Eliot. It evokes from Eliot his finest prose in the thesis, and it is that which connects with Eliot's ultimate commitment to religious belief. For Bradley's answer to the problem about how the different consciousnesses are related is that everything that occurs within what we think of as individual minds is really an aspect of a single comprehensive consciousness. There is, according to Bradley, nothing "over and above" human consciousness. Bradley totally rejected the idea of a super-rational or super-sensible reality. But to think—as we humans are obliged to—that this reality is divided up between, and carved up into, individual minds is error. Such a thought reflects Appearance, not Reality. In Reality, this division, like all other divisions, does not exist. There is the single seamless Absolute. And, interestingly, in keeping with the generally sceptical tone of his philosophy, Bradley arrived at this position not by mystical insight or by faith, but by an examination or analysis of the idea of the individual mind or personal consciousness. Philosophical criticism, Bradley thought, showed that any such idea is incoherent. The individual mind is a "false abstraction."

Later, when Eliot wrote about Bradley, he is not altogether frank about his relationship to the philosopher in whose ideas he once immersed himself. In the Notes to *The Waste Land* he quotes Bradley out of context and seems to give to a famous passage in *Appearance and Reality* an interpretation which ten years earlier he would have certainly rejected. And in his essay on Bradley—and in the much later introduction he provided for the reprint of his thesis—Eliot writes about Bradley as though it was exclusively as a stylist that he had interested or influenced him.

Certainly in his acceptance of religion and the idea

of a transcendent God, Eliot departed from Bradley's philosophy. For to Bradley the division between God and the world, a Creator and his Creation, represented an abstraction false like, though not so false as, any other abstraction. Nevertheless, even when Eliot added a belief in God, he retained the Bradleyan conviction that individual consciousness as it is ordinarily conceived is not an ultimate fact of reality: and for this conviction he retained the Bradleyan argument that you cannot arrive at truth or reality by simply adding up these individual consciousnesses—for your starting point is rooted in abstraction, therefore in error.

The famous quotation "out of context" in the Notes to *The Waste Land* runs as follows: "My external sensations are no less private to my self than are my thoughts or my feelings. In either case my experience falls within my own circle, a circle closed on the outside; and, with all its elements alike, every sphere is opaque to the others which surround it. . . . In brief, regarded as an existence which appears in a soul, the whole world for each is peculiar and private to that soul."
The lines to which this refers are:

> . . . *I have heard the key*
> *Turn in the door once and turn once only*
> *We think of the key, each in his prison*
> *Thinking of the key, each confirms a prison*
> *Only at nightfall, aethereal rumours*
> *Revive for a moment a broken Coriolanus*

If, as Mr. Wollheim indicates, the total effect of the lines and the Note is to misrepresent Bradley's philosophy, this is because the purposes of poetry and philosophy are different. Eliot was extremely aware of this difference and frequently discussed it in his criticism.

From the point of view of the poet, a philosophy or belief, like any other experience he may have, is to be regarded simply as something from which he may take whatever is material for his poetry. In his dealings with philosophy a poet's responsibility is to transform ideas into objects of language, not to represent a system of philosophic thought. If it were his duty to remain faithful to the logic of an abstract argument, then it would be better for him to write philosophy than poetry, since logical prose exposition is the only form of expression in which a philosophy can be stated without confusion. It is evident from Mr. Wollheim's summary that Eliot was occupied in exploiting Bradley for the purposes of writing his own poetry, not using his poetry to represent the philosophy. Interestingly enough, in our discussion about this, Mr. Wollheim remarked that he thought Eliot developed a certain terror of philosophy as he grew older: a comment which at first I thought excessive but which, on reflection, I find illuminating. Eliot was in his youth divided between philosophy and poetry, just as he was later divided between poetry and criticism. He was extremely conscious of the distinctions which had to be made between the rules governing different forms of organization of language. The imagination develops a logic of the emotions, consistent within its own terms, which is different from the intellect's logic of abstractions which is divorced from emotions. A poet who is addicted to abstract thinking is liable to use his imaginative material as illustration of an underlying abstract argument in his poetry, with the result that the line of abstract logic, acting like an acid, eats through the poetic imagery. Eliot was very aware that Matthew Arnold—to take an outstanding example—thought too crudely and too obviously in his poetry; and beyond Arnold he was aware of the sad figure of Coleridge, a poet whose inspiration is frozen by his philosophical thinking.

As a philosopher Eliot thought of Bradley as dry, logical, and, in the most exemplary and transparent sense, a thinker in prose. It is significant that in later life he should forget the purely philosophic side not only of Bradley, but of the young philosopher Eliot, writing his thesis about him. There were aspects of Bradley which appealed to Eliot not as philosopher but as poet. The most important of these was, as Mr. Wollheim indicates, Bradley's analysis of the relation of consciousness to reality. This was of fundamental concern to Eliot as poet. "Consciousness" is probably the word he most frequently uses in his discussion of poetry. In quotations which Eliot isolated from their contexts, and which often seem strangely close to his own poetry, Eliot found statements in Bradley which fed his imagination. After he had become a Christian, he tended to discard Bradley as a philosopher and to concentrate on praising him as a writer of polemical prose. The essay on Bradley, which he wrote in 1926, is largely devoted to this. In it, he remarks that Bradley is at his best in his comments on Matthew Arnold's ideas about the "will of God," after quoting which, Eliot suddenly breaks off and quotes a passage from Bradley as revealing, in its way, of what really touches the roots of Eliot's sensibility as are his quotations from Tourneur or Middleton in his essays on Elizabethan poets. Bradley, commenting on Arnold, asks:

> How can the human-divine ideal ever be my will? The answer is, Your will it can never be as the will of your private self, so that your private self should become wholly good. To that self you must die, and by faith be made one with that ideal. You must resolve to

give up your will, as the mere will of this or that man, and you must put your whole self, your entire will, into the will of the divine. That must be your one self, as it is your true self; that you must hold to both with thought and will, and all other you must renounce.[7]

. Bradley is here correcting Matthew Arnold, but in doing so he touches the chord of Eliot's deepest belief. Eliot comments: "The distinction is not between a 'private self' or a 'higher self,' it is between the individual as himself and no more, a mere numbered atom, and the individual in communion with God." This reflects Eliot's whole cast of mind.

[7] Quoted in "Francis Herbert Bradley," in *Selected Essays*, p. 452.

False Grails

● ● ●

III

Frédéric Moreau . . . is constructed partly by negative definition, built up by a great number of observations. We cannot isolate him from the environment in which we find him; it may be an environment which is or can be universalized; nevertheless it, and the figure in it, consist of very many observed particular facts, the actual world. Without this world the figure dissolves. The ruling faculty is a critical perception, a commentary upon experienced feeling and sensation.

—T. S. ELIOT, "Ben Jonson" (1919)[1]

"The Love Song of J. Alfred Prufrock" is the dramatic monologue of a man of uncertain age who speaks out of a life whose center is a society drawing room approached through streets, the description of which provides metaphors for the squalor (also the mystery and beauty) of a city, unnamed, which nevertheless seems representa-

[1] *Selected Essays*, p. 152.

tive of other great cities (and which merges into the
Paris of Baudelaire—itself a metaphor for Dante's hell).
It is the universal temporal city of modern Western
civilization.

The poem opens on the note of such a tour of exhibited symptoms:

> *Let us go then, you and I,*
> *When the evening is spread out against the sky*
> *Like a patient etherised upon a table;*
> *Let us go, through certain half-deserted streets,*
> *The muttering retreats*
> *Of restless nights in one-night cheap hotels . . .*

There is a parallel here with Dante's journey under
the guidance of Virgil, which is a conducted tour through
various human exhibits illustrating degrees of damnation, purgatory, or beatitude. Such a journey has the
character of an exploratory surgical operation. Symptoms are observed from the outside, by spectators, the
visitors to this circle of the Inferno. The inhabitants of
the room which is the object of the visit are also seen
from the outside:

> *In the room the women come and go*
> *Talking of Michelangelo.*

Entering the room and wandering among the women,
the spectator sees from inside "The yellow fog that rubs
its back upon the window-panes." Then there is a shift,
like that of a movie camera panning to the outside of
the house again where the fog has

> *Licked its tongue into the corners of the evening,*
> *Lingered upon the pools that stand in drains . . .*

In the next stanza, or section, the themes of outside
and inside, spectator and inmates of the drawing room
are brought together in a sequence of thoughts which
have not yet crystallized into the identity of Prufrock,

who is thinking them. What is introduced, however, is the theme of time, which recurs throughout the poem like the reiteration of a note in a Beethoven sonata:

> *And indeed there will be time*
> *For the yellow smoke that slides along the street*
> *Rubbing its back upon the window-panes;*
> *There will be time, there will be time*
> *To prepare a face to meet the faces that you meet;*
> *There will be time to murder and create,*
> *And time for all the works and days of hands*
> *That lift and drop a question on your plate;*
> *Time for you and time for me,*
> *And time yet for a hundred indecisions,*
> *And for a hundred visions and revisions,*
> *Before the taking of a toast and tea.*

There is here a gradual resolution, as in the sonata, of themes which have a development different from the satiric outside point of view of the poem's opening. "We" are now inside the room. After a recurrence of the lines "In the room the women come and go / Talking of Michelangelo," the "I" character who has been, as it were, in abeyance since the opening of the poem acquires the attributes and stage properties of Prufrock. Instead of being the satiric observer, he is the observed ("the observed of all observers"), transferring the contempt with which he believes the women in the room regard him onto himself in the form of self-irony. Prufrock represents a state of mind, but he is also (I would say) decidedly a person.

Prufrock's recital defines his characteristics but as narration is negative. He sees himself as existing passively in the minds of those whose society he frequents. It is they who remark that his arms and legs are growing thin, they who conversationally have him "sprawling on a pin." His negative motivation is that he dare not transgress the boundary of opinion which they have drawn round him. To do so would be to presume. So he dares not eat a peach or ask a universal question or make a proposal of love.

At the end of the poem Prufrock has his lyrical yet depressed, blunted vision of the mermaids. He does not think that they will sing to him.

Alongside all this negativeness of statement there is the paradoxical nature of the life of dream or imagination. The imagination *qua* imagination does not know any negatives. If I think that mermaids will not sing to me, but I have walked to the beach and envisioned them in imagination "Combing the white hair of the waves blown back," then in imagination they have sung to me. Thus Prufrock, considered as a consciousness, or imagination, situated in a world which has become phantasmagoric to him, negates negation. He has, after all, a positive aspect. He is more than the inhabitants of the drawing room precisely because he knows that he is less than they. He knows what he lacks. This is more than they know, because they are incapable of knowing or really experiencing what they have.

In his surroundings Prufrock is like an eel at the bottom of a tank. He knows the depths and the darkness which the deceived creatures who swim around in their artificial light do not know. This self-knowledge becomes realization of what psychically he is:

> *I should have been a pair of ragged claws*
> *Scuttling across the floors of silent seas.*

By negation he even has a certain grandeur. He knows he is not Prince Hamlet, which means that in the driven-down world of his isolated imagination he is one of his courtiers. Prufrock is superior to the inhabitants of his world because he is conscious of being inferior. He *suffers*, which means that he is one of those who

knows that he is in a Baudelairean hell. He glimpses
boredom and horror.

In the context of the development of Eliot's poetry,
Prufrock is a searcher, and his quest, like that of other
individuals in Eliot's poems, is for a grail. The grail,
however, is fantasy, artefact, not the real supernatural.
The mermaids are related to the grail of *Parsifal* or to
Siegfried conversing with the Rhine Maidens.

It is true that Prufrock is not a "character" who could
be taken out of one set of circumstances and put into
another, and who would behave independently of both,
like Mr. Pickwick, or Well's' Mr. Kipps, or a Hemingway
hero, or even like one of Browning's Renaissance aristo-
crats, painters, or bishops in his dramatic monologues.
But, in order to be an individual life portrayed, Prufrock
does not have to be a three-dimensional personage of
this kind. He is real in the manner of Frédéric Moreau,
Flaubert's antihero in *L'Education sentimentale*, whose
life is the projection of the conditions that surround him.

Prufrock is, then, a person of the kind who might
appear in a novel by D. H. Lawrence or Virginia Woolf.
His failure, for which he despises himself, is failure to
relate either with another person or with the Absolute.
He is isolated, he cannot communicate. Although the
fact that he is *conditioned* by the society in which he
lives may account for his spiritual and sexual enerva-
tion, this does not excuse his moral cowardice. The fact
that he is able to see his character as the projection of
circumstances is still no excuse for his inertia.

The epigraph from *Inferno*, Canto XXVII, casts light
on his case. Prufrock's sin of *"acedia"* is that he does
not act in some way which would transform his passive
condition of being the object of his circumstances into
an active one. He knows that he is in hell and, morally,
he takes this as a reason for not acting upon his knowledge. Like Guido, who says to Dante,

Ma per ciò che giammai di questo fondo
non tornò vivo alcun, s'i'odo il vero,
sensa tema d'infamia ti rispondo . . .
(but because no one ever returned alive from
this depth, if what I hear is true, I will
answer you without fear of shame . . .)

he speaks out of the depths from which no one returns. He has betrayed truth in that, being aware of the surrounding corruption and, at the same time aware that he himself is conditioned by it, he thinks he will not be held responsible for being as he is. Guido's offense was that he had attempted to "repent and will a thing at the same time." He had committed an act of treachery at the command of the Pope who assured him that he would be absolved at the very moment of committing it.

I emphasize the reality of Prufrock in his situation, because there is a tendency among critics today to present Eliot purely as a "symbolist." A generation and more ago Eliot's early poetry was seen as being closer to reality and less "literary" than it is today. "Where in modern poetry are there characters realised with such effectiveness as Prufrock and Sweeney?" asked F. O. Matthiessen in his book on Eliot first published in 1935.[2] Virginia Woolf thought that in Leopold Bloom and Prufrock "life" was put at the center of our time (for "human nature had changed in 1910"), whereas only the externals of life (such matters as the age of the characters) were given in the works of those like Arnold Bennett and H. G. Wells, whom she called "materialist" novelists. Ezra Pound considered that Prufrock was partly a self-portrait of the author, just as Hugh Selwyn Mauberley was partly his own self-portrait, though neither character was identical with Pound or Eliot.

The tendency I am opposing is that of certain critics

[2] F. O. Matthiessen, *The Achievement of T. S. Eliot*, p. 104.

to drain "Prufrock" of its considerable realism. An example of this is Bernard Bergonzi's remark in his informative, useful book on Eliot that in "Prufrock" it is impossible "to see any way in which the evening is really like a patient etherised upon a table, or in which the fog resembles a domestic animal wandering outside a house."[3] In fact these similes are very different, one being an example of what might be called "symptomatic" imagery (of which there are many examples in early Auden), the other being an example of close, naturalistic, very original observation. I shall consider each in turn. First:

> *When the evening is spread out against the sky*
> *Like a patient etherised upon a table . . .*

This simile (or perhaps metaphor) is not capable of being visualized, unless as a burning aura of smog above a city (it might have been drawn by Paul Klee). I call it "symptomatic" because the "patient" is the "soul" of the city. The simile or metaphor hangs on the word "etherised" which is ambiguous, suggesting, of course, "ether" (used for anesthetics) but also having many connotations in romantic poetry—for instance "ethereal." The combination of clinical and romantic connotations suggest the state of suspended consciousness of the "patient" and the head of the dreamer, full of the night sky and stars. One has only to substitute the word "anesthetized" for "etherised" to see how "anesthetized" would make the image rigid, anchored, grotesque. "Etherised" untethers it—makes it float, witty, dreaming. But this is to describe the effect, not to explain away how it so miraculously "works."

Mr. Bergonzi's inability to see any resemblance between a fog drifting through a street and a domestic

[3] Bernard Bergonzi, *T. S. Eliot*, p. 15.

animal makes me grateful for the Clean Air Act. Evidently he belongs to a generation who has never seen a real city fog. Along the street, the fog can be shredded by a lifting or lilting wind which will ultimately disperse it. It can be packed, sculpted, hollowed, rolled, like raw wool fretted by the elements. It can move in a curtain down a street and lift its skirt in order to avoid a puddle.

One very conscious effect in "Prufrock," as also in "Portrait of a Lady," is that of irony. This overlays everything like a varnish spread over a wide area of a painting with a very broad brush. If Prufrock's vision of himself as a "pair of ragged claws" seems out of key with the rest of his monologue, it is not because it is psychologically false or even that the lines seem too close to Websterian horror-fantasy, but because they drop the mask of irony. They are psychologically true of Prufrock's state—Prufrock is as nearly as possible psychoanalyzed in them—but the tone of self-mockery is not subtle enough to admit of Prufrock being seen as analogous to a hero of a tragedy by Webster or Tourneur, any more than as Prince Hamlet. The mood cannot shift convincingly from jeering self-contempt to tragic introspection.

The ironic note is even more pervasive in "Portrait of a Lady." Remy de Gourmont's account of Laforgue conveys very well its tone: "What dominates these first notes is irony. He mocks or pretends to mock. Perhaps, at bottom, he plays the dupe, but he does not want it to seem so—not even to himself."[4]

"The Portrait of a Lady" is about the failure of communication between a hostess and her guest in the course of three visits to her which he makes in one year. The embarrassed yet ironically mocking guest sees

[4] Remy de Gourmont, *Real Life and Poetry*.

the lady from the outside. To him she is exotic and absurd, self-dramatizing in her stage setting—"an atmosphere of Juliet's tomb." Hostessing being an artificial situation, the fact that she is constantly trying to step out of her social role and reveal her real self, a spiritual and emotional sensitive whose values are friendship and art, forces the visitor still further back on his own role of malicious, ironic, though also insidiously sympathetic, observer. He has a sensibility deeper than his social self—acting the role of visitor—which perceives that under the artificial setting and the affected speech of this lady there is a suffering human being, trapped in her situation: and, his young-man malice being stronger than his sympathy, he watches her writhing in this trap. He exploits the hostess-guest relation in order to keep interchange on his side polite, obsequious even, but not communicative at the level on which she wishes it to be. The poem analyzes the anguish, the guilt and self-reproach, the barbarity that lies just under the surface of the social visit.

The analogy here is with music—a frustrated harmony. The visitor has music he does not want to hear forced upon him, and within the music he detects notes of real anguish:

> *Among the windings of the violins*
> *And the ariettes*
> *Of cracked cornets*
> *Inside my brain a dull tom-tom begins*
> *Absurdly hammering a prelude of its own,*
> *Capricious monotone*
> *That is at least one definite "false note."*

(The tom-tom, incidentally, is an early example of the savage and the jungle which Eliot senses ever more insistently under the mask of so-called civilization.) The lady represents another kind of falsity:

The voice returns like the insistent out-of-tune
Of a broken violin on an August afternoon:
"I am always sure that you understand
My feelings, always sure that you feel,
Sure that across the gulf you reach your hand. . . ."

The young man is all satirist, with his sharp ear detecting the false notes in this score. But he also cannot avoid hearing the suffering which is real under the falsity:

"Yet with these April sunsets, that somehow recall
My buried life . . ."

For her this "buried life" is her own youth, of "Paris in the Spring." She is trying to talk the language of the "buried life" in Matthew Arnold's poem of that name. Under the words she uses, are the words she does not use; and the satire that the young man turns against himself, is against his own refusal to respond to this deeper language.

Eliot, like Arnold before him, is haunted by the contrast between the modern world of distraction, journeyings to and fro, traffickings in values purely material, money-making, work-routines, which form a surface, like a moving platform, carrying us along upon it, and, underneath, the real life. In Arnold's poem of that name, "The Buried Life" is the occasional but very rare situation in which lovers communicate their deepest feelings, needs, and aspirations consequent on the very condition of being alive, knowing they have to die, needing love—a fundamental, mutually-meeting seriousness, that is to say. On this seriousness is based joy as well as sorrow. And without this recognition there is neither joy nor grief, only a numbing and hurrying frustration.

The idea of an alternative life in which people really speak to one another releases the most spontaneous lyricism in Arnold. In "The Buried Life" he tries to trace the idea of the alternative life back to sources of experience:

> *Yet still, from time to time, vague and forlorn,*
> *From the soul's subterranean depth upborne*
> *As from an infinitely distant land,*
> *Come airs, and floating echoes, and convey*
> *A melancholy into all our day.*
> *Only—but this is rare—*
> *When a belovéd hand is laid in ours,*
> *When, jaded with the rush and glare*
> *Of the interminable hours,*
> *Our eyes can in another's eyes read clear,*
> *When our world-deafened ear*
> *Is by the tones of a loved voice caressed—*
> *A bolt is shot back somewhere in our breast,*
> *And a lost pulse of feeling stirs again.*

If "Portrait of a Lady" were a play, the comedy of the situation would be that the Boston hostess talks the language of "The Buried Life" while her visitor studiously refuses to respond with anything but conventional politenesses. Embarrassment and guilt provoke in him the language of self-hatred—the self-mirrored objection of one who refuses love:

> *And I must borrow every changing shape*
> *To find expression . . . dance, dance*
> *Like a dancing bear,*
> *Cry like a parrot, chatter like an ape.*

The end of "Portrait of a Lady" is particularly revealing. The narrator contemplates the death of the lady. He thinks that, if she dies, he will have to give her the advantage in the game of the emotions. Death is, after all, proof of sincerity, the final surfacing of the buried

life, checkmate. At the same time the young man is
suddenly revealed as the writer of the poem. This does
not mean that he is Eliot. But it does characterize the
literary character of his outsideness, the young poet's
detached malice with which he at once understands the
lady with his imagination but declines to understand
her on the level of their social intercourse. This is the
malice of young writers who regard those who entertain
them as their prey, material for their literature:

Well! and what if she should die some afternoon,
Afternoon grey and smoky, evening yellow and rose;
Should die and leave me sitting pen in hand
With the smoke coming down above the housetops;
Doubtful, for a while
Not knowing what to feel or if I understand
Or whether wise or foolish, tardy or too soon . . .
Would she not have the advantage, after all?
This music is successful with a "dying fall"
Now that we talk of dying—
And should I have the right to smile?

In Eliot's early work, there are no direct love poems.
When the poet writes about love he does so indirectly
and obliquely, with artifice that distances the feeling
from the object which is the poem. An example of this
strategy is "La Figlia che Piange," a poem to which the
poet seems to have attached a personal importance.
The occasion which suggested it was Eliot's visiting a
museum in northern Italy, to which he had been advised
to go by a friend, in order that he might see a stele of a
young girl weeping. He failed to find the stele and wrote
the poem, which has the quality of a *tableau vivant* of a
statue assuming a pose and then coming to life. It is a
poem of much artifice, in the Laforguean manner, including a line, "Simple and faithless as a smile and

shake of the hand," which is a free rendering of one by Laforgue. The poem has that pieced-together look of several of Eliot's early poems in which the poet's own lines are welded together with those of the French model he so much admired, and in which the emotion is twisted to suit the change of tone. The epigraph from Virgil, "*O quam te memorem virgo*," is one to chisel on stone. The stele was presumably Hellenistic, but the picture in the first stanza is curiously Victorian:

> *Stand on the highest pavement of the stair—*
> *Lean on a garden urn—*
> *Weave, weave the sunlight in your hair—*
> *Clasp your flowers to you with a pained surprise—*
> *Fling them to the ground and turn*
> *With a fugitive resentment in your eyes:*
> *But weave, weave the sunlight in your hair.*

This is more reminiscent of the Victorian classicism of a painter like Alfred Moore than of an Attic frieze.

The mood is artificial, as of the poet adopting the role of the painter and telling the model how to pose. The obvious clichés—"pained surprise," "fugitive resentment"—have an irony that protects the writer from revealing his feeling by preventing the reader taking this quite seriously. The strategy is Laforguean. The last stanza, which opens with the beautiful lines

> *She turned away, but with the autumn weather*
> *Compelled my imagination many days,*
> *Many days and many hours:*
> *Her hair over her arms and her arms full of flowers.*

returns to the *tableau vivant* in which the poet sees the third-person lover with whose feelings he identifies his own, leaving the girl. The spectatorial poet is left with a sense of loss:

And I wonder how they should have been together!
I should have lost a gesture and a pose.
Sometimes these cogitations still amaze
The troubled midnight and the noon's repose.

The elaboration, as of a frame around a picture which turns out itself to be a frame, and the irony do not quite remove the impression that a voyeur's experience, and perhaps his deep frustrations, are being covered over. In a gravely sophisticated way, the poem is Pierrotesque, giving the sense of tears behind the artificiality of the marble pose.

Real Life and Poetry

IV

"I have *lived* through material for a score of long poems in the last six months," Eliot wrote to his friend Conrad Aiken in January 1916. He listed his wife's illness, the death of his friend Jean Verdenal, and his own financial worries. "But I am having a wonderful time neverthe-less. . . . Cambridge seems to me a dull night-mare now." (By "Cambridge" he was referring to Harvard University.)[1]

If the time, though in many ways horrific, was wonderful this was because instead of enduring his education, he was living his life. He had come to England in June 1914 to continue his thesis at Merton College, Oxford, under Harold Joachim. (Bradley was a Fellow at Merton, but had long been a recluse; Eliot never met him.)

[1] *The Waste Land: A Facsimile and Transcript,* Valerie Eliot, ed., p. x.

He did not like Oxford, perhaps because he was tired of being educated. He dreaded returning to Harvard. He wanted to go to London and study at the British Museum.

The transition from "education" to "life" was accelerated by his marrying an English girl, Vivien Haigh-Wood. She was the daughter of a portrait painter who had inherited some money and retired early. In the absence of any authenticated biography of Eliot, rumors and legends surround this marriage. Ezra Pound, befriending Eliot and wishing to set him on an expatriate course (for poetry, he said, could not be written in America), apparently encouraged it, thinking to keep him in England. According to my friend who used to dance with Eliot at the Hammersmith Palais de Danse, Vivien was fresh, innocent, a chatterbox, pretty. She was known among Eliot's social English friends (who included Lady Ottoline Morrell, St. John Hutchinson and his wife, Virginia and Leonard Woolf, the Sitwells, the Aldous Huxleys) as "the river girl." There seems a trace of mockery in this name. She had a history of illness and "nerves."

Whatever the reasons, the marriage had a disastrous, progressively worsening effort on Vivien Eliot's "nerves" and only a slightly less disastrous one on those of her husband. From the account given by Valerie, Eliot's second wife, in her introduction to the manuscript of *The Waste Land*, it seems clear that most of the symptoms from which the two suffered during the years following this marriage were psychosomatic. The marriage was a failure.

Eliot's parents disapproved of Vivien, and of their youngest son living in England. The allowance his father gave him was not enough to provide the increasingly large sums necessary for the care of his wife. Eliot's father made arrangements that any property left to

Eliot would in the event of his death revert to the family trust and not go to Vivien Eliot. To make money, Eliot taught at High Wycombe Grammar School, then at Highgate Junior School (where John Betjeman, who knew him as "the American master," presented him with a volume called *The Best of Betjeman*). He did a great deal of literary journalism and also university extension lecturing. In March 1917 he obtained work in the Colonial and Foreign Branch of Lloyds Bank. This excited sympathy among his Bloomsbury literary friends who had gathered from the fiction of E. M. Forster that to be a bank clerk (and they thought of Eliot as one) was the most soul-destroying of occupations. In fact, Eliot was fascinated by what he called "the science of money" and was given jobs to do—such as dealing, after the war, with pre-war debts between Lloyds Bank and Germany. He was not altogether pleased when, in 1922, a group of well-meaning friends and admirers, at the instigation of Ezra Pound, formed a fund called Bel Esprit which was meant to release him from the sordidness of employment in a bank. Eliot declined this offer, the money raised was returned to the donors, and he stayed with the bank.

In January 1919 Eliot's father died, and in May *Poems 1919* was published by Leonard and Virginia Woolf at the Hogarth Press (which was still at this time a hand press on which they themselves set type). Within a year Alfred Knopf brought out *Poems by T. S. Eliot* in the United States—largely thanks to the advocacy and support of Eliot by the collector John Quinn, who, without their ever having met, was consistently generous to him. The same collection came out in London under the title *Ara Vos Prec*. Soon after this his collection of essays *The Sacred Wood* was also published.

Eliot was now started on his career. He was famous but his private life was no happier. His wife became more and more ill. Shortly after Eliot's mother and sister had come to visit them in London, Eliot himself, in September 1921, was ordered to take a complete rest, as he was on the verge of a nervous breakdown. He went first to Margate and later to a specialist in Lausanne. It was here that he wrote most of *The Waste Land*, though, as was the case with the writing of "Prufrock," several sections of it had been written many years earlier, some of them perhaps even at Harvard.

Eliot's material problems were largely solved in 1922, when he became editor of *The Criterion* (for which he received no salary as editor, however, while he was still at the bank) and won the annual *Dial* award of $2000. In 1925, when Lady Rothermere withdrew her support from the magazine, the publishing firm of Faber and Gwyer (later to become Faber and Faber) took it over, taking Eliot into the firm. In 1927 he was received into the Church of England, and, during the same year, he was naturalized. Valerie Eliot tells me that he regarded these two important steps, of becoming an English citizen and being received into the English Church, as one. In 1932 he went to Harvard University to give the Charles Eliot Norton Lectures. While at Harvard he took the decision to leave his wife. (After years of insanity, Vivien Eliot died in 1948, in a home.)

Although in one way England provided him with an extremely good setting for the development of his poetry (just enough encouragement, just enough resistance, and the entertaining companionship of people who cared deeply for literature), it may not have been the best background for marriage in which this extremely intelligent, but in some ways very unsure, young American was at times socially embarrassed by his wife—especially at Bloomsbury parties. The qualities of patience and forbearance which her hysteria brought out in him may not have been the best thing for either of them. Although Eliot by all accounts put up an extremely good show among the English literati, underneath he was too shy, too little cynical, too serious, too dedicated, too devout, for them. He had reserve, but the fact that he had was too obvious. His caginess became a bit of a joke: and Vivien had no reserve. London literary society acted as a sounding board or whispering gallery for the many anecdotes which this misalliance provided. Those that I have heard all point to one fact: that while Vivien's health may have made a normal marriage relationship difficult, she was totally and irrevocably dedicated to him. Indeed, in her case, the cliché, she worshiped him, seems to have been quite literally true.

Whatever Eliot's feelings toward her when they married may have been—and the marriage seems to have begun lovingly—at this stage in his life the difficulties of the relationship were overwhelming. There was his parents' disapproval; there were the years of overwork at journalism in order to support his wife in her illness; there was the bitter sense of not fulfilling his vocation. It must have been particularly galling to an American poet who despised the English Georgians because they had a "weekend" attitude toward writing poetry that he himself had so little time for writing.

The intervention of Bertrand Russell in the Eliots' marriage cannot have been helpful, though doubtless it was well intended. Russell, who, with his very abstract and logical mind, felt drawn to writers of poetic imagination (is not his complicated, catastrophic relationship with Lawrence an example of this?), interested himself in his ex-pupil and his wife and tried to help them in their difficulties. His attempts ceased, he commented later, when he made the discovery that the Eliots enjoyed being unhappy. Russell's help was generous, practical, and very rational. It revealed his distinterested and philosophical benevolence. He handed over £3000 in debentures to Eliot, the income from which greatly helped him in his difficult circumstances (Eliot later returned these). Russell wrote to Lady Ottoline Morrell of Eliot, "It is quite funny how I have come to love him, as if he were my son. He is becoming much more of a man. He has a profound and quite unselfish devotion to his wife, and she is really very fond of him, but has impulses of cruelty from time to time."[2] Russell took Vivien off her husband's hands by accompanying her to Torquay for a holiday, where Eliot later joined them.

There is no reason here to speculate about the relations between Russell and Vivien Eliot. What is significant in Eliot's poetic development is his ambivalent attitude toward Russell. "Mr. Apollinax," the poem which he wrote about Russell's visit to Harvard, is taken by most critics to be a genial enough piece of mild satire. It certainly has a grinning surface, yet I think that underneath there is a revulsion which Eliot only equals in the "Sweeney" poems—there is even something of Sweeney in the portrait of Mr. Apollinax:

In the place of Mrs. Phlaccus, at Professor Channing-
Cheetah's
He laughed like an irresponsible fœtus.
His laughter was submarine and profound
Like the old man of the sea's
Hidden under coral islands
Where worried bodies of drowned men drift down in the
green silence,
Dropping from fingers of surf.

The undersea world is always one of death and horror —of eyes eaten by crabs—in Eliot's poetry. As he was

[2] Bernard Bergonzi, *T. S. Eliot*, p. 33.

to write some years later in the first version of *The Waste Land,* before it had been edited by him and Pound:

> *Full fathom five your Bleistein lies*
> *Under the flatfish and the squids.*
>
> *Graves' Disease in a dead jew's eyes!*
> *Where the crabs have eat the lids . . .*

Whatever Eliot's feelings of personal obligation to Russell, he thought of him as rationalist materialism incarnate and felt the same resistance to his philosophy as Blake had for Newton, Yeats for Bernard Shaw, and Lawrence (also) for Russell. In his attacks on liberals Eliot sometimes employs the term "Whig" which would certainly apply to Russell and his ancestry.

Eliot was perhaps too restrained to be a satirist, too considerate of persons to make enemies. His polemics were severe but they were parliamentary. However, when he writes about the state of modern society, or about politics, or about the Jews, he borrows sometimes the rhetoric of reaction of writers like Charles Maurras, Paul Claudel, or Pound.

Eliot's support for extreme right-wing politics was curbed after 1927 by his Christianity. In editing *The Criterion* he became, despite his conservative views, almost liberal in admitting writers who expressed a great variety of opinions, including those of the young Communists. In his dealings with younger writers he was gentle, helpful, and tolerant, and never expressed disapproval of their politics. Auden once remarked to me that of all the older writers with whom we had dealings, Eliot was the most consistently friendly, the least malicious, envious, and vain.

However, it would be doing less than justice to Eliot

as poet and critic to present him simply as a figure of universal benevolence. Under the kindness there was a penetrating intelligence, under the intelligence irony, and under the irony an almost Swiftian ferocity. The ferocity was closely allied to his daimon and to attitudes of a severity alien to most modern minds: for instance, his goal of love beyond that of created human beings. He knew extremes of ice and fire, and of the dark night of the soul. He is most a poet when he is describing extreme conditions, and the Dantesque circumference which is drawn around his work is of consciousness always at the most extreme state of awareness of horror or boredom or glory.

The mood of "Ode" (full title: "Ode on Independence Day, July 4th, 1918," a poem first published in *Ara Vos Prec* in 1920 and not republished in *Poems, 1920*) is one of ferocity and despair. Evidently the events to which it refers are of an intensely personal kind and are given a deliberately hermetic form. The fact that each section, or division, of the poem begins with a word expressing anguish is significant. These key words are: "Tired," which precedes the first section (of four lines); "Misunderstood" the second (of two lines); "Tortured" the third (of six lines); "Tortuous," the concluding section (of seven lines).

The first section runs:

> *Tired.*
> *Subterrene laughter synchronous*
> *With silence from the sacred wood*
> *And bubbling of the uninspired*
> *Mephitic river.*

The third section:

> *Tortured.*
> *When the bridegroom smoothed his hair*
> *There was blood upon the bed.*

Morning was already late.
Children singing in the orchard
(Io Hymen, Hymenaee)
Succuba eviscerate.

The poem is arid, dead almost, yet it is like a message scribbled on the back of an envelope which contains the first sketched idea of a great invention. This method will later explode in *The Waste Land.* The key idea is that the private failure of the sacrifice and sacrament, which is ritual between bride and bridegroom, is the result of the public failure of creativity within the civilization. The association is made between the ceremony that is poetry and that derives from rituals of culture, and the personal relationship between two people.

"Ode" is, as I say, scarcely more than arid notes, but it contains the secret of a method. The other poems in *Ara Vos Prec* are in quatrains derived from Gautier's *Emaux et camées* and used with great effect by Pound in *Hugh Selwyn Mauberley.* The quatrains do not come naturally to Eliot. In them he is very consciously writing for the eye, not so much imagist poetry, as poems based on metaphors from the visual arts. The scenario of "The Hippopotamus" is like a primitive religious wall painting:

I saw the 'potamus take wing
Ascending from the damp savannas,
And quiring angels round him sing
The praise of God, in loud hosannas.

"Whispers of Immortality," with "the skull beneath the skin," where ". . . breastless creatures under ground /Leaned backward with a lipless grin," belongs to funeral monuments, dark engravings, and woodcuts of tombstones, or the famous seventeenth-century engraving of Donne's monument in St. Paul's cathedral. In "Mr. Eliot's Sunday Morning Service" the picture by a painter of the Umbrian School, is, I suppose, suggested by *The Baptism of Christ* by Piero della Francesca in the National Gallery of London. "Sweeney Erect" evokes directly the painter's art: "Paint me a cavernous waste shore / Cast in the unstilled Cyclades." "Sweeney Among the Nightingales" is some ghoulish *Sweeney Todd* or *Murder in the Red Barn* stage set.

The "Sweeney" poems, then, have a stiff, rigid, static quality not characteristic of Eliot's other poems, perhaps because the others are based on metaphors with music.

In *The Achievement of T. S. Eliot*, to which I have already referred, F. O. Matthiessen shows himself eager to defend Eliot from the charge of making, in the "Sweeney" poems, crude comparisons of life today with the past—much to the advantage of the past. He writes of "Sweeney Among the Nightingales":

> The contrast that seems at first to be mocking a debased present as it juxtaposes Sweeney with the hero of antiquity, ends in establishing also an undercurrent of moving drama: for a sympathetic feeling for Sweeney is set up by the realization that he is a man as well as Agamemnon, and that his plotted death is therefore likewise a human tragedy, as the end of Agamemnon's career was also sordid.[3]

This seems too defensive. It also seems misleading to interpret this savage caricature as a picture in which "Apeneck Sweeney," who "spreads his knees / Letting his hands hang down to laugh, The zebra stripes along his jaw / Swelling to maculate giraffe," meets the tragically butchered Agamemnon on the grounds of a common humanity. Agamemnon, for Eliot, belongs to

[3] F. O. Matthiessen, *The Achievement of T. S. Eliot*, p. 129.

the opaque primitive Greek world of murder and vengeance, not the luminous Virgilian one of Roman civilization. It is the Greece of Nietzsche's *The Birth of Tragedy*—eyes cut open onto frightful darkness. If there is common ground, it is perhaps of horror and violence—indeed, of inhumanity. Matthiessen is right, however, in pointing out that Eliot is not, in these poems, crudely comparing the present and past. He is not nostalgic in the manner of, say, the German poet Stefan George, who simply sees the past as a terrible sermon delivered by inscriptions on Roman monuments to the debased present. Eliot paints in these pictures the past and the present as though they shared one plane of time. There is no nostalgia and no archaism. Sweeney is depicted sprawling in the foreground of the canvas, and Agamemnon is seen, as it were, through a door or at the end of a corridor. The contrast is between the rituals of contemporary violence and those of Greek tragedy. There is not any feeling—as there would be in nostalgic poetry—that the poet or reader can choose between them: could choose, in feeling and imagination, to renounce the present and live spiritually in the Greek past. What is stated, within the context of the modern, is the clash of rituals of the Greek tragedy, of the sacraments of the Convent of the Sacred Heart, and of the ignoble, debased, mock-rituals of modern life. Sweeney and Agamemnon share the horror and violence of their ancient and modern melodrama.

"Sweeney Among the Nightingales" is, then, a violent cartoon, depicted with a ferocity which foreshadows the work of Francis Bacon (who has painted a triptych recording his impressions of Eliot's fragmentary play *Sweeney Agonistes*). The hatred for life in some of these poems approaches that of Swift, horrified by the flesh when he reiterates in a poem the phrase "Celia shits!" But there is also the extraordinary precision and

beautiful art of wit, which fixes these poems with a
sharpness and clarity unequaled in any other of Eliot's
writings. One aspect of his virtuosity is to cram these
poems with allusions and quotations from other writers
(and from paintings). The very epigraph of "Burbank
with a Baedeker: Bleistein with a Cigar" contains excerpts strung together from Gautier, Henry James,
Byron, Shakespeare, Browning—and also the Latin in-
scription written in Mantegna's hand on his portrait of
Saint Sebastian in the Accadèmia in Venice ("nothing
endures except that which is divine; all else is smoke"
[beautiful, the Latin: *"nil nisi divinum stabile est;
caetera fumus"*]).

This poem is about the visit of an American (a
cultivated Henry James character) called Burbank, to
Venice, where he falls prey to a certain Princess Volupine. In a satirically pompous and ironic passage, the
fall of Burbank is compared to that of Mark Antony
enamored of Cleopatra (with its sequel of defunctive
music and the departure from Antony of the God
Hercules). However, Bleistein, "Chicago Semite Viennese," arrives and carries off the Princess Volupine. The
victory of Bleistein over Burbank is regarded as symptomatic of the decline of Venice (studied by Ruskin,
to whom there is reference).

> *A lustreless protrusive eye*
> *   Stares from the protozoic slime*
> *At a perspective of Canaletto.*
> *   The smoky candle end of time*
>
> *Declines. . . .*

This, with its allusion to Mantegna's *"caetera fumus,"*
leaves us with little doubt that Burbank reads the situation as a symptom of the decline of the culture. He ends
with a Jamesian or an Eliotian traveler's thought:

> *. . . Who clipped the lion's wings*
> *And flea'd his rump and pared his claws?*
> *Thought Burbank, meditating on*
> *Time's ruins, and the seven laws.*

The answer to this question is already conveyed and, in the widest context, it is political:

> *The rats are underneath the piles.*
> *The jew is underneath the lot.*
> *Money in furs. . . .*

The stanza quoted has (together with other such asides by Eliot) aroused great indignation on account of its flash anti-Semitism. I shall not attempt to put up any defense of Eliot about this. It scarcely helps to say that in 1918 or 1919 such a reference to the Jew as a symbol of capitalist-industrialist exploitation was hardly more prejudicial than it would be today to refer to the "Scot" as cheese-paring. However, I respect Eliot for not having tried to edit out of his early poems views which he himself later came to regard as reprehensible. (I might add that in the thirty-five years of my acquaintance with him I never heard him utter an anti-Semitic remark.)

These poems give the effect of being painted in primary colors, with each section being contrasted stridently with another to which it sometimes seems very obscurely related. The most obscure is "A Cooking Egg," which begins:

> *Pipit sate upright in her chair*
> *Some distance from where I was sitting;*
> Views of Oxford Colleges
> *Lay on the table, with the knitting.*
>
> *Daguerreotypes and silhouettes,*
> *Her grandfather and great great aunts,*

> *Supported on the mantelpiece*
> *An* Invitation to the Dance.

The poem then switches abruptly to an ironic vision of
the author transported to heaven. After reflecting on
the pleasures of an immortality shared with Sir Philip
Sidney and Coriolanus for Honour, Sir Alfred Mond (a
well-known Jewish financier of that time) for Capital,
and Lucretia Borgia (to be his bride) for Society, the
poet reflects that he will "not want Pipit in Heaven,"
because Madame Blavatsky will instruct him "In the
Seven Sacred Trances" (a swipe at W. B. Yeats). The
poem then rockets into a shower of brilliant questions:

> *But where is the penny world I bought*
> *To eat with Pipit behind the screen?*
> *The red-eyed scavengers are creeping*
> *From Kentish Town and Golder's Green;*
>
> *Where are the eagles and the trumpets?*
>
> *Buried beneath some snow-deep Alps.*
> *Over buttered scones and crumpets*
> *Weeping, weeping multitudes*
> *Droop in a hundred A.B.C.'s*

This conclusion is a great rhetorical and technical
success—the explosive questions breaking beyond the
form, so that an extra line is interpolated between the
two concluding stanzas, with the effect of a voice, or a
great patch of light, clanging brassily between clouds.

"Whispers of Immortality," with its magnificent opening:

> *Webster was much possessed by death*
> *And saw the skull beneath the skin;*
> *And breastless creatures under ground*
> *Leaned backward with a lipless grin.*

is the greatest success among the poems of this first phase. In four stanzas of sustained stark imagery Eliot enters into that sensuality of the post-Elizabethan era which identifies passionate feelings about love with those about death—flesh and skeleton. The parallel with a modern situation "works" here where in the other poems it seems a bit imposed; for Eliot at times seemed to see the decadence and disillusionment, the horror and sensationalism of the seventeenth-century imagination and his own modern vision as a historic unity. The part of the poem dealing with the contemporary scene, with Grishkin of the uncorseted bust giving "promise of pneumatic bliss," introduces, of course, the note of the "tawdry cheapness" of our days which is in contrast with the sensual horror of Webster and Donne. But the two pictures are fused in the concept of dryness of bones, dryness of abstraction in the last two lines:

> But our lot crawls between dry ribs
> To keep our metaphysics warm.

The "Sweeney" poems are the narrations of an extremely detached ironic observer. They have the essential quality of satire, which is that they are by an outsider who makes glaring caricatures of contemporary life, occasionally contrasting them with flashbacks—backward glances—from the New Testament or from Greek tragedy.

With "Gerontion" there is a complete and dramatic change of attitude. The "I" who is narrator of the poem is no longer an outsider. Quite the contrary, he is the very center of the poem. His narration consists of the laying bare of his symptoms, which are indistinguishable from those of contemporary civilization. He is the decay of history become conscious in him. Gerontion has no character apart from the attitudes and symptoms he reveals, which are those of Christian civilization in its senescence. The poem is about what the man—who is as old as the civilization itself—sees. The reader does not stand outside "Gerontion" in the way that he does outside the "Sweeney" poems. He is drawn into the vortex of conscious history. He is made to see that he also is corrupted by living within the decadent civilization, and that he cannot be other than corrupted by it. All he can do is attain to that degree of consciousness, which includes both the past and the present, where he can see himself, through the eyes of Gerontion, as belonging to the senescent stage of its life—history. By looking at himself from a point of view which includes the past, he can see that he is conditioned by circumstances which have destroyed the values of the past.

"Gerontion" is an important stage in Eliot's development, leading toward *The Waste Land*, in which he wished to include it: but was dissuaded from so doing by Ezra Pound, on the grounds that *The Waste Land* was already "the longest poem in the English language." A better reason for excluding it might be that Eliot was experimenting in this poem which, after thirty-two lines, becomes enwebbed in the style which Eliot borrows from the Jacobean playwright Cyril Tourneur.

The opening of the poem comes near to creating Gerontion as a mythical character from antiquity, like Tennyson's Ulysses. One can almost see Gerontion seated in Hades, in these lines:

Here I am, an old man in a dry month,
Being read to by a boy, waiting for rain.
I was neither at the hot gates
Nor fought in the warm rain
Nor knee deep in the salt marsh, heaving a cutlass,
Bitten by flies, fought.

The picture of Gerontion as a historic-mythical character is immediately dissipated by our being told that he lives in "a decayed house, /And the jew squats on the window sill, the owner . . ." Gerontion has moved from an undefined antiquity into an undefined later, perhaps quite modern, time. Nevertheless, something Rembrandtesque about the stage properties of the opening lines—the cutlass, being read to by a boy, Antwerp, Brussels, London, the goat, the woman "poking the peevish gutter"—stretches across time and holds the picture together up to this point.

In the lines that follow, any picture that we may have been forming in our minds of Gerontion as a character disintegrates, as it were, into the atoms of the fragmented civilization, held together now only by memories of exhortations, rather than by the exhortations themselves, and by a ghostly rhetoric. The thoughts of Gerontion are the dreams of the civilization that burst on the world, with Christ—"Christ the tiger." The true rituals have become dissolved in the decadence of history.

Signs are taken for wonders. "We would see a sign!"
The word within a word, unable to speak a word,
Swaddled with darkness. In the juvescence of the year
Came Christ the tiger

The line about "The word within a word" is taken from a Nativity sermon of 1618 by Bishop Lancelot Andrewes, a theologian and writer, subject of an admiring essay by Eliot.[4] Bishop Andrewes, to his believing audience, preached the wonder of the Incarnation realized in the wordless child, the Word of God. Eliot is quoting him with bitter irony to contrast "the juvescence of the year" of the beginning of the Christian era signified by "Christ the tiger" with the contemporary

---

[4] See "Lancelot Andrewes," in *Selected Essays*, pp. 349–53.

world that makes a mockery of the true rituals. "Came
Christ the tiger"

*In depraved May, dogwood and chestnut, flowering
    judas,*
To be eaten, to be divided, to be drunk
Among whispers; by Mr. Silvero
With caressing hands, at Limoges
Who walked all night in the next room;

By Hakagawa, bowing among the Titians;
By Madame de Tornquist, in the dark room
Shifting the candles; Fräulein von Kulp
*Who turned in the hall, one hand on the door. Vacant
    shuttles*
Weave the wind. I have no ghosts,
An old man in a draughty house
Under a windy knob.

Eliot excels in this poem in an effect at which he
always shows great brilliance: condemning attitudes
by attaching to them names and gestures which are in
themselves prejudicial. By merely inventing a name
like Fräulein von Kulp he can evoke in us the punishing
hatred we have felt in a lodging house, say in Vienna,
for some unknown person in the next room who keeps
us awake all night by expectorating in a peculiarly dis-
gusting manner which we involuntarily seize upon as
being the expression of her Central European personality. Eliot invents names for such targets of what seems
an atavistic righteous indignation. Cosmopolitans, who
signify for him the debasement of the sacraments of
religion and art, are encapsulated in these thumbnail
sketches.

Halfway through the poem, with the question "After
such knowledge, what forgiveness?" Eliot introduces a
passage which is haunted by lines from Tourneur's *The*

Revenger's Tragedy (c. 1606). In this dark and horrify-ing scene, Vindice, the hero, addresses the skull of his mistress:

> *Does the silkworm expend her yellow labours*
> *For thee? For thee does she undo herself?*
> *Are lordships sold to maintain ladyships*
> *For the poor benefit of a bewildering minute?*

Eliot enters so thoroughly into the idea that the deca-dence, violence, intrigues, villainy, and deviousness of the Jacobean world of corridors and mirrors correspond to the post-1918 Europe, that the parallel of the post-Elizabethan disillusionment, with its haunting decayed poetry, takes over the rest of the poem. "History" would perhaps be a very good subject of rhetoric for a character in a play by Webster or Tourneur; Gerontion now assumes the voice of such a character in *The Revenger's Tragedy* or Webster's *The White Devil*:

>   *Think now*
> *History has many cunning passages, contrived corridors*
> *And issues, deceives with whispering ambitions,*
> *Guides us by vanities. Think now*
> *She gives when our attention is distracted*
> *And what she gives, gives with such supple confusions*
> *That the giving famishes the craving. Gives too late*
> *What's not believed in, or if still believed,*
> *In memory only, reconsidered passion. . . .*

The lines are obscure in the sense that cunning pas-sages and contrived passages are dark. It is the obscurity, grasped by the imagination, which makes what is being said relevant. For it needs imagination to grasp the idea that the history of a civilization is a process of aging which results, among those who live in it, in the cor-ruption of faith and will, the frustration and perversion of action. There is not merely a loss of faith in the myths

and virtues on which the civilization originally flourished, but it becomes impossible to believe in them except vicariously, through remembering the past, now
completely inaccessible as springs of present action.

If the second half of "Gerontion" doesn't really convince on the levels of imagination or of intellectual
argument, this is because the attempt to draw a parallel
between Jacobean plays about political intrigues at small
Italian courts and the situation of Europe at the time of
the signing of the Treaty of Versailles doesn't work. The
modern political theme, which affects the whole world,
is being forced through too narrow a channel. The
sinister backstairs post-Elizabethan atmosphere is hypnotic rather than illuminating. Critics have suggested
that "contrived corridors" and, some lines later, "a
wilderness of mirrors" are images suggested by the intrigues of the peacemakers in 1918 in the Versailles Hall
of Mirrors to establish a "Polish corridor." If this is so,
it seems less silly to say that the Polish corridor and the
Versailles mirrors put a Jacobean poetic thought in
Eliot's head than that the pastiche Jacobean poetry sig-
nificantly evokes the Europe of Clemenceau and Lloyd
George. In this poem, for once, Eliot has gone back to
the past without discovering there an idiom which he
transforms into something as modern as the present.
The failure becomes obvious, I think, if one compares
"Gerontion" with Yeats's poem "The Second Coming,"
written at much the same time, and also about the collapse of the Western civilization whose origins are indicated as the coming of Christ. Yeats states in six lines
what Eliot conveys indirectly through his long passage
of Jacobean pastiche:

> *Things fall apart: the centre cannot hold;*
> *Mere anarchy is loosed upon the world,*
> *The blood-dimmed tide is loosed, and everywhere*

> *The ceremony of innocence is drowned;*
> *The best lack all conviction, while the worst*
> *Are full of passionate intensity.*

The tone of these lines is Biblical, apocalyptic, and Aeschylean, and it is this which Eliot was to adopt in *The Waste Land*:

> *What are the roots that clutch, what branches grow*
> *Out of this stony rubbish? . . .*

"Gerontion" loses direction when Eliot goes down that dangerous, insidious, tempting, post-Elizabethan tunnel: the same that Shelley lost himself in, in *The Cenci*. Eliot attempts to pull the poem back to its starting point by repeating themes of "Christ the tiger" and the "rented house"; but they seem dragged in and obstruct the Jacobean flow:

> *The tiger springs in the new year. Us he devours. Think*
> *   at last*
> *We have not reached conclusion, when I*
> *Stiffen in a rented house . . . .*

The tone and the speaking character change again in the lines that follow, which seem contemporary and personal though tricked out in Jacobean brocade and grease paint:

> *I would meet you upon this honestly.*
> *I that was near your heart was removed therefrom*
> *To lose beauty in terror, terror in inquisition.*
> *I have lost my passion: why should I need to keep it*
> *Since what is kept must be adulterated?*
> *I have lost my sight, smell, hearing, taste and touch:*
> *How should I use them for your closer contact?*

Contemporary private neurosis is here being attributed to historic causes. The corruption of the time is such that, removed from that spring when Christ the tiger came, it is impossible within a decayed and senile history, to think, act, judge, taste, other than corruptly. This idea, whether or not historically justified is a development perhaps of the "decadence" which characterized the French literature Eliot so greatly admired. Decadence is seen as the "decline of the West" corrupting the whole society, and the lives of the individuals living in it. This was, of course, a view very prevalent after the World War I. It takes the form not so much of concentrating, like the poets of the 1890s, on the effeteness and decadence of a particular period, as of surveying the whole civilization and seeing every period, particularly in its art and culture, as symptomatic of its history. Thus Yeats relates the phases of European history to the metaphor of the changes of the moon extending over the 2000 years of Western civilization, from the birth of Christ to the present century. Pound sees the introduction of usury and the modern banking system into Florence in the fourteenth century as a moral fissure which corrupted the once-pure lines drawn by Italian artists of the early Renaissance. This way of looking at civilization led to the personification of history (become at that time heavily political) in the 1930s. It seems to receive its apotheosis as farce in Auden's line about his generation: "History seems to have struck a bad patch."

After the strong first part of "Gerontion," the poem becomes lost in its own corridors and dark passages. It is not so much obscure as cryptic. Eliot is not, of course, writing a didactic poem about the effects of history and the decay of the Christian faith on his life and culture. The subject of the poem is only an occasion which becomes transformed into the poetry. The trouble is that the subject becomes not so much transformed

as entangled in the highly metaphorical style of Tourneur's *Revenger's Tragedy.* The poem is strange, weird,
wonderful, but ultimately private to Eliot's view of the
parallel of modern Europe with the Machiavellian scene
of Italian courts as depicted by the post-Elizabethan
dramatists. Given the tragic content of the poetry—
which is about the breakdown of civilization reflected in
the breakdown of the personal life—the poet is *enjoying*
—or indulging—himself a bit too masochistically: as
though turning his favorite horror stories of contemporary life into his favorite Jacobean horror stories. The
last part of "Gerontion" hovers ambiguously between
tragic statement and black farce, with high "camp"
thrown in at the end. The difficulty is that the reader
does not know on what level of tragedy or farce to take
the ending:

> *What will the spider do,*
> *Suspend its operations, will the weevil*
> *Delay? De Bailhache, Fresca, Mrs. Cammel, whirled*
> *Beyond the circuit of the shuddering Bear*
> *In fractured atoms. Gull against the wind, in the windy*
> *   straits*
> *Of Belle Isle, or running on the Horn*
> *White feathers in the snow, the Gulf claims,*
> *And an old man driven by the Trades*
> *To a sleepy corner.*
> *   Tenants of the house,*
> *Thoughts of a dry brain in a dry season.*

These are statements in which the comical *almost*
merges with the tragic, just as the tragic does completely merge into the heartbreakingly, cosmically funny
at the end of *King Lear,* or in that scene in *War and
Peace* when Pierre Bezukhov rushes into a house in burn-

ing Moscow to rescue a baby—who turns around and bites him. The end of "Gerontion" is a bit too "literary," too much of a *tour de force* to achieve an explosive fusion of the farce with the tragedy of the civilization in decline. This fusion takes place in the last section of *The Waste Land.*

Poet-Critic, Critic-Poet

V In 1961, in a lecture entitled "To Criticize the Critic," Eliot offered some opinions about his early criticism, with something of that air of a man reflecting on his life in some previous incarnation which so amused Wyndham Lewis. On the whole, this young fellow Eliot, while providing him with some surprises, did the sexagenarian more credit than he had expected: "I am happy to say that I did not find quite so much to be ashamed of as I had feared." But, Eliot added, in words which Lewis might have relished, "There are statements the meaning of which I no longer understand." He deplored, too, certain errors of judgment, "errors of tone: the occasional note of arrogance, of vehemence, of cocksureness or rudeness, the braggadocio of the mild-mannered man safely entrenched behind his typewriter." "Yet," he concluded, "I must acknowledge my relationship to the man who

made these statements, and in spite of all these excep-
tions, I continue to identify myself with the author"
(*To Criticize the Critic*, p. 14). The ghost of the younger
Eliot must have felt grateful for these kind words.

He describes his criticism as a "by-product" of his
"creative activity" and observes that in his early critical
writings he was "implicitly defending the sort of poetry
that I and my friends wrote. . . . I was in reaction, not
only against Georgian poetry but against Georgian criticism; I was writing in a context which the reader today has either forgotten, or has never experienced"
(*ibid.*, p. 16).

He divides his early essays into "the essays of gen-
eralization (such as "Tradition and the Individual
Talent") and "those of appreciation of individual
authors" and says that he prefers the latter, and of
them, the essays on minor Elizabethans to those on
Shakespeare, because it was "from these minor dramatists that I had learned my lessons."

But the division scarcely holds. In fact, some of the
most striking generalizations appear in essays on individual writers: for example, the famous theory of the
"objective correlative":

> the only way of expressing emotion in the form of
> art by finding an objective correlative; in other words,
> a set of objects, a situation, a chain of events which
> shall be the formula of that *particular* emotion; such
> that when the external facts, which must terminate in
> sensory experience, are given, the emotion is im-
> mediately evoked. . . . (*Selected Essays*, p. 145)

appears in the essay on *Hamlet*. Here the poet, writing
criticism, invents metaphors describing the *process*
which results in a poem, the *measuring* which relates
the new work of art to the works of the past tradition,

the *mechanism* of poetic inevitability—the scientific exactness of the process. Eliot may, when he was old, have pretended that he had not the faintest idea what the young Eliot meant by the "objective correlative," but for most readers it is a critic's poem about what happens when a poet produces a phrase which seems inevitable:

> If you examine any of Shakespeare's more successful tragedies, you will find this exact equivalence; you will find that the state of mind of Lady Macbeth walking in her sleep has been communicated to you by a skilful accumulation of imagined sensory impressions; the words of Macbeth on hearing of his wife's death strike us as if, given the sequence of events, these words were automatically released by the last event in the series. (*Ibid.*)

What Macbeth says on hearing of his wife's death, "She should have died hereafter," certainly has an appropriateness of genius but does not, as a response, without Eliot's analysis, absolutely convince one that Shakespeare might not have put some other observation into Macbeth's mouth that would strike the audience as being equally appropriate. It does not detract from the excitement of visualizing. The fact is that one is left dubious by theories of poetic inevitability, even when they are called the "objective correlative," the operation of poetic logic as the performance of an exquisitely organized and functioning machine—a matter of wheels and pistons or cells working harmoniously to issue the exact but completely surprising result.

In these early essays Eliot invents metaphors that enable one to *see*, in the mind's eye, the relation of the new work of art to the whole past tradition. To say that he has a tendency to see these functions, relations, and logical performances as mechanical models, may make his criticism sound unpoetic. But the reverse is true. Just as Jean Cocteau's title for his modern version of the tragedy of Oedipus, *La Machine infernale*, is a convincing poetic metaphor for the system that is Greek tragedy, so Eliot's metaphors are a kind of prose poetry. What adds to all this is that the young poet brings a certain romantic excitement to bear on scientific metaphor—for the ideas, even, of the poet as scientist, of poetry as a science, and of criticism as scientific analysis. He made the idea of scientific criticism alive to a generation of new critics.

He can, of course, be brash in his terminology. The crudest use of the scientific metaphor in his criticism occurs when, in "Tradition and the Individual Talent" (1919), he compares the poet's mind to "a receptacle for seizing and storing up numberless feelings, phrases, images, which remain there until all the particles which can unite to form a new compound are present together" (*Selected Essays*, p. 19). The analogy is to the process of depersonalization, which reduces the poet's sensibility to chemical reaction to material fed into it in a manner approaching "the condition of science." The comparison is with the "action which takes place when a bit of finely filiated platinum is introduced into a chamber containing oxygen and sulphur dioxide" (*Selected Essays*, p. 17). This is probably the most pretentious and most questionable of his scientific analogies. The scientific model tends to distract from the poetic behavior it is supposed to describe and focuses the reader on the model itself—and on the young Mr. Eliot held up before the reader as a white-coated laboratory assistant.

Much more compelling is the famous metaphor set up to demonstrate the relation of the new work of art to past monuments. In "Tradition and the Individual Talent," the passage runs:

No poet, no artist of any art, has his complete meaning alone. His significance, his appreciation is the appreciation of his relation to the dead poets and artists. You cannot value him alone; you must set him, for contrast and comparison, among the dead. I mean this as a principle of aesthetic, not merely historical, criticism. The necessity that he shall conform, that he shall cohere, is not onesided; what happens when a new work of art is created is something that happens simultaneously to all the works of art which preceded it. The existing monuments form an ideal order among themselves, which is modified by the introduction of the new (the really new) work of art among them. The existing order is complete before the new work arrives; for order to persist after the supervention of novelty, the *whole* existing order must be, if ever so slightly, altered; and so the relations, proportions, values of each work of art toward the whole are readjusted; and this is conformity between the old and the new. Whoever has approved this idea of order, of the form of European, of English literature will not find it preposterous that the past should be altered by the present as much as the present is directed by the past. And the poet who is aware of this will be aware of great difficulties and responsibilities. (*Selected Essays*, p. 15)

The poet is looked on here as a depersonalized mind measuring the past monuments and relating to their scale the new work produced, while the tradition is seen as an organic system of relations established in the past which adapts itself in an evolutionary way to new conditions through objective procedures taking place in the mind of the living artist.

This picture of the tradition as a system like a functioning mechanism can be taken seriously on the imaginative level but not literally as a scientific working model. It is both serious and witty, in the manner of metaphors of the metaphysical poets. Eliot is not making a blueprint, diagrammatically explaining the relations between the tradition and the creativity of the contemporary artist, in the manner of a model of atomic structure in a science museum. His dogmatically stated metaphors are modified or softened by the introduction of mysteriously qualifying words—puzzling or baffling as these may be. The word "really" in the parenthesis "the really new" is teasing. For if what is new is objectively measurable, there would be no need to qualify it by the word "really."

Eliot the critic-poet-scientist is also a mystifier. Put the mystifier and scientist together, and he acquires some of the characteristics of the priest pronouncing a ritual. Very characteristic of such mystification is the passage in which Eliot qualifies the "scientist's" severe view that poetry is not a turning loose of emotion but an escape from emotion, not an expression of personality but an escape from personality, with the remark "But, of course, only those who have personality and emotions know what it means to want to escape from these things" (*Selected Essays*, p. 21).

Another example of Eliot's use of metaphor is the famous passage in his essay on "The Metaphysical Poets" (1921) that the difference "between the time of Donne or Lord Herbert of Cherbury and the time of Tennyson and Browning . . . is the difference between the intellectual poet and the reflective poet. Tennyson and Browning are poets, and they think; but they do not feel their thought as immediately as the odour of a rose. A thought of Donne was an experience; it modified his sensibility" (*Selected Essays*, p. 287).

Eliot goes on to develop the metaphor, or illustration,

into a theory that "the poets of the seventeenth century, the successors of the sixteenth, possessed a mechanism of sensibility which could devour any kind of experience. They are simple, artificial, difficult, or fantastic, as their predecessors were; no less nor more than Dante, Guido Cavalcanti, Guinicelli, or Cino" (*Selected Essays,* pp. 287–88). (The names of Guinicelli and Cino, are, I suspect, a bravura Poundian touch, thrown in to alarm and dismay the reader.) The "theory," which turns out to be another metaphor drawn from seeing the sensibility acting like an organism that devours things, has been much disputed. For it is as little demonstrable that Donne felt his "thought as immediately as the odour of a rose" as that something called the "organic community" flourished in the English countryside at one time: an idea which sprang perhaps from Eliot's metaphor for the organic, natural, sensuous connection between thinking and feeling which existed up to the seventeenth century.

These metaphors crystallize the idea of sets of relations between the poetic sensibility and the material it works on. Like poems they have a power of survival even when the theories which arise from them are disputed. Matthew Arnold, writing that Shelley was "an ineffectual angel beating in the air his luminous wings in vain," was writing a poem of this kind (in a metaphor which finds an echo in lines of *Ash Wednesday:* "Because these wings are no longer wings to fly / But merely vans to beat the air / The air which is now thoroughly small and dry"). To be told that Shelley had considerable influence on English Socialists does not alter the fact that Arnold's beautiful quip stings to the heart of Shelley's rose.

The personal drama concealed in Eliot's early criticism (in this respect again he resembles Keats in his letters) is of the young poet seeing himself under the cliff of the whole great tradition of poetry and choosing his ancestors. His traditionalism becomes creative when, with his eye on his own poetry he selects, for example, the passage from *The Revenger's Tragedy*, quoted above (p. 63), in which the reader recognizes the rhythm and the sepulchral convolutedness—ghostly corridors—of "Gerontion." Knowing Eliot's poetry doubles one's pleasure in his essays on *Four Elizabethan Dramatists* (1924). One reads into them—and especially in the passages quoted—not only the poetry discussed but also *The Waste Land* and the "Sweeney" poems. And this is a pleasure one rarely gets from the later criticism.

The polemics of the early criticism—in step here with Ezra Pound—are directed not only against Georgians, or post-Swinburneans but also against Milton, Shelley, Swinburne, and, in certain respects, the "provincial" Blake.

Eliot's polemical strategies gave rise to fear, envy, and resentment among some of his contemporaries. Illustration of this hostility is to be found in a story by Richard Aldington, called *Stepping Heavenward*, which includes a caricature of an American poet called Cibber who conquers England and the world by subtle self-promotion, a portrait clearly based on the career of T. S. Eliot. Among much which is as obtuse as it is envious and spiteful, Aldington does make a pointed analysis of Cibber's polemical criticism. He describes the "oblique method," "which Cibber made so formidable," in these words: it is "always to create by destruction, to seek truth for oneself by exposing the errors of others." Eliot's essay on "Euripides and Professor Murray" (1920) is perhaps an example of what Aldington had in mind. Eliot attacks Murray's translations of Euripides on the grounds that the great scholar, "the most conspicuous Greek propagandist of the day . . .

almost habitually use(s) two words where the Greek language requires one" (*Selected Essays*, p. 61), and he gives examples of Murray introducing striking phrases into his translation which are not in the Greek. What is surprising about this attack is that the demolition of Gilbert Murray for introducing unnecessary words and home-made English phrases into his translations is used as the occasion for promoting the far less accurate ones of Ezra Pound. There is certainly something "oblique" about this. To those capable of comparing Pound's scholarship with Murray's, it must have seemed grossly unfair. However, Eliot is really attacking Murray not on account of his ignorance of Greek but because his versions of Euripides are fitted into "the loose frame of William Morris" and "blur the Greek lyric to the fluid haze of Swinburne." He wants to destroy Murray's translations because he sees them as themselves destructive: both of the Greek and of the English into which they are rendered and which is, as language in the modern circumstances, not equivalent of the Greek in the Euripidean circumstances. This leads Eliot to one of his strongest affirmations. After remarking that to translate the Greek classics "we need a digestion which can assimilate both Homer and Flaubert" (a bone thrown to James Joyce) and "we need a careful study of Renaissance Humanists and Translators, such as Mr. Pound has begun," he pronounces: "We need an eye which can see the past in its place with its definite differences from the present, and yet so lively that it shall be as present to us as the present. This is the creative eye; and it is because Professor Murray has no creative instinct that he leaves Euripides quite dead" (*Selected Essays*, p. 64).

It is significant here that Eliot views translation as being identical with creative writing. For translating was essential to the program of re-creating the past in its pastness within the presentness of the present. The idiomatic modern translation—as old as the original, as new as the mind of the contemporary translator— provided a model for that re-creation of the tradition within the contemporary which was the aim of Eliot and Pound, then very consciously intent to be modern, as also to be traditional. In translation the poet made himself midwife of the past born into the present. Thus Pound, the most proselytizing of moderns, made a great many translations in which he was concerned far more with carrying forward the spirit of the old into the idiom and form of the modern, than with the meaning.

There was an element of translation in many works which were not imitations. In *Ulysses*, James Joyce, making a parallel between events in the *Odyssey* and those in modern Dublin, was translating episodes from the Homeric world into his plot of Leopold Bloom/Odysseus and Stephen Dedalus/Telemachus. In *The Waste Land* the quotations from works in several languages— torn out of their original contexts to be pieced into those of modern London life—are, in a very literal way, translations—carryings over. The method of "collage" is a form of translation.

In his early essay "The Function of Criticism" (1923), we see Eliot struggling with the problem of what standards of judgment should be applied to literature. He is divided between the view that literature provides its own standards (which may be discovered by analyzing and comparing a great many works) and the view that there are values outside it—called those of Classicism and Catholicism—to be applied. At the end he comes down (provisionally, I think) in favor of what he calls fact: that a great many facts about the work itself and the conditions from which it arose (its conditions, its setting, its genesis) should be mastered and then brought to bear on the work. Then we shall have not "opinion or fancy," which is corrupt, but the truth about the work, and in that truth there will lie judgment.

"The sense of fact," Eliot writes, "is something very slow to develop, and its complete development means perhaps the very pinnacle of civilization" (*Selected Essays*, p. 31). Coming from a writer who always raised eyebrows at any exalted claim for literature (Matthew Arnold's remark that poetry at bottom is criticism of life causes him to comment, "at bottom: that is a great way down; the bottom is the bottom"), this pinnacle seems too exalted. Through his appeal to fact as a basis of literary judgment, Eliot is, indeed, in danger of falling into the trap of a utilitarian argument. Comparison of facts leads us to discriminate between what is good and bad. Agreed, but the criterion of good and bad cannot simply be the facts themselves. Why approve one fact more than another if there are no standards but facts? Some other standard is being appealed to when we call the sense of fact the "pinnacle of civilization."

We are left with the impression that in this essay Eliot is striving toward some principle of judgment which he has not found. The essay is indeed important in laying so much stress on close analysis, and it germinated the New Criticism. Eliot certainly was justified in emphasizing the importance of analysis in fact-finding and comparison, even in the idea that facts should provide the basis of cooperative activity between like-minded critics. The idea of shared research and the application of shared principles of comparison appealed to the side of him that liked at this time to think of criticism—even, in large part, of creativity— as shared laboratory tests and experiments. The fusion of criticism and creativity would be a fusion of poetry with science: "Probably . . . the larger part of the

labour of an author in composing his work is critical
labour; the labour of sifting, combining, constructing,
expunging, correcting, testing: this frightful toil is as
much critical as creative" (*Selected Essays*, p. 35). He
goes on to say that "some creative writers are superior"
to others solely because their critical faculty is superior.
And it is "Whiggery" to suppose anything else. ("Whiggery" is an evil which can merely be detected, like a
bad smell, without resource to any great accumulation
of fact.)

Having brought creation and criticism together in the
fusion of the creative act, Eliot is anxious to separate
them again. "The critical activity finds its highest, its
truest fulfilment in a kind of union with creation in the
labour of the artist." But "a creation, a work of art, is
autotelic," whereas "criticism, by definition, is *about*
something other than itself. Hence you cannot fuse
creation with criticism as you can fuse criticism with
creation" (*Selected Essays*, pp. 30–31).

The essay is remarkable for an "oblique" attack on
John Middleton Murry. (The 1920s seem to have been
declared by Eliot, Lawrence, and various other writers
as an open season for hunting Murry. You were allowed to do anything but shoot him.) Murry is given
high praise: the oblique method is again in evidence.
"To Mr. Murry I feel an increasing debt of gratitude."
But having discharged this debt in one paragraph, Eliot
then swoops down and demolishes him in four merciless
pages. Murry's offense is that he speaks up for something which he calls the Inner Voice; Murry has attacked Catholicism and Classicism because they "stand
for the principle of unquestioned spiritual authority
outside the individual." This, of course, is exactly the
authority toward which Eliot is gravitating. However,
while defending Classicism and Catholicism against
Middleton Murry's Inner Voice, Eliot does not as yet

see them as having values applicable to literature. If a classical work is better than a romantic one, this is because it can be shown to be so simply by comparing the two works by values purely internal to literature. Everything must be kept separate, compartmentalized. In the following passage, the Church is sandwiched between politics and poetry as though to prevent its getting out of its place:

If . . . a man's interest is political, he must, I presume, profess an allegiance to principles, or to a form of government, or to a monarch; and if he is interested in religion, and has one, to a Church; and if he happens to be interested in literature, he must acknowledge, it seems to me, just that sort of allegiance which I endeavoured to put forth in the preceding section. (*Selected Essays*, p. 27)

The allegiance is to the idea of dealing with literature exclusively as literature. However, at the very end of the essay, Eliot strikes the note I have already drawn attention to, reaching toward values outside literature but so authoritative that they apply to it as to every other sphere of human activity:

For the kinds of critical work which we have admitted, there is the possibility of cooperative activity, with the further possibility of arriving at something outside of ourselves, which may provisonally be called truth. But if anyone complains that I have not defined truth, or fact, or reality, I can only say apologetically that it was no part of my purpose to do so, but only to find a scheme into which, whatever they are, they will fit, if they exist. (*Selected Essays*, p. 34)

In all these early essays Eliot insists on the objectivity of art. He gives a picture of the artist as craftsman, working upon given material, which is, for the purposes of his art, outside himself, even if it is his own life, his own feelings. The artist who does not seek directly to express his own personality does so "indirectly through concentrating upon a task which is a task in the same sense as the making of an efficient engine or the turning of a jug or a table-leg." The attitude of the artist toward his material is exemplified in the extreme example of a Russian ballet dancer who "exists only during the performances . . . a vital flame which appears from nowhere, disappears into nothing and is complete and sufficient in its appearance" (*Selected Essays*, p. 113).

The idea that the subject of a work of art is simply material worked upon to produce an object in a particular medium gives rise to difficulties when Eliot is discussing the poet's beliefs in his early criticism. The view he struggles to maintain is that when a poet is writing about a philosophy of life or a faith, the poetry is not the vehicle for ideas or religion. These subjects are, rather, occasions which provide material for art. The work of art is the result of an emotion which the poet has about ideas or religion, not an expression of a philosophy or a faith. If the poet puts thoughts into a poem it is because he has feelings about those thoughts, not because he is using poetry to express them.

In his essay on "Shakespeare and the Stoicism of Seneca" (1927), Eliot declares himself unable to see any reason for believing that Dante or Shakespeare did any thinking of his own. "The people who think that Shakespeare thought, are always people who are not engaged in writing poetry, but who are engaged in thinking, and we all like to think that great men were like ourselves" (*Selected Essays*, p. 136). Eliot was defending the poet against contemporary pressures on him to have a philosophy or religion or deep meaning. Criticizing Wyndham Lewis for having written that we "have a great deal of evidence as to what Shakespeare thought of military glory and martial events," Eliot asks: "Do we? Or rather, did Shakespeare think anything at all? He was occupied with turning human actions into poetry." Nothing, then, should be demanded of the poet except that he turn experiences into poetry. If the poetry produces the impression on readers that it is about ideas or any of the human activities which have been so transformed, then this is just an illusion. "All great poetry gives the illusion of a view of life." But it is only an illusion.

With one side of him—that which had devoured the poetry of Mallarmé—Eliot did believe that poetry was self-enclosed. But with the other side—that which was potentially the Christian mystic—he was not sure. In the same essay Eliot takes up again the question of the relationship of poetry to the prevalent "climate of ideas" (as it would be called today). He now states a position that is not so absolute as that poets do not think. They do no *real* thinking, he now says, they have no original thoughts. Poets can have emotions about the ideas which lie around them in their time—which, in Elizabethan times, were largely those resultant from the immense esteem in which Seneca was held. This echoes the view put forward by Matthew Arnold in *The Function of Criticism at the Present Time* (1864), that "this creative power works with elements, with materials . . . which . . . are ideas; the best ideas, on every matter which literature touches, current at the time." The thoughts upon which Dante worked were those of Thomas Aquinas, "a man as great and lovely as Dante himself," Eliot writes. But the thoughts behind Shakespeare are "of men far inferior to Shakespeare." Dante had better luck than Shakespeare in having the thoughts of Saint Thomas behind him, and not those of Seneca, Montaigne, and Bacon.

One might deduce from this that Dante was a greater poet than Shakespeare because of the superior thought behind him. But it would be wrong to do so:

> In truth neither Shakespeare nor Dante did any real thinking—that was not their job; and the relative value of the thought current at their time, the material enforced upon each to use as the vehicle of his feeling is of no importance. It does not make Dante a greater poet, or mean that we can learn more from Dante than from Shakespeare. We can certainly learn more from Aquinas than from Seneca, but that is quite a different matter. When Dante says
> > *la sua voluntade e nostra pace*
>
> it is great poetry, and there is a great philosophy behind it. When Shakespeare says
> > *As flies to wanton boys, are we to the gods;*
> > *They kill us for their sport.*
>
> it is *equally* great poetry, though the philosophy behind it is not great. But the essential is that each expresses, in perfect language, some permanent human impulse. Emotionally, the latter is just as strong, just as true, just as informative—just as useful and beneficial in the sense in which poetry is useful and beneficial, as the former.
>
> What every poet starts from is his own emotions. And when we get down to these, there is not much to choose between Shakespeare and Dante. (*Selected Essays*, pp. 136–37)

One notices in this passage a shift from the view that poetry expresses nothing except the poetry to the view that it expresses "in perfect language, some permanent human impulse." This seems at odds with the symbolist view that out of whatever material of feelings or ideas of experiences the poetry derives, it creates an independent object of language. The argument or arguments are like those of a needle on a dial quivering in response to the pull of opposite forces—poetry and religion. One is at first surprised to find uncertainties in a critic with so authoritative a manner as Eliot, but this, on second thought, may be one of the most valuable qualities of his criticism. Shortly after the passage quoted above, he writes: "If Shakespeare had written according to a better philosophy, he would have written worse poetry; it was his business to express the greatest emotional intensity of his time, based on whatever his time happened to think."

What, then, have we been told? (a) poets do not think; (b) they express emotions in their poetry about the thoughts which are current in their time; (c) Dante was lucky because he had the greatly superior thoughts of Thomas Aquinas behind him; (d) Shakespeare only had behind him the watered-down Elizabethan idea of the stoicism in Seneca's plays—keeping a stiff upper lip and trying to cheer oneself up by striking stoical attitudes—which was bad luck in Shakespeare; (e) nevertheless, in their best poetry Dante and Shakespeare are equals; (f) as a matter of fact, Shakespeare would have been a worse poet if he had had better thinkers behind him; (g) "the great poet, in writing himself, writes his time" (but the reader should realize by now how many qualifications accompany those phrases "in writing himself" and "his time"); (h) "Dante, hardly knowing it, became the voice of the thirteenth century"; (i) Shakespeare, hardly knowing it, became the representative of the end of the sixteenth century, "of a turning point in history." It is curious to find Eliot appearing to think that it is the function of the poet, at any period, to be "representative of his time." If this is so, what are we to think about the modern poet? There is a sense, of course, in which one can be representative of one's time in opposing it.

The significance of Eliot's argument lies in the bewilderment—what I call the vibration. As so often, what he is really concerned with is to maintain the independent function of poetry, which has to be rescued from responsibility to everything except itself. The passages I have quoted conclude with the reflection that poetry is not a substitute for philosophy and religion: "it has its own function. . . . We can say that it provides 'consolation': strange consolation, which is provided equally by writers so different as Dante and Shakespeare."

The fundamental cause of bewilderment is, I think, a certain wavering between two attitudes: first, his wish to keep the poet, in the moment of creating his poetry (a very vivid moment in Eliot's mind), independent of all claims that he should be acting as interpreter of values other than purely poetic ones; and second, his feeling that there are absolute values—final causes— to which poetry relates. This division did not disappear even when he became a convinced Christian and wrote the *Four Quartets*. For tension is maintained there between the mystical-religious view, which uses language in such a way that it tends to disappear into the state of ecstatic belief communicated, and the view that poetry is about poetry.

Eliot writes in the Seneca essay some sentences which he can hardly have agreed with a year after he wrote them, when he entered the Christian communion:

> I doubt whether belief proper enters into the activity of a great poet, *qua* poet. That is, Dante, *qua* poet, did not believe or disbelieve the Thomist cosmology or theory of the soul: he merely made use of it, or a fusion took place between his initial emotional impulses and a theory, for the purpose of making poetry. (*Selected Essays*, p. 138)

This seems an almost desperate attempt to separate the poetic consciousness from the man who believes in Christianity. It is followed by a passage extremely revealing (in the second sentence) of Eliot himself at the time:

> In making some very commonplace investigations of the "thought" of Donne, I found it quite impossible to come to the conclusion that Donne believed anything. It seemed as if, at that time, the world was filled with broken fragments of systems, and that a man like Donne merely picked up, like a magpie, various shining fragments of ideas as they struck his eye, and stuck them about here and there in his verse. (*Selected Essays*, pp. 138–39)

Well, perhaps at the time of writing this, in a world filled with fragments of systems, the thought at the back of Eliot's mind was that in relation to his age he was like Donne. However, within two years, in his essay on Dante (1929), he starts discussing Dante's thought as integral with his poetry. A difficulty for the modern reader, he now argues, may be that he cannot think as Dante thought or enter into his beliefs. We are told here that Dante "not only thought in a way in which every man of his culture in the whole of Europe then thought, but he employed a method which was common and commonly understood throughout Europe" (*Selected Essays*, p. 242). The method was allegory, and the nature of Dante's imagination was visual. He literally, as part of his life, had visions. Allegory, based on visions, Eliot calls a "mental habit, which when raised to the point of genius can make a great poet as well as a great mystic or saint." One does not feel here that the poet, mystic, and saint are compartmentalized. Nevertheless, Eliot is still concerned not completely to identify the philosophy of Aquinas with the beliefs expressed by Dante. He considers the possibility that Dante wrote *The Divine Comedy* without belief but only "with understanding," though he thinks this improbable even in the case of "so great a poet." Next, he draws a distinction between "what Dante believed as a poet and what he believed as a man." "Dante could [hardly] have composed the *Comedy* merely with understanding and without belief; but his private belief becomes a different thing in becoming poetry. It is interesting to hazard the suggestion that this is truer of Dante than of any other philosophical poet" (*Selected Essays*, p. 258). Reading Goethe's poetry Eliot finds himself thinking: "This is what the man believed." And this is written as adverse criticism of Goethe.

By 1935, Eliot had gone far toward handing over autonomous art to religion. In "Religion and Literature" he writes:

> In ages like our own, in which there is no such common agreement [on ethical and theological matters], it is the more necessary for Christian readers to scrutinize their reading, especially of works of imagination, with explicit ethical and theological standards. The "greatness" of literature cannot be determined solely by literary standards; though we must remember that whether it is literature or not can be determined only by literary standards. (*Selected Essays*, p. 388)

Herbert Read wrote that after *The Hollow Men* Eliot's poetry became for the post part moralistic. "All the poetry that follows, including the *Four Quartets*, is, in spite of flashes of the old fire, moralistic poetry."[1] I

[1] See *T. S. Eliot: The Man and His Work*, Allen Tate, ed., p. 34.

believe this to be wrong, and the peculiar tension of the *Four Quartets* the result of the poet's refusal to be moralistic while, at the same time, as a Christian recognizing that religion is more important than the poetry "which does not matter." But to say it does not matter is also a kind of sublime joke. The inner drama of *Four Quartets* consists of a serious jocular confrontation between the autonomy of language in poetry and the divine word of religion, between the word and the Word. The two opposed attitudes fuse in the concept (God's joke) of the Word made flesh.

The Temporal City of Total Conditioning

•

VI

In my opening remarks I drew attention to the changing role of the witnessing "I" that is the center of consciousness in Eliot's poems. In "Prufrock" and "Portrait of a Lady" the narrators reveal their attitude to the drawing-room society they inhabit by portraying themselves both as self-despising victims and as intellectually or aesthetically superior, ironic outsiders. They may feel themselves condemned by the society in which they move but, nevertheless, in their deepest being they feel themselves not to be part of it (though unable, of course, to escape from its clutches). If the people in the drawing room can hold Prufrock "formulated on a pin," there is also a sense in which he passes judgment on them. He has something private to him: if not vision, at least the knowledge that he has no vision. Aestheticism is the last refuge of the in-effective. Prufrock is an individualist: driven

down, detritus, fag end of history, but with a little spittle
if no spunk in him.

The escape route is left open in Eliot's early poems
into some private solution of the problem of the soul
conditioned by the history in which it lives. E. M.
Forster, who was very conscious of the bolt-holes possible for individuals in a hostile society, gave as his
reasons for liking Eliot's early poems that the poet did
not say "Avaunt! to Armadillo-Armageddon." Reading
Eliot in wartime Cairo in 1914 he reflected: "Here was
a protest and a feeble one, and the more congenial for
being feeble. For what, in that world of gigantic horror,
was tolerable except the slighter gestures of dissent?"
Fourteen years later, reading *The Waste Land*, he was
shocked. He felt that the poet had been overwhelmed by
horror: "The earth is barren, the sea salt, the fertilising
thunderstorm broke too late." He believes that the poet
"cannot say 'Avaunt!' to the horror, or he would crumble
into dust." Forster does not accept the view which was
then held by several of Eliot's contemporaries that Eliot's
poem passed judgment on Western civilization. On the
contrary, "it is just a personal comment on the universe, as individual and as isolated as Shelley's *Prometheus*."[1] This oddly anticipates Eliot's own retrospective
comment that his poem was "just a piece of rhythmical
grumbling," one man's grouse.

(Much later, in 1936, another significant reaction to
The Waste Land was that of John Cornford, a sixteen-
year-old schoolboy who as a result of reading it joined
the British Communist Party. He took it to be a poem
about the collapse of capitalist society. And this is indeed
a possible Marxist interpretation.)

[1] E. M. Forster, "T. S. Eliot," in *Abinger Harvest* (London,
1936), pp. 88, 91, 92.

In *The Waste Land* there is no route of escape into the aesthetic life or the values, dear to Forster, of the private life of personal relations. Everything private is exposed as symptoms of the neurosis which is that of the civilization itself. The individual has become symptomatic of the state of the civilization, his consciousness the expression of its fragmentation.

The Waste Land was completed in early 1922. But Eliot had been accumulating over a number of years sketches of scenes of modern life. Some of these went back for more than ten years, to 1911. For example, as a Harvard undergraduate he had published a poem called "The Death of St. Narcissus," in which the following lines appear:

Come under the shadow of this gray rock
Come in under the shadow of this gray rock,
And I will show you something different from either
Your shadow sprawling over the sand at daybreak, or
Your shadow leaping behind the fire against the red rock.

These reappear in *The Waste Land,* transformed into the famous lines:

                       Only
There is shadow under this red rock,
(Come in under the shadow of this red rock),
And I will show you something different from either
Your shadow at morning striding behind you
Or your shadow at evening rising to meet you;
I will show you fear in a handful of dust.

The likelihood is that Eliot regarded the scenes he had written as material which could be incorporated in a long poem once he had a central theme which would draw it together. As late as September 1920 he was writing to his mother that he longed for "a period of tranquility to do a poem that I have in mind."[2] He complained in a letter to his patron John Quinn early in 1921 that he lacked "*continuous* time . . . for turning out a poem of any length." Yet various things were happening which, if brought to a climax, might precipitate the work. Eliot had seen James Joyce in the autumn of 1920 and a bit later read "the latter part of *Ulysses*," which he declared in the same letter to Quinn to be "truly magnificent."[3]

Events in his private life, while making it more difficult to get down to writing his long poem, probably enabled him to have a clearer idea of the theme of public and private catastrophe which was to fuse these fragments into a whole. In addition to Vivien's bouts of illness, he was also having complications with the parents on both sides of the marriage. Vivien's father was very ill (two operations). Eliot's mother and his sister Marian came to London, and the Eliots had to move out of their own flat in order that these relations, probably alarmed at the idea of Vivien, might occupy it. Eliot, in fact, praised Vivien whenever he mentioned her in the letters he wrote from England to his parents, but they seem to have remained suspicious of her. Old Mrs. Eliot had all the scarifying energy of the octogenarian on her last sightseeing tour before the eternal darkness. All this was only two years after the death of Eliot's father, an event which doubtless preyed on his mind. He was probably deeply affected by the fact that his father left his family money in trust so that if he,

<hr />

[2] *The Waste Land: A Facsimile and Transcript*, Valerie Eliot, ed., p. xx.
[3] *Ibid.*

Tom Eliot, died, it could not be inherited by his wife. In September 1921 Eliot's health collapsed, and a London specialist ordered him to go on holiday. From Margate, where he went, he wrote to Julian Huxley and obtained from him the address of a nerve specialist (Dr. Roger Vittoz) in Lausanne. In November he went to Lausanne, leaving Vivien in Paris.

Much of *The Waste Land* was written in December 1921 in Lausanne. Eliot then took it to Paris, where Ezra Pound was living, and showed the drafts to him. Perhaps when they were together, and certainly later, in correspondence, Pound worked on the drafts, slashing out whole sections and suggesting alterations, some of which Eliot did not agree to. What Pound did essentially was to release the energy of the poem and suppress what was distracting, superfluous, slovenly, or rhythmically or imagistically obstructive in it. He cut through the undergrowth. Eliot, though not always agreeing with him, acted on the same principle; and if he insisted on retaining a line which Pound had deleted, this was because he saw that the deletion was contrary to Pound's own principle of retaining what was dynamic. It is possible to regret the omission of some lines, but of remarkably few.

The brilliance of Pound's and Eliot's collaboration in editing is exemplified in the operations they performed on the scene in the third section, "The Fire Sermon," which describes the "small house agent's clerk" and "the typist." In the final version this is a masterpiece of incisiveness. In the draft, much too much is said. The typist is given the background of

> *A bright kimono wraps her as she sprawls*
> *In nerveless torpor on the window seat.*

The young man when he leaves the apartment:

> *. . . at the corner where the stable is,*
> *Delays only to urinate, and spit.*

Where everything should be—and is, in the final version—left precise, bold, suggestive, and simple, the original scene was a 1920s period piece.

Another scene of contemporary squalor which Pound removed is the sketch of a lady called Fresca (a sordid "portrait of a lady"), depicted in couplets imitating Pope, as she makes her toilet. Eliot here shows a disgust for female physical functions which competes with that of Swift (and owes something perhaps to the ablutions and jakes visiting of Bloom in *Ulysses*):

> *This ended, to the steaming bath she moves,*
> *Her tresses fanned by little flutt'ring Loves;*
> *Odours, confected by the cunning French,*
> *Disguise the good old hearty female stench.*

In contrast to this there is a passage which has the holidaying sense of pastoral release of certain allegrettos of Beethoven:

> *Kingfisher weather, with a light fair breeze,*
> *Full canvas and the eight sails drawing well . . .*

linked (perhaps with some straining of intellectual purpose), with Dante's account in the *Inferno* of the last voyage of Ulysses. The omission of this is, poetically speaking, the only long passage to be regretted.

Undoubtedly the most dramatically decisive change was the scrapping of the scene with which the poem opened, of Sweeney-like buddies having a night out on the town, drinking and going to a brothel and seeing the dawn. This opening was already entitled "The Burial of the Dead." The draft began rather archly with the lines:

First we had a couple of feelers down at Tom's place,
There was old Tom, boiled to the eyes, blind

and continued in this vein of daredevil slightly embarrassing heartiness. Characters called "Silk Hat Harry," "Old Jane" (Tom's wife), "Myrtle" (a brothelkeeper) are introduced, there is a fracas with the police, and so on. On its merits the scene did not deserve to be retained. But even if it had been much better, the fact that a long "real life" sketch of this kind introducing the poem would have given the whole work the character of a sequence interrupted by glimpses, like flashbacks, of the unconscious and the Buried Life, of the Dantesque and Baudelairean hell. By beginning the poem with the arresting "April is the cruellest month," Eliot affected a decisive reversal in the presentation. The statement of underlying, terrible, prophetic truth became its main theme, the "scenes" became secondary, illustrative material. They took their place as caricature illustrations, like, say, illustrations by Cruikshank for a Dickens novel. Mention of Dickens is relevant here because, as Valerie Eliot in her introduction to the published manuscript of *The Waste Land* explains, the original title of the "long poem" was intended to be a quotation from Dickens, "He Do the Police in Different Voices." If the poem had begun as was adumbrated in the order of the sketches which Eliot took to Pound it would have been a sequence of scenes in the manner of "Prufrock" or "Portrait of a Lady." By putting the prophetic statement first, Eliot makes it prophecy and not social satire. The contemporary voices become illustrative symptoms of the state of the civilization.

There are many voices which say "I" in *The Waste Land*. But those which speak out of their living characters are of the surface, objects of the prophetic or witnessing voices. Even when they speak in the first person, dramatically, they are third-person voices of people looked at from the outside, while they utter their confessions which demonstrate the theme of the breakdown of values. One easily recognizes these secondary voices:

And I was frightened. He said, Marie,
Marie, hold on tight. And down we went. . . .
I read, much of the night, and go south in the winter.

or:

"My nerves are bad to-night. Yes, bad. Stay with me. . . .
"I never know what you are thinking. Think."

or:

When Lil's husband got demobbed, I said—
I didn't mince my words, I said to her myself . . .

or:

"Well now that's done: and I'm glad it's over."

Such voices are symptoms: symptoms of attitudes, reflexes, neuroses, which are the results of the state of the civilization to which deeper voices, voices of the Biblical and Greek world, bear witness. There is one other voice—the voice of the poet in the poem, who suffers. The prophetic voices either make impersonal statements, such as that with which the poem opens, or ask questions:

What are the roots that clutch, what branches grow
Out of this stony rubbish? . . .

Or they are projected onto a figure of the past—Tiresias —whose consciousness is not only prophetic from the past as of the future but inclusive of the other voices in the poem.

The relationship of the underlying (literally) to the superficial voice is shown in the scene in "The Fire Sermon" section, between the typist and the "young man carbuncular," the "small house agent's clerk," with whom she makes squalid love on the divan ("at night her bed"), an episode witnessed from his place in the underworld by Tiresias:

> *I Tiresias, old man with wrinkled dugs*
> *Perceived the scene, and foretold the rest—*
>
> *I who have sat by Thebes below the wall*
> *And walked among the lowest of the dead.*

This situation—typist and clerk on divan, Tiresias seeing from under the divan, as it were, and foreseeing, out of his past—is a model of Eliot's interrelating of past and present consciousness in *The Waste Land*.

As Eliot points out in his Notes: "Tiresias, although a mere spectator and not indeed a 'character,' is yet the most important personage in the poem, uniting all the rest. . . . What Tiresias *sees*, in fact, is the substance of the poem." The mind of Tiresias connects the fragments of a civilization scattered through time and space. For the purpose of holding the poem together it is the linchpin or knot.

The same device of bringing things together within a seeing consciousness is achieved as satire or parody— caricature—in the first section, "The Burial of the Dead," by Madame Sosostris, clairvoyante. The emphasis is again on voyeurism:

> *Madame Sosostris, famous clairvoyante,*
> *Had a bad cold, nevertheless*
> *Is known to be the wisest woman in Europe,*
> *With a wicked pack of cards. Here, said she,*
> *Is your card, the drowned Phoenician Sailor . . .*

With her hand of cards she connects up the main symbolic characters in the poem, a service rendered which Eliot underlines in a note:

> The Hanged Man, a member of the traditional [Tarot] pack [of cards], fits my purpose in two ways: because he is associated in my mind with the Hanged God of Frazer, and because I associate him with the hooded figure in the passage of the disciples to Emmaus in Part V. . . .

The introductory note to *The Waste Land* has been seized on by expositors, source hunters, and so on. In this Eliot writes, "Not only the title, but the plan and a good deal of the incidental symbolism of the poem were suggested by Jessie L. Weston's book on the Grail legend: *From Ritual to Romance*." He also records his indebtedness to Sir James Frazer's *The Golden Bough*. Eliot indirectly acknowledged a further debt in *The Dial* (November 1923), when reviewing *Ulysses*, earlier episodes of which he had read in *The Egoist*:

> In using the myth, in manipulating a continuous parallel between contemporaneity and antiquity, Mr. Joyce is pursuing a method which others must pursue after him. They will not be imitators any more than the scientist who uses the discoveries of an Einstein in pursuing his own, independent, further investigations.

I have already observed how attracted Eliot was to the idea of introducing what he regarded as scientific methods or models for writing poetry. Where Joyce used the Homeric myth as the parallel brought into illuminating relation with the modern, Eliot turned to anthropology. The parallel derived from his anthropological studies was of vegetation myths of early religions in which the land becomes sterile on account of the sexual wound inflicted on the Fisher King. The best summary of this is contained in Cleanth Brooks's essay *"The Waste Land*: Critique of the Myth" from which I quote:

> In the legends which she [Miss Weston] treats there, the land has been blighted by a curse. The crops do not grow and the animals cannot reproduce. The plight of the land is summed up by, and connected with, the plight of the lord of the land, the Fisher King, who has been rendered impotent by maiming or sickness. The curse can be removed only by the appearance of a knight who will ask the meanings of the various symbols which are displayed to him in the castle. The shift in meaning from physical to spiritual sterility is easily made, and was, as a matter of fact, made in certain of the legends.[4]

In *Ulysses*, Joyce uses the *Odyssey* as a schematism which he traces very closely, episode by episode, in his story of the Dublin of Leopold Bloom and Stephen Dedalus. There is also a sense in which his protagonists, being equivalents, *are* Odysseus and Telemachus. Where Eliot develops and extends the "scientific" invention of Joyce is in introducing the figure of a Tiresias, who, while remaining confined within his pastness, sees what happens in the later time. It is as though there were in *Ulysses* a character from Homer's *Odyssey*, still living in antiquity, who was a witness of Bloom and Stephen.

Eliot cites Einstein in connection with *Ulysses*. Although there is a suggestion of the relativity of time in the nature of Tiresias, with hindsight one can suggest that, considered as a model of consciousness, he is better found in Freud. Part of Freudian theory is that in grow-

[4] In Cleanth Brooks, *Modern Poetry and the Tradition* (Chapel Hill, 1970), p. 138.

ing up the individual traverses in his own life all the stages of the development of the civilization. If this is so, the completely conscious and unrepressed individual would preserve in his mind a reflection in miniature of all the stages of the development of civilization. Part of his consciousness would be that which is symbolized by the figure of Tiresias.

In a very extended and highly imaginative metaphor in *Civilization and Its Discontents*, Freud compares the "unconscious" of the individual with that of Rome, supposing that all phases of development of the history of the Eternal City were simultaneously coexistent and present. If we interpret the metaphor not as concerning the individual but the civilization itself imagined within a poetic consciousness, the following passage describes the *seeing* prophetic consciousness of Tiresias in *The Waste Land*:

Now let us, by a flight of imagination, suppose that Rome is not a human habitation but a psychical entity . . . in which nothing that has once come into existence will have passed away and all the earlier phases of development continue to exist alongside the latest ones. This would mean that in Rome the palaces of the Caesars and the Septizonium of Septimius Severus would still be rising to their old height on the Palatine and that the castle of S. Angelo would still be carrying on its battlements the beautiful statues which graced it until the siege by the Goths, and so on. But more than this: in the place occupied by the Palazzo Caffarelli would once more stand— without the Palazzo having to be removed—the Temple of Jupiter Capitolinus; and this not only in its latest shape, as the Romans of the Empire saw it, but also in its earliest one, when it still showed Etruscan forms and was ornamented with terracotta antefixes. Where the Coliseum now stands we could at the same time admire Nero's vanished Golden House. On the Piazza of the Pantheon we should find not only the Pantheon of today, as it was bequeathed to us by Hadrian, but, on the same site, the original edifice erected by Agrippa; indeed, the same piece of ground would be supporting the church of Santa Maria sopra Minerva and the ancient temple over which it was built. And the observer would perhaps only have to change the direction of his glance or his position in order to call up the one view or the other.[5]

The whole history of Rome was in fact happening in Freud's mind when he wrote this passage, which is, as it were, an impressive poem by Freud-Tiresias. Civilization survives to the extent that it is not the past but the present within living consciousness.

If all pasts are contemporaneous as consciousness, then to compare the past and the present civilizations is not merely to make odious comparisons. For both past and present are happening as mental imaginative and psychological events all the time in the minds of the living. So to compare the present with the past is like placing side by side epochs that are contemporary within consciousness. The state of the civilization is a sum of consciousness at various epochs, all of which are present in it. And if the most recent additions to the sum reveal a decadence which is the contemporary world, then all pasts are decadent (as they have always to some extent been), within consciousness. Tiresias in what seems his remote past is, nevertheless, part of the whole contemporary consciousness. If he at his end of

[5] *Standard Edition of Sigmund Freud,* James Strachey, ed. (London, 1961), XXI, 70.

time foresees our world, we also, at ours, look back through his.

He is the character in whom all the others meet because his consciousness is like the underlying stratum of his Thebes upon which numerous later Thebes have been built—Thebes I, Thebes II, up to Thebes VII, let us say. Other levels are superficial, and, for that reason, the "characters" they contain are illustrative of behavior which Tiresias sees and foresuffers. You could cut a shaft through the stratifications of behavior within the civilization and on a vertical axis above Tiresias's foresuffering all "Enacted on this same divan or bed," see:

> *Elizabeth and Leicester*
> *Beating oars*
> *The stern was formed*
> *A gilded shell*

and, at a still more superficial stratum of a later history:

> *". . . Highbury bore me. Richmond and Kew*
> *Undid me. By Richmond I raised my knees*
> *Supine on the floor of a narrow canoe."*

And of course "the young man carbuncular," and the typist, are also enclosed in this consciousness:

> *I Tiresias, old man with wrinkled dugs*
> *Perceived the scene, and foretold the rest—*

Tiresias is the carbon that, bearing the weight of centuries upon it, is crushed into diamond. In him subjectivity has been acted upon by all that has happened in history between his Thebes and modern times. He has become its objective voice, with nothing left of his own subjectivity.

This, then, is the fundamental voice of *The Waste Land*: that of the consciousness totally acted upon and conditioned. The situation expressed is much more *serious* than that treated in Eliot's earlier poetry, where the conscious individual finds himself in an environment which he regards ironically while being at the same time ironic about himself. Instead of a society which the individual can remain outside of, there is now the absolute conditioning of which he himself is a symptom. Hence satire is hammered into tragedy. The consciousness realized is not that of the poet who stands outside the society in which he lives, but that of the whole civilization realized through him. The difference between the consciousness of the poet and that of other contemporaries in this world of sterility is that the poet alone is conscious of being in his own body and soul fragmented by the fragmented state of the civilization. The others illustrate through their behavior that of which he is aware as a state of mind.

This finally means that the contemporary consciousness which says "I" is also an object in the mind of Tiresias. But Tiresias is dependent for his projection into the present on having a contemporary voice. He needs a living voice of a poet that can turn his pastness into newness. We need an eye which can see the past in its place with its definite differences from the present. "This is the creative eye" (*Selected Essays*, p. 64), Eliot wrote in the essay in which he lambasted Gilbert Murray's renderings of Euripides. The creative eye (or "I") in *The Waste Land* is a voice which provides a modern idiom for a voice from antiquity. In this sense they are one. But to accept the experiences of the modern "I" as those of Tiresias is to verge on absurdity, which is surely what Eliot's most distinguished exegesist does in treating the poem as the autobiography of Tiresias.

Grover Smith comments on the opening passage: "Tiresias, who is speaking, has been content to let winter cover him 'in forgetful snow.' "[6] This is to take Eliot's notes very much *au pied de la lettre.* Why does Tiresias say "winter kept *us* warm"? Perhaps he is employing the editorial "we" in providing an information sheet for the inhabitants of *The Waste Land.* But common sense does not permit such a literal interpretation of the famous opening:

> *April is the cruellest month, breeding*
> *Lilacs out of the dead land, mixing*
> *Memory and desire, stirring*
> *Dull roots with spring rain.*
> *Winter kept us warm, covering*
> *Earth in forgetful snow, feeding*
> *A little life with dried tubers.*

"Us," I think, here means "us": "You and I" (like "us" in the opening of "Prufrock") are appealed to on the grounds of an experience which is or can be shared. "It was like this," the poet is saying, "we survived the winter." But of course the use of "we" here is only the tip of the iceberg included in "us":

> *I will show you fear in a handful of dust.*

And, before this, "us" has been particularized and at the same time given a more historic dimension in the lines:

> *Summer surprised us, coming over the Starnbergersee*
> *With a shower of rain; we stopped in the colonnade,*
> *And went on in sunlight, into the Hofgarten . . .*

"Us" now introduces an illustrative example, the voice of the countess who tells of her experiences being driven in the sled with her cousin the archduke. Yet such a meeting in a park abroad, with a stranger, is possible

[6] Grover Smith, *T. S. Eliot's Poetry and Plays,* p. 72.

to the "us" who is "you and I," and to whom an invisible narrator appeals, like Joseph Conrad's Marlow (or Hamlet's father's ghost) starting a yarn into which we are drawn convivially but which, within a few minutes, will make our hair stand on end.

The voice which is the deepest "I," that of a witness, a contemporary voice melting into that of the most ancient—the Biblical here perhaps more than Tiresias —addresses to us a quite different appeal, that of an Old Testament prophet:

What are the roots that clutch, what branches grow
Out of this stony rubbish? Son of man,
You cannot say, or guess, for you know only
A heap of broken images, where the sun beats,
And the dead tree gives no shelter, the cricket no relief,
And the dry stone no sound of water. . . .

Having flung at us his handful of examples, the speaker becomes impatient with these trivia, this stuff of "Prufrock" and "Portrait of a Lady," and plunges to the depths of such a well as that out of which Saint John the Baptist might have preached in *Salome*. He has appealed to our eyes and ears, now he appeals to our heart and conscience. As Eliot's Notes inform us, the voice is Ezekiel and Ecclesiastes. What matters more is the voice speaking directly into the heart, of "Those who have crossed /With direct eyes, to death's other Kingdom"—an appeal to be repeated in a different key of poignant memory a few lines farther on:

—Yet when we came back, late, from the hyacinth gar-
    den,
Your arms full, and your hair wet, I could not
Speak, and my eyes failed, I was neither
Living nor dead, and I knew nothing,
Looking into the heart of light, the silence.

Tiresias may see or foresee this, but this is not his voice. It is the contemporary guilt-ridden voice, but still the voice of a particular individual, one who sees into the heart of light. This voice is prodigiously present throughout "A Game of Chess," leaves a visiting card from the poet himself on us in "The Fire Sermon": ("By the waters of Leman I sat down and wept . . ." Eliot wrote much of *The Waste Land* at Lausanne, on Lac Léman). It is certainly that of the "I" who exclaims:

> *O City city, I can sometimes hear*
> *Beside a public bar in Lower Thames Street,*
> *The pleasant whining of a mandoline*
> *And a clatter and a chatter from within*
> *Where fishmen lounge at noon: where the walls*
> *Of Magnus Martyr hold*
> *Inexplicable splendour of Ionian white and gold.*

It is the voice of poignant regret which cries out near the end of the poem:

> *your heart would have responded*
> *Gaily, when invited, beating obedient*
> *To controlling hands*

Of all modern poems, *The Waste Land* is that which has received the greatest burden of analysis and explication. I do not intend therefore to attempt to relate the mythology of the Fisher King to the poem, nor to discuss sources and references. I shall limit myself to considering the method of presenting the scenes of which the poem is composed and of their relation to its main themes.

A problem for Eliot in all his longer poems is that he is essentially a poet of fragments. The impulse by which he is able to see and organize his material as poetry is not very sustained. In "Prufrock," for example, the development of the poem is from scene to scene and symbol to symbol: first, the journey ("Let us go then, you and I") through the city; then the fog; then the symbols of time; then of eyes.

However, if his inspiration is fragmentary, Eliot's themes are not. They are obsessive. His problem, which he resolves, is to bind together the fragmentary passages of poetry with the obsessive themes. The central theme of *The Waste Land* is the breakdown of civilization, and the conditioning of those who live within it by that breakdown, so that every situation is a symptom of the collapse of values. This theme is prevented from being journalistic (expressing the despair of a postwar generation merely) by the vision of the whole past civilization within which the contemporary examples of modern life are enclosed. Further, there is an elegiac theme. Although the personal grief is transcended, it is felt with a poignancy reminiscent of *In Memoriam*.

Finally, Eliot makes a virtue of what might be seen as a defect: fragmentariness. The poem is about a fragmented culture, so the fragmentariness seems suited to it. Fragmentariness, when projected into many scenes, with shifts of center of attention and mood, lends force to the obsession, gives the poem its apocalyptic visionary force. Lastly, the fragments are organized in order to stress the contrast between prophetic and contemporary voices.

The Waste Land falls into five sections which, following the musical analogy, might be compared to movements. The first movement, "The Burial of the Dead," is exposition, in which Eliot establishes both the theme of the "stony rubbish" of modern life set against the prophetic Biblical questioning, and also the pattern of his method and procedure, followed in other sections. It begins with a statement ("April is the cruellest month"), rapidly proceeds to cite symptoms ("Summer surprised us, coming over the Starnbergersee"), raises the most terrifying questions ("What are the roots that clutch"), then declares its "handful of dust." From there it proceeds to the accusation of the wound—failure of sexuality and, more than that, of love. Madame Sosostris (a hit at Madame Blavatsky and perhaps also at Yeats's own spiritualism) serves, as we have seen as junction and nodular connecting system of the poem's symbolism, and also is herself prime symptom of the decay of religion into superstition. This connects with the epigraph of the poem, the quotation from Petronius about the Sibyl hanging in a cage who, being asked what she wished for, answered, "I wish to die." "The Burial of the Dead" ends with a Dantesque vision of London as a city of the dead and a strange encounter with the past of antiquity in the form of a soldier who was the narrator's companion in the naval battle at Mylae, and to whom he addresses sinister questions that seem from a tragedy of Webster or Tourneur. Finally, the poet addresses Baudelaire's famous appeal to the hypocritical reader: "You! hypocrite lecteur!—mon semblable,—mon frère!" Being in the same situation as the poet who addresses him, the reader belongs to the general conspiracy of the civilization which has at its center the sexual wound.

The second section, "A Game of Chess" provides deeper insight into the failure of love. In the magnificent opening lines the poet, with a kind of buried irony, portrays a lady sitting at her dressing table. He brings to bear all the forces of past great art upon this woman. She seems painted with the brush of Titian, evoked with the poetry of Shakespeare describing Cleopatra seated in her barge. The whole passage seems orchestrated with an overrich corrupt music like that of Richard Strauss in *Salome*.

In this description Eliot brings all the resources of his aesthetic sense of the past to lines of original invention which nevertheless convey a sense of pastiche, as though all these phrases assembled were fragments from wonderful masterpieces of the past. This very rich and complex introduction encloses the theme of sexual violence and sterility ("The change of Philomel, by the barbarous king / So rudely forced . . ."), and suppresses, as under a very dense impasto of paint, the scene of a modern woman sitting at her dressing table brushing her hair. In every way the material is organized so as to give the impression of a densely orchestrated Prelude of a post-Wagnerian kind which mixes all the arts. As a result of this, the poem does not distintegrate into its scenes.

The dialogue that follows, spoken hysterically by the woman, not answered except by incommunicable and terrible thoughts by the man, is where the poem touches the poet most closely. It is the poem's innermost sanctum. This is the wound, the heart of the suffering. The poet is here brought up against the exhibited conditioned behavior of the woman who speaks aloud: "What shall we do tomorrow? / What shall we ever do?" His unspoken comments have that immediacy of speech for which the only possible language is poetry. It is the poetry of real situations and projects a character which can only be Eliot himself. Comments such as "I think we are in rats' alley / Where the dead men lost their bones" are the poetry of immediate reaction to experience. But beyond this Eliot indicates the process whereby such *lignes données* become transformed into a different kind of poetry. The line "Those are pearls that were his eyes," from Ariel's song in *The Tempest* is followed in Shakespeare by:

> *Nothing of him that doth fade,*
> *But doth suffer a sea-change*
> *Into something rich and strange.*

lines of mysterious import for Eliot, because they signify
for him the mystery of the transformation of experience
into poetry. Eliot once referred to *The Waste Land* as
an elegy. Whose elegy? His father's? Jean Verdenal's—
mort aux Dardanelles in the war? Anyway the elegiac
line from Shakespeare is here the deepest hidden thought
of the silent interlocutor answering the woman's question: "Do you remember / Nothing?" and at the same
time it suggests the process of past poetry moving into
the poetry of the jazz age:

> *But*
> *O O O O that Shakespeherian Rag—*
> *It's so elegant*
> *So intelligent*

This dialogue of only twenty immensely pregnant
lines is followed by thirty-three lines of conversation
everheard in a London pub. Their character and equality
is, I suppose, the nearest in the poem to the Ur-*Waste
Land* scenes from modern life. They are little more than
programmatic. They establish that the married life of a
demobilized soldier and his working-class wife can be
sordid. They do very little beyond this, though they are
brought back into the frame of the past impinging on
the present in the quotation from Ophelia's farewell to
the ladies of the court of Denmark in the last line.

The opening of the third section, "The Fire Sermon,"
like that of "A Game of Chess," has breadth of orchestra-
tion, weaves together the themes of past and present,
and is a prelude before the curtain has gone up on the
drama of the clerk and typist. In the opening lines,
Eliot's method, the scientific mode, developed from
Joyce, of portraying the past parallel with the present,
is very much in evidence. The part of the River Thames
here wryly celebrated is that invoked by Edmund
Spenser in "Prothalamion," a poem which sets up echoes

in these lines: "Sweet Thames, run softly, till I end my song." But this is the modern Thames and the nymphs have departed to be replaced by girls whose "friends, the loitering heirs of City directors;/ Departed, have left no addresses."

Different times and histories and states of consciousness fuse, and Eliot employs a characteristic device for making them melt into one another: by making a negative statement which with the imagination one reads as both negative and positive:

> *The river bears no empty bottles, sandwich papers,*
> *Silk handkerchiefs, cardboard boxes, cigarette ends*
> *Or other testimony of summer nights. . . .*

In its Spenserian context, this is of course true. In the modern context, which is also here implied, the river does bear all these things. The same fusion of negative and positive occurs in Prufrock's remark about the mermaids: "I do not think that they will sing to me." Similarly, in *The Hollow Men*, the poet writing in the first person:

> *Eyes I dare not meet in dreams*
> *In death's dream kingdom*
> *These do not appear . . .*

which makes those eyes very real in the imagination. In the first section of *Ash Wednesday*, when the poet is hesitating between belief and unbelief, he develops with much complexity this kind of ambiguity of negative and positive throughout.

The Thames is historical in the first fourteen lines of "The Fire Sermon." With the fifteenth line the scene changes to a "dull canal" which is symbolic, conveying the state of civilization and mingling the elegy with Ferdinand's grief in *The Tempest* because he believes his father, Alonso, to be drowned:

Musing upon the king my brother's wreck
And on the king my father's death before him.

Grover Smith writes that at this time the "I" whom he refers to as "the quester" has long become the Fisher King. Perhaps it is helpful to think this, or, rather, perhaps it is impossible to paraphrase the symbolism without doing so.

There is the further example of sexual inadequacy in Mr. Eugenides, the Smyrna merchant who

Asked me in demotic French
To luncheon at the Cannon Street Hotel
Followed by a weekend at the Metropole.

This passage makes me wonder about the appropriateness of labeling the "I" the Fisher King. One hardly thinks of even a Smyrna merchant having the temerity to invite a Fisher King to a night of homosexual love in Brighton.

"The Fire Sermon" then focuses on the scene between the small house agent's clerk and the typist, on the divan, exposed to the prophetic sight of Tiresias. There follow three scenes of London, one of which, about Elizabeth and Leicester, resumes the scene of the Thames in the time of Spenser's England. After a reference to Eliot's nervous breakdown, there are lightning flashes from a life outside the temporal city—theme of Eliot's poetry after *The Waste Land*. The reference is to Saint Augustine's arrival at Carthage and his account of this in his *Confessions*:

Burning burning burning burning
O Lord.Thou pluckest me out
O Lord Thou pluckest

burning

When Eliot was persuaded by Pound that he should cancel from the original draft the lines about a voyage and shipwreck, he supposed that he should also cancel "Death by Water," about Phlebas the Phoenician. However, Pound insisted on his retaining these. On the analogy of musical form they are entirely justified, breaking the mood of the first three sections, opening onto a world which, despite their sadness, is pure and filled with light. They recall the intaglio-like elegies of certain poems in *The Greek Anthology*—for example, these lines of Leonidas of Tarentum:

. . . I, Callaeschrus, wrenched from life
As I sailed the mid-Lybian waters, my bones
Now thread the sea, as the fish and the tides turn
   them . . .[7]

"Death by Water" crystallizes the hidden elegy that is in *The Waste Land*—hinted at, as we have seen, in "Those are pearls that were his eyes." The passage has, however, an innocence of cleansing waters which seems outside both the sordidity and the apocalyptic fire of the rest of the poem. It seems an escape from a mood, and perhaps that is its virtue. Eliot's attempt in the Notes to make Mr. Eugenides, the one-eyed merchant, seller of currants, melt into the Phoenician sailor, seems forced, although in "Dans le Restaurant" (1917), one of his French poems, in which Phlebas appears as "Phlébas, le Phénicien, pendant quinze jours noyé," Phlebas seems associated with a peculiarly dirty-minded waiter who tells a customer—narrator of the poem—about his chastising when he was seven years old a small girl who was still younger than he and his experiencing a

[7] Clive Sanson, trans. *The Greek Anthology*, Peter Jay, ed. (London, 1973), p. 106.

moment "de puissance et de délire." Yet even in the French poem the lines about Phlebas seem to have no connection with what goes before.

Eliot seems to have written the last section of *The Waste Land*, "What the Thunder Said," with extreme rapidity—almost as if it were automatic writing. It is visionary poetry written out of intense suffering and transforms the poet into seer. It is very close to the state of mind described by Rimbaud in his famous letter to Paul Démeny (May 15, 1871). Bearing in mind that Eliot wrote "What the Thunder Said" while he was recovering from a nervous breakdown, Rimbaud's words throw much light on this poetry.

> I say that one must be a *seer*, make oneself a *seer*.
> The poet makes himself a *seer* by a long, prodigious, and rational *disordering* of *all the senses*. Every form of love, of suffering, of madness; he searches himself, he consumes all the poisons in him, and keeps only their quintessence. This is an unspeakable torture during which he needs all his faith and superhuman strength, and during which he becomes the great patient, the great criminal, the great accursed—and the great learned one!—among men. For he arrives at the unknown! Because he has cultivated his own soul—which was rich to begin with—more than any other man! He reaches the unknown, and even if, crazed, he ends by losing the understanding of his visions, at least he has seen them![8]

In "What the Thunder Said" the "I" which is the consciousness of the poet has become his theme of the Fisher King:

[8] *Rimbaud, Selected Verse*, Oliver Bernard, trans. (Harmondsworth, 1962), pp. 10–11.

> *I sat upon the shore*
> *Fishing, with the arid plain behind me*
> *Shall I at least set my lands in order?*

The voice that says "I" in this concluding section is naked consciousness acted upon by events. The "I" has become the depersonalized witness of the world which has become it. This is the process Keats imagined in *Hyperion* and *The Fall of Hyperion* as that of the poet becoming Apollo. For Keats as for Rimbaud, the poet as seer was essentially Greek. The Greek attitude to poetry is described by Nietzsche in *The Birth of Tragedy*:

> The "I" of the lyrist therefore sounds from the depth of his being: its "subjectivity," in the sense of modern aestheticians is a fiction. When Archilochus, the first Greek lyrist, proclaims to the daughters of Lycambes both his mad love and his contempt, it is not his passion alone that dances before us in orgiastic frenzy; but we see Dionysus and the Maenads, we see the drunken reveler Archilochus sunk down in slumber— as Euripides depicts it in the *Bacchae*, the sleep on the high mountain pasture, in the noonday sun. And now Apollo approaches and touches him with the laurel. Then the Dionysian-musical enchantment of the sleeper seems to emit image sparks, lyrical poems, which in their highest development are called trage-dies and dramatic dithyrambs.[9]

"What the Thunder Said" consists of a succession of visions in the desert of the world without God, dominated by the absence of Christ, the God who has not risen and whom the disciples cannot see:

[9] F.Nietzsche, *The Birth of Tragedy and The Case of Wagner*, Walter Kaufmann, trans. (New York, 1967), pp. 50–51.

> *He who was living is now dead*
> *We who were living are now dying*

These visions are all of the agony in the garden, the desert, the lack of water which is only a mirage of the sound of water, the hallucination of "the third who walks always beside you" in the extremity of the North or South Pole. Eliot finds confirmation for the waste land in the modern world. It is contained in "the account of one of the Antarctic expeditions" in which "the party of explorers, at the extremity of their strength, had the constant delusion that there was *one more member* than could actually be counted." Everything here is the vision of extremes: extremes of agony, thirst, adventure, victims, cities—extremes which are the result of the absence of significant reality in life but which result also in disasters in the world of actuality: unreal. The poem ends not with an affirmation of faith so much as with gestures of resignation which fall back on Buddhism: the Oriental religion of the acceptance of the world as suffering, the world in which everything is consumed by fire. Christianity—Saint Augustine— and the Buddha are brought together only as the teaching of asceticism in a civilization which is reduced to a flurry of quotations: "These fragments I have shored against my ruins." The madness of Hieronymo, the hero whose son has been murdered in Kyd's *The Spanish Tragedy* can only be hushed by the words Shantih shantih shantih, "The Peace which passeth understanding."

The surface state of the civilization which is the sum of all its stages—all its pasts enclosed within its present— is the waste land of the modern world. The long result of time comes out like a sum at a particular moment in history. Eliot—who tended to take a historic view of his work—once said to me that *The Waste Land* could not have been written at any moment except when it was written—a remark which, while biographically true in regard to his own life, is also true of the poem's time in European history after World War I. The sense that Western civilization was in a state which was the realization of historic doom lasted from 1920 to 1926. It emanated from the revolutionary explosions and still more from the monetary collapse of central Europe. Money is, after all, life blood; and no grotesque spectacle of misery has been more completely one of negation than that of Germans in the early 1920s having to fill suitcases and perambulators with currency in order to buy bread. Compared with this, the period between the English General Strike (1926) and the beginnings of the Great Depression (1929) was one of resurgence of hope, like the very terrible birth pangs of a new world coming into being.

In a brilliant essay on the original drafts of *The Waste Land*, William Empson suggests that Eliot wrote over a number of years a collection of sketches which he let "pile up in the hope of finding a theme for them." Empson then asks: "What is this theme?" and finds the answer to be, "London has just escaped from the First World War, but it is certain to be destroyed by the next one, because it is in the hands of international financiers. The very place of it will be sown with salt, as Carthage was, and forgotten by men; or it will be sunk under water." He points out that the poetry is obsessed with the theme of the doomed city and that Carthage comes into sections I, III, and IV (but Carthage signifies redemption as well as destruction, because it was at Carthage that the author of the *City of God* was plucked by the hand of God).[10]

10 William Empson, "My God There's Bears on It," *Essays in Criticism*, XXII (October 1972), 417–29.

I agree with Empson that the theme of the poem is doom, and that at the time of writing it Eliot was certainly influenced by the idea of the end of European civilization. London provides the dominating symbol for this, but surely it was of Europe as much as London that Eliot was thinking. After the war he was occupied in studying international financial arrangements between England and Germany under the terms of the Treaty of Versailles, and, being fascinated by the "Science of money," he must have had considerable insight into the economic disaster—no mere abstraction but grim reality in the plight of refugees, the starvation of children—after 1918. The most immediate lines in the poem record the plight not of London but of Germany and Austria:

> *What is that sound high in the air*
> *Murmur of maternal lamentation*
> *Who are those hooded hordes swarming*
> *Over endless plains . . .*

This is the world of Kokoschka's and Käthe Kollwitz's posters of the period appealing for help for refugees. In his Notes, Eliot quotes from Hermann Hesse's *Blick ins Chaos*, "Schon ist halb Europa, schon ist zumindest der halbe Osten Europas auf dem Wege zum Chaos" ("Already half of Europe, at any rate the Eastern half of Europe is on the way to chaos"). Hesse describes this Europe as in a state of Dionysian drunkenness and ecstasy singing *"betrunken und hymnisch"* as Dimitri Karamazov sang. "The bourgeois, enchanted, laughs at these songs, the saint and seer hears them with tears."

There is much evidence that Eliot thought that Western civilization was confronted by impending ruin. Many of his writings at the time and for some years afterward, including his *Criterion* Commentaries, show how convinced he was that the civilization would collapse. In

1929, when I myself as a very young man had lunch with him for the first time, I asked him what form he had thought the collapse would take. "Internecine warfare," he answered. Puzzled by this, I pressed him for a more precise answer. He said, "People killing one another in the streets."

The Waste Land is "placed" in contemporary history. It arises out of unique sets of circumstances which were catalytic to Eliot, public ones combining with others private to him, which made it possible for him to write the poem.

The images of parched land, rocks and deserts, water that only drowns, trees that are dead, are all terrifying to Eliot, as are also, in a different way, ancient Greece, and vegetation rites—the scientific anthropological view of the world. So much has been written about The Waste Land that there is a tendency for the poem itself to have become made abstract by all the explanations. But a quotation from Joseph Conrad—"The horror! The horror!"—was originally the epigraph to the poem until Pound persuaded Eliot to remove it.

Conrad's Heart of Darkness is of course one of the "influences" in The Waste Land. It seems to me, though, much more than this. Conrad's story is of the primitive world of cannibalism and dark magic penetrated by the materialist, supposedly civilized, world of exploitation and gain; and of the corruption of the mind of a man of civilized consciousness by the knowledge of the evil of the primitive (or the primitive which becomes evil through the unholy union of European trade and Congolese barbarism). The country of the mind described by Conrad is a country of pure horror. Eliot is usually thought of as a sophisticated writer, an "intellectual." For this reason, the feeling of primitive horror which rises from the depths of his poetry is overlooked. Yet it is there in the rhythms, often crystallizing in some phrase which suggests the drums beating through the jungle darkness, the scuttling, clawing, shadowy forms of life in the depths of the sea, the spears of savages shaking across the immense width of the river, the rough-hewn images of prehistoric sculptures found in the depths of the primeval forest, the huge cactus forms in deserts, the whispering of ghosts at the edge of darkness. Probably this is the most Southern (in the American sense) characteristic of Eliot, reminding one that he was a compatriot of Edgar Allan Poe and William Faulkner. And Conrad's *Heart of Darkness* is a landscape with which Eliot is deeply, disquietedly, guiltily almost, familiar, and with which he contrasts effects of sunlight, lips trembling in prayer, eyes gazing into the heart of light or hauntingly into other eyes, a ship answering to the hand on a tiller as a symbol of achieved love and civilization.

The theme of *The Waste Land*, as of all Eliot's poetry, is the quest. In making his parallel between the grail legend and the myth of the wounded God, Eliot added a new dimension of the imagination to the drama of the quest in the modern world. But what is not as yet realized is the nature of the true grail. The need for redemption is passionately realized in Eliot's poems, but, in terms of the symbolism employed, the vision of redemption if realized would be as delusory as Prufrock's vision of the mermaids who did not sing to him (and who, if they did sing, would be singing the wrong song). One cannot imagine the resurrection of the Fisher King and the restoration of his lands being any more positive a solution to the problem of attaining supernatural values than was the singing of the mermaids. What *The Waste Land* does on the positive side is to replace the aesthetic with anthropological myth.

There is, therefore, a certain hollowness at the center

of the poem. This is not just that of the civilization described: it is the hollowness of describing civilization in terms of the temporal city when the true quest is for the eternal city, the *civitas dei*. This search does, it is true, haunt the poem like a rumor of eternity. There are flashes of a supernatural which is of a Dantesque order, not that of vegetation mythology—especially in "The Fire Sermon":

> *Burning burning burning burning*
> *O Lord Thou pluckest me out*
> *O Lord Thou pluckest*

The Waste Land might be described as a poem about its own hollowness, the sense of which is wonderfully realized in "What the Thunder Said":

> *In this decayed hole among the mountains*
> *In the faint moonlight, the grass is singing*
> *Over the tumbled graves, about the chapel*
> *There is the empty chapel, only the wind's home.*

It is impossible to proceed beyond this negation because the terms on which the search for

> *Jerusalem Athens Alexandria*
> *Vienna London*
> *Unreal*

could be transcended within the search for the *civitas dei* are not stated. In this respect the poem is like an argument in logic with the middle term left out, which explains the hysteria—sublime though it may be—of the ending. The middle term is the doctrine of the Incarnation, and it is toward this that Eliot's poetry moves after *The Waste Land.*

Toward the City Outside Time

• •

VII

The Hollow Men is a kind of coda to *The Waste Land*. The effect is of a *danse macabre*, a pure lyric sequence of fragments sinister in themselves and yet floating like smoke and sparks from a bonfire. It pushes to its poetically logical conclusion one idea implicit in *The Waste Land*: that in the temporal city of modern life those who are contemporaries and physically alive may be less truly living than the dead.

> *Shape without form, shade without colour,*
> *Paralysed force, gesture without motion;*

This is the world of those whom the truly living, who have "crossed /With direct eyes, to death's other Kingdom," do not remember as being damned—"lost / Violent souls, but only/As the hollow men /The stuffed men."

The rituals here are parodies of true rituals, though it might be said that, in the context of

Eliot's whole spiritual development in his art, they are an advance in not being an evasion. They are not rituals of aestheticism or of some cultural concept of the whole civilization. They parody worship, but of a pagan kind without a church:

> *Here the stone images*
> *Are raised, here they receive*
> *The supplication of a dead man's hand*
> *Under the twinkle of a fading star.*

In the line about the twinkling star, the parody of religion becomes parody in poetry, recalling "twinkle, twinkle, little star." This parody suggests its opposite, however, the unparodiable, the true religion which the hollow men dare not meet: they dare only ask,

> *Is it like this*
> *In death's other kingdom*
> *Waking alone*
> *At the hour when we are*
> *Trembling with tenderness*
> *Lips that would kiss*
> *Form prayers to broken stone.*

There is an almost obsessive preoccupation with imagery connected with eyes. Eyes symbolize various things. (1) They suggest eroticism connected with feelings of guilt. These are the eyes of the shades of the sodomites who stare at and embrace one another— ("*ciascun ombra e baciarsi una con una*")—in Canto XXVI of the *Purgatorio*. These surely are the "eyes I dare not meet in dreams." But (2) in "death's dream kingdom"

> *These do not appear:*
> *There, the eyes are*
> *Sunlight on a broken column . . .*

(3) In the fourth section eyes become sightless and unseen—the opposite of vision. (4) There are the eyes of those who are without fear and gaze directly into the light of truth:

> *Those who have crossed*
> *With direct eyes, to death's other Kingdom . . .*

(5) But truly to see would be to have spiritual sight opened onto the eyes in which the seen and the seeing become one in the beatific vision:

> *Sightless, unless*
> *The eyes reappear*
> *As the perpetual star*
> *Multifoliate rose*
> *Of death's twilight kingdom*
> *The hope only*
> *Of empty men.*

The many meanings attached to eyes—seeing, being seen, not seeing, not being seen—could hardly be developed further. The complexity of vision, physical and spiritual and blinded, contributes to the poem's uncanny effects, hovering light and shadows among many revelations. Stars, in looking like eyes, and in being the most distant luminous brilliant objects, are on the edge of the twilight kingdom.

This is a poem that trembles on the verge of many things, not least that of Shelleyan romanticism. We are not far from the stars in Shelley's "To a Skylark," a poem which is all the more likely to have haunted Eliot because he criticized its vagueness: "like a star of Heaven, /In the broad daylight"; and "that silver sphere /Whose intense lamp narrows /In the white dawn clear, /Until we hardly see, we feel that it is there." Shelley's star expresses the unifying of visibility and invisibility—

seeing, as it were, not with the eyes but with the feelings.

The Hollow Men is the poetry of pure dissolution, the individual dissolved into the temporal world which is conditioned so that the living are the dead, the dead the living. The only hope lies in acceptance, dissolution beyond dissolution, death within the world, so as to meet in twilight (the half-light, half-darkness, therefore the meeting of light and dark, a merging of one into the other) the life-in-death of the "other kingdom" of the dead who see.

The fifth section of the poem abandons the symbolist imagery of the preceding sections which is at once elusive and stark ("Rat's coat, crowskin, crossed staves /In a field . . .") and, after the first stanza, which parodies a nursery rhyme ("*Here we go round the prickly pear*"), contrasts a world of ghostly abstractions (a Bradleyan dance of bloodless categories) with the remoteness of the repeated phrase from the Lord's Prayer, printed in italics in the right-hand margin of the poem like a withheld promise:

> *Between the idea*
> *And the reality*
> *Between the motion*
> *And the act*
> *Falls the Shadow*
>> *For Thine is the Kingdom*

And the poem ends with the famous throw-away

> *This is the way the world ends*
> *Not with a bang but a whimper.*

It is difficult to say how appropriate this is as comment on a world likely to end with a very big bang indeed (metaphorically, of course, an H-bomb might be considered a very small whimper), but within the context of Eliot's imagination, it draws a very decisive line between the temporal city of European civilization become the waste land, which is the main subject of his poetry up to these two lines, and the spiritual world of the City of God, not dependent on the condition of civilization, which becomes his concern from now on.

With *Ash Wednesday* (published in 1930, but Part II had already appeared under the title "Salutation" in 1927 and Part I as "Perch'io non spero" in 1928) Eliot's poetry moves toward uplands of increasing light, like those concluding cantos of the *Purgatorio*, in which Virgil leaves Dante to pursue his upward journey toward Paradise alone, and Dante then perceives the lady, later to be called Matilda, who answers his eager questions.

Ash Wednesday seems saturated in this Dantesque light, from which much of its imagery derives. Its imagery constantly suggests musical and visual analogies. It is a poem in which lines stand out and create pictures like monkish illuminations painted on parchment:

At the first turning of the third stair
Was a slotted window bellied like the fig's fruit
And beyond the hawthorn blossom and a pasture scene
The broadbacked figure drest in blue and green
Enchanted the maytime with an antique flute.

*   *   *

While jewelled unicorns draw by the gilded hearse.

*   *   *

Till the wind shake a thousand whispers from the yew

*   *   *

The "I" is no longer aesthetic, nor is it conditioned by the state of the civilization, nor is it representative of a state of consciousness the result of social circumstances, nor is it the voice of Tiresias—of the past, the dead. This conscious self is personal, though divested of most of the attributes which we connect with personality. It is the self naked in the presence—or the absence—of God. This is the very center of the poet's own consciousness, where he crosses over from being involved with the world through fear, ambition, contempt, literature, society, to his faith in the Church.

This divestiture leads to the abandonment of hope. The first section of the poem conveys the self's renunciation of all to which it was attached—"The vanished power of the usual reign," "The infirm glory of the positive hour." Knowledge that "time is always time / And place is always and only place / And what is actual is actual only for one time," is knowledge of time and place and actuality as a zero condition.

Nevertheless, the lines that strike to the center in this section are:

Because I cannot hope to turn again
Consequently I rejoice, having to construct something
Upon which to rejoice

In divesting himself of this hope, the self has also discarded the things that hope is involved in. These include not only personal ambition and the struggle for personal happiness but also caring about civilization. An immense burden which weighed on the past poetry has fallen from *Ash Wednesday*, and the result is the sense of alleviation and flowing streams and the air of high places. The poet of *The Waste Land* was weighed down by taking upon himself the burden of civilization; the poet of *Ash Wednesday* asks to be taught to "care and not to care /Teach us to sit still." Despair is not an abdication of responsibility but it is a refusal to be crushed by it for the sake of trust in powers that are delusory.

I have said that the last two lines of *The Hollow Men* draw a line under the whole development of Eliot's poetry up to that point. The chief characteristic of this work is that it was involved with consciousness conditioned by the state of the civilization at this time in history: first seeking for an escape from it into aesthetic and individualist separateness; and then acceptance of being totally conditioned. Despair means the abandonment of hopes connected with the conditioned world. It is the starting point for a Pascalian leap on to the conditionless world of faith in supernatural values.

Instead of the kind of responsibility which is associated with the highest tasks of criticism, Eliot—though not, as a matter of external obligation, abandoning these tasks—now accepts a different kind of responsibility, which is prayer. Prayer has two aspects: one is prayer for oneself, one's life in eternity for which one alone is responsible; the other is prayer for one's neighbor, which is inseparable from this. Hence in Eliot's later poetry he discriminates between "I" and "we" in his poetry under the aspect of praying:

> *Lord, I am not worthy*
> *Lord, I am not worthy*
>
> *but speak the word only.*

"I" is the individual soul's entirely separate relationship ("I and Thou") with God. In the following passage "we" shifts from meaning the bones of the "I" who entreats the Lady as intercessor—bones which are left to whiten in the desert—to meaning, in the Biblical sense, the people:

Under a juniper-tree the bones sang, scattered and shin-
* ing*
We are glad to be scattered, we did little good to each
* other,*
Under a tree in the cool of the day, with the blessing of
* sand,*
Forgetting ourselves and each other, united
In the quiet of the desert. This is the land which ye
Shall divide by lot. And neither division nor unity
Matters. This is the land. We have our inheritance.

Prayer is subject and hero of *Ash Wednesday.* It is
the connecting link between despair and hope, unbelief
and belief. For in order to pray you do not have to have
hope or faith, though you will not be able to do so unless you pray to have both. Thus the poet can at one and
the same time "renounce the blessèd face / And renounce the voice . . . And pray to God to have mercy
upon us." He can, following the precedent which he
finds in Dante, pray through the intercession of the
Lady. He must also (as happens in Section III) endure
lapses back to the desires of the senses which he believes
himself to have renounced. Such is the scene beyond "a
slotted window bellied like the fig's fruit."

Perhaps the least successful section of the poem,
rather contorted in expression, is Section V. Its theme
is the relation between the word and the Word. But,
despite a certain laboredness, it is most interesting in
showing Eliot's preoccupation with the relationship of
the Word considered as Incarnation and the word considered as poetry.

The Word is the Word made flesh, the Incarnation.
This is the end of the quest which has, until *Ash
Wednesday,* been the theme of all his poetry. The Word
as the Symbol is unlike other symbols in poetry. For in
it the supremely poetic idea coincides with the greatest

mystery of the intersection of eternity—the supernatural —with a moment in history.

To accept the literal truth of the Incarnation not only altered Eliot's life but also altered his attitude to poetry. Until now he had thought that philosophic and religious ideas in poetry were for the poet simply material about which he had those emotions which enabled him to write poetry. He did not have to believe a religion or philosophy in order to write poetry about it. However, the Word (with the first letter a capital) was only a significant symbol in poetry if the poet believed in the Incarnation, which it symbolized in the world.

Thus the introduction of the symbol of the Word into his poetry was different even from introducing other Dantesque symbolism, such as the Rose or the Garden (both of which are present in *Ash Wednesday*). It means introducing a symbol which carries the same truth inside the poetry as outside it. Moreover, the Word is not subject to the same law of needing constant renewal for the purposes of its use in poetry as, for example, the rose. The Word is an absolute and exists with the same compressed intensity of meaning in poetry as in religion.

However, to be accepted as absolute the Word has to find words. It has to be recognized, and this can only be done through words. The word has to be spoken and heard in order that the Word may be spoken and heard.

The poet is, then, still struggling with his unbelief in *Ash Wednesday*. In Section IV the "silent sister veiled in white and blue" who intercedes for the poet "bent her head and signed but spoke no word"

> *But the fountain sprang up and the bird sang down*
> *Redeem the time, redeem the dream*
> *The token of the word unheard, unspoken*

The word has not been spoken and therefore the Word is not heard. This is the opening of Section V:

If the lost word is lost, if the spent word is spent
If the unheard, unspoken
Word is unspoken, unheard;
Still is the unspoken word, the Word unheard,
The Word without a word, the Word within
The world and for the world;
And the light shone in darkness and
Against the Word the unstilled world still whirled
About the center of the silent Word.

The reason for the silence of the Word is that in the conditions of the world the word cannot speak, become united with it:

Where shall the word be found, where will the word
Resound? Not here, there is not enough silence

In *Ash Wednesday* the poet cannot identify the word with the Word. The alternative to the world of "those who walk in darkness" can only, at this stage, be prayer, and the prayer beyond prayer, that the prayer will finds its object: "And let my cry come unto Thee."

I have mentioned that *Ash Wednesday* contains lines and images which seem like illuminations in a missal. It also offers an example of Eliot's invention of forms that seem analogous with music. When I first read this poem, it struck me that Section II has a form reminiscent of the mysterious second movement of Beethoven's Quartet in A Minor, opus 132. I wrote to ask Eliot whether he had heard the late Beethoven quartets. He replied on March 28, 1931, that he was very glad I was listening to them, and continued:

I have the A Minor Quartet on the gramophone, and find it quite inexhaustible to study. There is a sort of heavenly or at least more than human gaiety about some of his later things which one imagines might come to oneself as the fruit of reconciliation and relief after immense suffering; I should like to get something of that into verse before I die.

Here is perhaps the place to relate some anecdotes, two of which concern *Ash Wednesday*. In the following I am quoting from the account I wrote shortly after Eliot's death:

> Eliot could be less than helpful if one tried to "explicate" him. In 1929, there was a meeting of the Oxford Poetry Club at which he was the guest of honour. . . . An undergraduate asked Eliot: "Please, sir, what do you mean by the line: *'Lady, three white leopards sat under a juniper-tree?'*" Eliot looked at him and said: "I mean, *'Lady, three white leopards sat under a juniper-tree.'*"[1]

A year previous to this, on Wednesday, May 16, 1928 (to be precise), Eliot addressed an undergraduate club, The Martlets, at University College, Oxford. He declined to give a lecture, but agreed to answer questions. The question was raised whether there was any ultimate criterion for judging a work of art. How can we be certain that *Antony and Cleopatra* and the Acropolis continue always to be beautiful? T., an undergraduate, who in his cups would often call on me late at night and talk about the philosophy of Santayana, said that surely it was impossible to believe in aesthetic values being permanent, unless one believed in God in whose mind beauty existed. Eliot bowed his head in that almost praying attitude which I came to know well, and

[1] In *T. S. Eliot, The Man and His Work*, Allen Tate, ed., p. 46.

murmured words to the effect of: "That is what I have come to believe."

On one occasion I was having tea with Leonard and Virginia Woolf when Eliot was also a fellow guest. At their most "Bloomsbury-agnostic" they started needling him about his religious beliefs. "Tom, do you really go to church?" "Yes." "Do you hand round the collection?" "Yes." "Oh, really! What are your feelings when you pray?" They waited rather tensely for his answer to this question. Eliot leaned forward, bowing his head in that attitude which was itself one of prayer, and described the attempt to concentrate, to forget self, to attain union with God. The striving.

When I first met him in 1928 Eliot was going through a period of great unhappiness in his private life—this was before he separated from his wife. Her reactions to him took forms which exposed him to humiliation before strangers. I cite one example, from a later time, just after he had published *Murder in the Cathedral*. A friend of mine who did not know Eliot used to go to the same hairdresser as Vivien Eliot and sometimes found herself sitting side by side with her under the dryer. On one occasion, Vivien Eliot complained bitterly that when she was in the street coming to the hairdresser people persistently stared at her. My friend found this as unaccountable as Mrs. Eliot did, until she saw upon leaving the hairdressers, Mrs. Eliot put on her hat. This had stitched on it the rather garish purple and green dust-jacket of Eliot's play, with the letter-print MURDER IN THE CATHEDRAL very prominent round the rim. Eliot clearly felt that his wife's unhappiness and illness were in large measure his fault (though she had a history of nervous illness before she met him). The most personal feelings, revealed indirectly in his poetry (they are almost a matter of the sensibility present there), are of guilt and remorse. In the prose as well as the poetry which he wrote at this time, he showed a puritan distaste for the pleasures of the senses. It was in this mood that in *After Strange Gods* he attacked D. H. Lawrence as "spiritually sick" and in some of his stories an instrument of "the daemonic powers." But later he withdrew this book which he had called "a primer of modern heresy" from publication. On one occasion he told me that when he wrote *After Strange Gods* he was in a state of unhappiness which distorted his judgment. Empson quotes him as saying of some of his prose: "I was very sick in soul when I wrote that passage . . . and I wish now that I could rewrite such material entirely." Empson comments: "it seems to me that remarkably little attention has been paid to these reflections of his later years. However, he always gave great credit to his second wife for his eventual spiritual recovery."[2]

Disgust with the flesh finds its way into the poetry, of course, for example in a passage from "Marina" (lines beautiful in themselves and which therefore render ambiguous what intellectually they say):

Those who sharpen the tooth of the dog, meaning
Death
Those who glitter with the glory of the humming-bird,
*   meaning*
Death
Those who sit in the stye of contentment, meaning
Death
Those who suffer the ecstasy of the animals, meaning
Death

[2] William Empson, "My God There's Bears on It," *Essays in Criticism*, XXII (October 1972), 428.

The emphasis on the animals for which disgust is being expressed might make the reader reflect that after all men are animals, and that they have to die anyway. The condemnation expressed in these lines can mean one of two things: either that animal enjoyment of life by human beings is a form of death, or that we know we have to die. If it means the former, then for a human to delight in having the glory of the hummingbird means that he or she at least has not equated life with death. If it means (as Eliot sometimes seems to mean) that only very brief time separates us from death and that beds on which we make love are also our deathbeds, then the despised animals have a greater wisdom in their ignorance than we have with our knowledge of death.

Eliot in a good many of his writings was altogether too willing to condemn the ordinary living of ordinary people as a form of death. In the same passage about Lawrence from which I have quoted he observes, "most people are only very little alive; and to awaken them to the spiritual is a very great responsibility." He agrees with Lawrence in regarding "modern material civilization" as a "living death," "against which Lawrence spoke again and again"; but he does not agree with the form which Lawrence's protest took. The word "death" as a description applied to other people's lives is, in fact, thrown about with as great facility by Eliot as by Lawrence, though from different directions, as it were. They do a good deal to justify their contempt for dead humanity. Yet perhaps this willingness to pass poetic death sentences on millions of ordinary lives may tell us at least as much about the alienation from life of these writers as it does about the people they so despise.

Inevitably Eliot and Lawrence are, in their opposite ways, more interesting when they are writing about life as they see it than about death. Each of the poems written after *Ash Wednesday*—"Journey of the Magi" and "A Song for Simeon," "Animula," and "Marina"— is about a death and a birth: the Incarnation, which signifies the new life. The death is now of "the old dispensation," the birth that of Christ. The voices of the Magi and of Simeon are glad of the death which leads to this birth. "Animula" is the prayer for the simple soul at the hour of birth. "Marina" derives from the lost daughter of that name in Shakespeare's *Pericles* and, as the epigraph shows, the awakening of Heracles from sleep after scenes of madness in which he has killed his family, from a nightmare of a past world. The images of dog, hummingbird, swine, and animal ecstasy from the past life are now dissolved "By this grace dissolved in place," and the new life (symbolized by the daughter recovered from the sea) defines its different reality:

Resign my life for this life, my speech for that unspoken . . .

Again we have Eliot using the same word in the same sentence to represent opposites: life opposed to life, dream opposed to dream, word opposed to Word. This opposition derives its force from the idea that modern life is a kind of death and the death called life is installed in the seats of power. Words like "dream," "life," "word," "love," all relate to the question which writers like Eliot, Yeats, and Lawrence have put into the reader's mind—what is real? If the materialism which we take to be reality is unreal, then that which a utilitarian world considers unreal is reality. Yeats stressed opposites such as "life-in-death and death-in-life" defiantly, with an air of saber rattling. Lawrence made propaganda for his own doctrines of the dark gods of the unconscious. With Eliot the difference is between values of a fragmented secular civilization, which he first sees as those of death, partly redeemable by the absorption of the living within the values of the tradition (that is to say, the dead), and which he later comes to see as those of the temporal city which can only be redeemed through the *civitas dei* which is the Church.

Ideas of Poetry

● ● ●

VIII

Eliot not only thought that the best critics were those, like Dryden, Johnson, and Coleridge, who themselves wrote poetry but thought that a critic who was a poet should in his critical writings draw on his creative experience. He reproached Matthew Arnold for not having done so. Correcting Matthew Arnold was a lifelong preoccupation with him, and it is not surprising that in his criticism he, unlike Arnold, constantly drew on his own creative experience.

His remarks about writing poetry sometimes appear inconsistent, if not self-contradictory. Perhaps, though, Eliot does not so much contradict himself as submit to self-correction, an operation which sometimes seems to be performed under an anesthetic. He has become oblivious of some previous attitude.

The older he gets the more frequently he admits to his dislike of reading his earlier prose. If he does stumble on his opinions, it is usually to correct or repudiate them, as he does with those he once expressed about Milton, Goethe, and Shelley. In an essay on "Goethe as the Sage" (1955) Eliot sets himself the task of making the effort "to reconcile myself to Goethe: not primarily to repair an injustice done, for one has committed many such literary injustices without compunction, but because I should otherwise have neglected some opportunity of self-development, which it would be culpable to neglect." Eliot goes on to say that the very fact of his entertaining such a feeling is a kind of tribute to Goethe: "the admission that Goethe is one of the Great Europeans" (*On Poetry and Poets*, pp. 210–11).

In a passage from "The Three Voices of Poetry" (1953), which I shall discuss more fully later, Eliot writes that in poetry of the "first voice," there is "a simultaneous development of form and material." The poet is in the act of writing solely concerned with finding the words for some "thing" which, when the words have been found, disappears to be replaced by a poem. In each case for poetry of this kind the form is unique. Yet, in his essay on "Johnson as Critic and Poet" (1944) he writes, "structure I hold to be an important element of poetic composition," and criticizes Johnson for lacking structure. It is difficult to reconcile this idea of an external planned architecture—which seems essentially premeditated—with that of the "moment-to-moment struggle with angel and octopus" of the "first voice" of poetry. Yet the second view is surely corrective of the first rather than a contradiction of it. There is a fruitful dialogue between the French symbolist idea of poetry and the intellectually structured in Eliot's mind.

He places Goldsmith's "The Deserted Village" above any poem by Johnson or by Gray. His reasons for doing this is that Goldsmith writes with an instinctive sense of structure that develops from line to line. He has (Eliot writes) "a skill and concision seldom equalled since Chaucer."

There were, I think, certain relations between the intellectual and conscious and the unconscious and instinctual elements in poetry which Eliot felt to be extremely important and which he was continually trying to clarify. One of these was the relation between the creative and the critical faculties in the act of composition. He described the creative as acting unconsciously and the critical almost but not quite simultaneously saying "yes" or "no" to it. What he was far less certain about was the part played by the conscious mind in planning a poem before it was written.

This relationship between intellectualized structure and a distinctive form is centrally bound up with that of the status of the subject matter in a poem. As we have already seen, in his early criticism Eliot suggested that Dante need not have believed in the Thomist philosophy which was the subject of *The Divine Comedy*. With his conversion to Christianity, he no longer thought this. But he then considered that for some readers of his essay on Dante their inability to accept Dante's beliefs must be a problem. He advises the reader that while he cannot afford to ignore what Dante believes, he is not called on to believe it. All that is required is that he should understand it, and in order to do this the reader need not believe but must suspend his disbelief. In a note to the second edition of this essay he states his reactions to the attitude toward poetry and belief expressed by I. A. Richards in *Practical Criticism*. Eliot agrees with Richards that the reader can have "full literary or poetic appreciation without sharing the beliefs of the poet." If this were not so, there could be no literature and no criticism. Recalling his assertion that "we can distinguish between Dante's beliefs as a man and his beliefs as a poet," he now qualifies this by adding, "We are forced to believe that there is a particular relation between the two and that the poet 'means what he says.'"

He writes: "If we learned for instance that *De Rerum Natura* was a Latin exercise which Dante had composed for relaxation after completing *The Divine Comedy,* and published under the name of one Lucretius, I am sure that our capacity for enjoying either poem would be mutilated." Then he rejects Richards' description of *The Waste Land* as a poem in which the writer has effected "a complete severance between his poetry and *all* beliefs" (*Selected Essays,* pp. 269–71).

Returning to the idea that the reader can "understand" a belief which he does not share, when it is expressed by a poet, Eliot then produces an argument which is extraordinarily revealing of that inner logic which runs through all his prose and poetry and directs him inexorably toward positions where truth is asserted dogmatically and values are related to a "final cause."

> If you yourself are convinced of a certain view of life, then you inevitably and irresistibly believe that if anyone else comes to "understand" it fully, his understanding *must* terminate in belief. It is possible, and sometimes necessary, that full understanding must identify itself with full belief. A good deal, it turns out, hangs on the meaning, if any, of this short word *full.*

Quibbling about the meaning of the word "full" rings a bit comical, as though to say that, having stated an irrefutable position, let us now sit down and discuss what is meant by "irrefutability." The argument itself, though hedged round with qualifications, is clear. In the long run A, who thinks he understands the view of life of which B is convinced, can only complete such understanding by coming to believe what B believes. Anything short of this is merely to understand why B believes something that A cannot believe. It is an explanation of A's failure or refusal to understand the view of life which B thinks to be literally true.

The argument underlines Eliot's previously held positions; for, obviously, if by "understanding" is here meant understanding the views held by Dante, then fully to understand Dante is to enter into his view of life. Not to enter into it "fully" is to exhibit some degree of not understanding. Thus to argue, as Eliot did once, that Dante need not have believed in the philosophy which he put into *The Divine Comedy*, would show incomplete understanding of Dante: and complete understanding would mean not just appreciating the poetry, but coming to believe what Dante believed.

The argument had a force for Eliot which progressively he applied to himself. In the note to the second edition of his essay on Dante, from which I have already quoted, he goes on to dispute Richards' theory of "pseudo-statements" (i.e., statements which are accepted as true within the context of the poetry, but which are not true outside it) and remarks that Shakespeare's "Ripeness is all" has "profound emotional meaning" for him "with, at least, no literal fallacy"; while he accepts Dante's *"la sua voluntate è nostra pace"* as a statement which is *literally true*. If this is so, then the gap which divides "the illusion of reality" created inside the poetry and the reality of philosophical truth outside it, at certain points at least, becomes closed. What is literally true outside the poetry is literally true inside it. The word coincides with the Word.

Eliot was received into the Church of England on June 29, 1927. The change that his religion brought about in his prose writing is apparent in *For Lancelot Andrewes* (1928), a volume of essays which show his interest in Christian orthodoxy. The title essay is devoted to praise of an ecclesiastic who was eminent in the formation of the Church of England. In the same volume "Baudelaire in Our Time" contains, in the manner that characterizes so much of Eliot's prose, some concealed autobiography of the literary generation to which Eliot belonged. In attacking Arthur Symons' 1890ish renderings of Baudelaire, Eliot points out that "the 'nineties are nearer to us" (by whom he must mean himself and Ezra Pound) than "the *literary* generation which includes Mr. Bernard Shaw, and Mr. Wells, and Mr. Lytton Strachey. This generation, in its ancestry, 'skipped' the 'nineties: it is the progeny of Huxley, and Tyndall, and George Eliot, and Gladstone. And with this generation Baudelaire has nothing to do; but he had something to do with the 'nineties, and he has a great deal to do with us."

This is historically important. Pound and Eliot when they came to Europe before World War I were looking for the English literary scene which had connections with Paris, English poets with the French symbolists. What they found were the Georgians. To them these poets seemed a total irrelevance in the modern age, just as the English " '90s" poets, in turn, seemed childish and self-indulgent by the exacting intellectual standards of contemporary poets in France. Eliot writes in this essay that "the important fact about Baudelaire is that he was essentially a Christian, born out of his due time." He remarks also that Baudelaire's "tendency to 'ritual . . .' springs from no attachment to the outward forms of Christianity, but from the instincts of a soul that was *naturaliter* Christian." Here Eliot writes as one who has found his true grail.

Eliot takes up the question of the ideas in poetry again in *The Use of Poetry and the Use of Criticism* (his Charles Eliot Norton Lectures at Harvard, 1932). He admits that he cannot admire the poetry of Shelley which he liked so much when he was young. This may be because Shelley's ideas now excite his abhorrence. At the same time he questions whether one should condemn poetry on account of the ideas it contains. This question arises when he comes to discuss Yeats, whose poetry—at any rate that of his middle age—Eliot admires, for he found little to admire in Yeats's ideas.

He was very much fascinated by self-induced trance states, calculated symbolism, mediums, theosophy, crystal-gazing, and hobgoblins. Golden apples, archers, black pigs and such paraphernalia abounded. Often the verse has an hypnotic charm: but you cannot take heaven by magic, especially if you are, like Mr. Yeats, a very sane person. Then, by a great triumph of development, Mr. Yeats began to write and is still writing some of the most beautiful poetry in the language, some of the clearest, simplest, most direct. (*The Use of Poetry and the Use of Criticism*, p. 140)

Eliot later modified his views about Shelley, discovering, in "What Dante Means to Me" (1950), that Shelley's *The Triumph of Life* contained "some of the greatest and most Dantesque lines in English" (*To Criticize the Critic*, p. 130). He paid even greater tribute to Shelley in *The Cocktail Party* when, asked to explain his attitude to life, the gurulike psychoanalyst-priest Harcourt-Reilly asks if he may quote poetry, and embarks on Earth's speech in *Prometheus Unbound*:

> *Ere Babylon was dust*
> *The magus Zoroaster, my dead child,*
> *Met his own image walking in the garden. . . .*

However, the issue for Eliot in 1933 was Shelley's ideas. Shelley was especially repellent to him on account of his views about marriage expressed in _Epipsychidion_. Eliot deduced a general rule from his own reaction to these ideas:

> When the doctrine, theory, belief, or "view of life" presented in a poem is one which the mind of the reader can accept as coherent, mature, and founded on the facts of experience, it interposes no obstacle to the reader's enjoyment, whether it be one that he accept or deny, approve or deprecate. When it is one which the reader rejects as childish or feeble, it may, for a reader of well-developed mind, set up an almost complete check. (_The Use of Poetry_, p. 96)

Having entertained the thought that the ideas in poetry do after all affect one's view of the poet, Eliot develops it further. Following on his remarks about Shelley, he quotes with approval a remark by Aldous Huxley in his Introduction to _The Letters of D. H. Lawrence_ to the effect that Lawrence "loathed the Wilhelm-Meisterish view of love as an education, as a means to culture, a Sandow-exerciser for the soul!" Eliot echoes "precisely" and declares himself in this matter for once on the side of Lawrence, adding:

> That view runs through the work of Goethe. . . . Does "culture" require that we make (what Lawrence never did, and I respect him for it) a deliberate effort to put out of mind all our convictions and passionate beliefs about life when we sit down to read poetry? If so, so much the worse for culture. Nor, on the other hand, may we distinguish, as people sometimes do, between the occasions on which a particular poet is "being a poet" and the occasions on which he is "being a preacher." (_The Use of Poetry_, p. 97)

Eliot gives other examples of the relation (*relation* and *relatedness* are key words in this discussion) of poetry to philosophy. One is Landor, whom Eliot considers "one of the very finest poets of the first part of the nineteenth century" and who has yet never had a reputation to compare with that of Wordsworth, or even of Byron, Keats, and Shelley. The reason for this is that Landor is "only a magnificent by-product" of history, whereas with Wordsworth "there is something integral about such greatness, and something significant in his place in the pattern of history, with which we have to reckon." In fact, rather surprisingly, Eliot sees Wordsworth's greatness as that of the revolutionary: "When you find Wordsworth as the seer and prophet whose function it is to instruct and edify through pleasure, as if this were something he had found out for himself, you may begin to think that there is something in it, at least for some kinds of poetry" (*The Use of Poetry*, pp. 88, 75).

It is evident that in this book Eliot considerably enlarges his view of the importance of the subject in poetry. In embracing Wordsworth he has accepted the egotistical sublime, which surely means, among other things, expression of the poet's personality. However, he still insists that the purpose of the poetry is not to communicate this material, but to *be*, as poetry. Poetry cannot be bound—the word *bound* has force for Eliot. He objects to any theory of poetry which, in relating poetry to "a religious or social scheme of things," attempts to explain it in terms of those things. Such attitudes are "in danger of *binding* poetry by legislation to be observed—and poetry can recognise no such laws" (*The Use of Poetry*, p. 139).

Throughout his life Eliot insisted above all, as we have already seen, that poetry cannot, should not, and must not take the place of or be a substitute for religion.

He quotes approvingly Jacques Maritain: "It is a deadly error to expect poetry to provide the super-substantial nourishment of man," and: "By showing us where moral truth and the genuine supernatural are situate, religion saves poetry from the absurdity of believing itself destined to transform ethics and life: it saves it from overweening arrogance." Eliot attacks Richards when he echoes Matthew Arnold by remarking that in the chaos of ideas in the modern world "poetry is capable of saving us" (*The Use of Poetry*, pp. 137, 130). Eliot sums up his view of poetry in a way which nevertheless seems to make concessions to the social and psychological view of its use. Rather surprisingly he says nothing about tradition and nothing about the function of poetry as purifying and sustaining the language:

[Poetry] may effect revolutions in sensibility such as are periodically needed; may help to break up the conventional modes of perception and valuation which are perpetually forming, and make people see the world afresh, or some new part of it. It may make us from time to time a little more aware of the deeper, unnamed feelings which form the substratum of our being, to which we rarely penetrate; for our lives are mostly a constant evasion of ourselves, and an evasion of the visible and sensible world. (*The Use of Poetry*, p. 155)

The Use of Poetry and the Use of Criticism is, on the whole, liberal in tone, conciliatory, meeting opponents halfway, though firm in its opposition to attitudes of critics which Eliot traces to Matthew Arnold.

In "Goethe as the Sage" Eliot described himself as someone who combines "a Catholic cast of mind, a Calvinistic heritage, and a Puritanical temperament." All these, together with a rebulliency of patriotism for the reactionary South, are in evidence in *After Strange*

Gods: A Primer of Modern Heresy, three lectures which he gave at the University of Virginia in 1932. This was a time of extreme tension for him, when he was making up his mind to separate from his wife. Some of the unhappiness shows in the lectures which, after their first publication, he never allowed to be reissued. In them, while being careful to explain that what he is doing is not "literary criticism," he tries to relate the work of some modern writers—notably Joyce, Hardy, Kipling, and Lawrence—to the concept of orthodoxy, which he discovers in the Church. He applies to the writers discussed standards deriving from ideas such as original sin, the devil, the forces of evil, heresy. Sitting in judgment on his contemporaries, he declares them not guilty of blasphemy—for blasphemy is a sin he admires, Baudelaire frequently indulging in it. Lawrence is perhaps an exception—almost capable of sin. In some ways, Eliot regards Lawrence as an ally. He can certainly not be held to be tainted with liberalism: "That we can and ought to reconcile ourselves to Liberalism, Progress and Modern Civilisation is a proposition which we need not have waited for Lawrence to condemn; and it matters a good deal in what name we condemn it. I fear that Lawrence's work may appeal, not to those who are well and able to discriminate, but to the sick and debile and confused" (*After Strange Gods*, p. 61). Lawrence is on the side of the angels of reaction but perhaps for unsalubrious reasons. Eliot, as we have seen, came to think that when he expressed these views it was he and not Lawrence who was sick. But perhaps we are all sick.

Eliot was fascinated by Lawrence partly on account of his genius, but partly also because like himself Lawrence saw the modern world as a struggle between the forces of Life and of Death. Admitting that he has not read all Lawrence's "late and his posthumous works, which are numerous," Eliot remarks optimistically: "In some respects he may have progressed: his early belief in Life may have passed over, as a really serious belief in Life must, into a belief in Death" (*ibid.*, p. 60).

After Strange Gods is certainly in many respects a "sick" book, and Eliot was doubtless justified in withdrawing it. However, there are passages in it which are prophetic of the extremes of "confessional" writing and self-expression since. Who today, reading recent "turned-on" writings, would disagree with the following: "It is by no means self-evident that human beings are most real when most violently excited; violent physical passions do not in themselves differentiate men from each other, but rather tend to reduce them to the same state" (*After Strange Gods*, p. 55).

T. S. Eliot was distressed by the fact that so many of his readers prefer his early to his later criticism. One can agree that his sense of grievance was partly justified. He continued to write excellent literary criticism in which he extended his range beyond the Elizabethans to the eighteenth and nineteenth centuries. His essays on Dryden, Johnson, and Matthew Arnold—not to mention more general surveys, such as "What Is a Classic?" (1954), "Virgil and the Christian World" (1957), and "The Three Voices of Poetry" (1953)—are more mature and of wider interest than his early criticism. Nevertheless, some of the passion that involved the reader in the earlier essays has gone. The difference is, I think, that Eliot's earlier criticism flowed, with quotations and metaphors, into the poetry he was writing, and in its preoccupations with the tradition representing the communion of the dead, it pressed toward "the frontiers of metaphysics" (*Selected Essays*, p. 21). That writing was, in a word, the prose branch of the poetic quest. After *For Lancelot Andrewes* literary criticism became an activity of whose limitations he was very much aware and which interested him less than either poetry or theology. The difference can be detected by comparing his remarks about the relationship of the new work to the monuments of the past in "Tradition and the Individual Talent" (quoted earlier) with the following eminently sensible remarks about our relations to the past in "Johnson as Critic and Poet":

> The sensibility of any period in the past is always likely to appear to be more limited than our own; for we are naturally much more aware of our ancestors' lack of awareness to those things of which we are aware, than we are of any lack in ourselves, of awareness to what they perceived and we do not. We may ask then whether there is not a capital distinction to be drawn between a limited sensibility—remembering that the longer extent of *history* of which we have knowledge, makes all minds of the past seem to us limited—and a defective sensibility; and accordingly ask whether Johnson, within his proper limits, is not a sensitive as well as a judicial critic; whether the virtues he commended in poetry do not always remain virtues, and whether the kinds of fault that he censured do not always remain faults and to be avoided. (*On Poetry and Poets*, p. 166)

This is a very extended gloss on Eliot's terse apothegm written when he was a young man: "Someone said: 'The dead writers are remote from us because we *know* so much more than they did.' Precisely, and they are that which we know" (*Selected Essays*, p. 16). The young man's remark, which converts it into something concretely seen, has all the force of his poetry and the immanence of his religious passion. The older man's is made by the critic who has carefully separated literary criticism from religion and morals, and who makes his point abstractly and with an air of almost painful attention. Painful attention and abstract language also characterize Eliot's writings on education in *To Criticize the Critic* and nearly all of *Notes Towards the Definition of Culture.*

However, Eliot's late prose is shot through with passages of discreet, moving, and humble poetic autobiography, passages such as this one in the "Conclusion" of *The Use of Poetry and the Use of Criticism*:

> Why, for all of us, out of all that we have heard, seen, felt, in a lifetime, do certain images recur, charged with emotion, rather than others? The song of one bird, the leap of one fish, at a particular place and time, the scent of one flower, an old woman on a German mountain path, six ruffians seen through an open window playing cards at night at a small French railway junction where there was a watermill: such memories may have symbolic value, but of what we cannot tell, for they come to represent the depths of feeling into which we cannot peer. (*The Use of Poetry and the Use of Criticism*, p. 148)

Occasionally, too, he writes an essay in which he seems to forget theology, morality, education, sociology, and all his new interests and weighty responsibilities, and returns to that total absorption in poetry which must have remained with him always under everything that grew on top of it—for without it he could not have continued to be a poet. Such is the marvelous essay "From Poe to Valéry" (1948). Eliot seems to touch his own deepest preoccupations in discussing the "incantatory" quality of Poe and what Eliot calls "in the most nearly literal sense . . . 'the magic of his verse' " and in describing him not as an American but as "a displaced European" who lived in America and who was in some sense different from that in which the epithet would apply to Whitman, provincial; in examining the interest of Baudelaire and Mallarmé in Poe; in discussing those French symbolist poets who influenced him when he was young; and in considering the writing of Valéry as the last of all that tradition which begins with Poe and which includes Eliot himself. In the same essay Eliot goes on to consider the term "*la poésie pure.*" He writes of a "third state" in the historic development of poetry in which the poet, after caring first about the subject matter and then, second, the style, "the subject may recede to the background: instead of being the purpose of the poem, it becomes simply a necessary means for the realization of the poem." The goal of complete disappearance of the subject within the language, Eliot takes to be that of *la poésie pure*. Poetry, however, he thinks, has to be impure, that is, have sense as well as meaning. But the meaning exists for the sake of the poetry not the poetry for the sake of the meaning. Eliot thought that with Valéry the attempt to write "*la poésie pure*" had gone as far as it could go and that after him there would be a reaction—though in what direction he could not guess (*To Criticize the Critic*, pp. 37–42). Perhaps the *Four Quartets* in part realized the reaction.

More than forty years after writing "Prufrock" Eliot summed up his views about the way in which he wrote poetry in a lecture given for the National Book League in Cambridge in 1953 and later published under the title "The Three Voices of Poetry." He distinguishes between three distinct voices of poetry: first, the voice of the poet talking to himself; second, the voice of the poet addressing an audience; and, third, the voice of the poet when he attempts to create a dramatic character speaking in verse. The main distinction is between the first and the third voice, the introverted meditative voice of the past speaking to himself and the extroverted, dramatizing voice in which he speaks to an audience. And of these, it is the first which concerns us here.

Discussing the first voice, Eliot cites Gottfried Benn, who describes the beginning of a poem in the writer's mind as the fertilization of a creative germ (*"ein dumpfer schöpferischer Keim"*) by the language. The poet has, to use Eliot's paraphrase of Benn, "something germinating in him for which he must find words; but . . . he cannot identify this embryo until it has been transformed into an arrangement of the right words in the right order. When you have the words for it, the 'thing' for which the words had to be found has disappeared, replaced by a poem." Eliot writes that he agrees with Benn about this, and would take his remarks further. In a poem written in the voice of the poet talking to himself, "the poet may be concerned solely with expressing in verse—using all his resources of words, with their history, their connotations, their music—this obscure impulse." At this stage the poet is concerned with nothing but finding what for him— and for him alone—are the right, or the least wrong, words. "He is haunted by a demon, a demon against which he feels powerless, because in its first manifestation it has no face, no name, nothing; and the words, the poem he makes, are a kind of form of exorcism of this demon" (*On Poetry and Poets*, pp. 97–98).

This is not so much a theory of poetry as an account of how Eliot wrote what he calls poetry of the first voice, which corresponds curiously to the writing of romantic inspirational poetry. It also resembles modern imaginative writers—of fiction as well as poetry. James Joyce (in his *Scribble Books*), D. H. Lawrence, and Virginia Woolf give evidence of having written in much the same way. Eliot is particularly illuminating when he goes on to consider form:

It is misleading, of course, to speak of the material as creating or imposing its own form: what happens is a simultaneous development of form and material; for the form affects the material at every stage; and perhaps all the material does is to repeat 'not that! not that!' in the face of each unsuccessful attempt at formal organization; and finally the material is identified with its form. (*On Poetry and Poets*, p. 107)

By "material," in this context, Eliot means the "unknown, dark *psychic material*—we might say, the octopus or angel with which the poet struggles" (*ibid.*, p. 100). A poem of the "first voice" tends to discover its own form—so that in each poem written out of this voice, the form will be unique to that poem.

There is an important distinction to be noted here between Eliot's account of his "first voice" and rather similar accounts by Rimbaud and, later, by surrealist writers. Rimbaud, asserting that poetry is not written out of the will and consciousness, but is a process of submission by the writer to unconscious forces in him, advocated a complete surrender to the unconscious. He aimed not at that impersonality colored by the personal which one finds in Eliot's poetry but at the reduction of the poet, body and soul, to the condition of an instrument—violin or gong—played upon by external forces of violence and internal psychic ones. "So much the worse for the piece of wood which discovers itself to be a violin." Rimbaud's "*on me pense*" and "*je est un autre*" means that the poet is not a voice speaking to himself but a depersonalized sensibility acted upon by external or internal forces, like the scream of a victim which rings in his own ears as though uttered by someone not himself.

It is very clear, however, that by impersonality in

poetry Eliot does not mean depersonalization. Depersonalization would imply Rimbaud's *"dérèglement des sens"*—the programmatic disorganization of the senses. Some symbolists aimed at an equally depersonalized poetry in which the language becomes completely divorced from the subject matter of a poem and the poet becomes an instrument of sensibility through which the poem writes itself.

Eliot's position was different from that of writers in whom the struggle with the "octopus or angel" is envisaged as one in which the octopus or angel wins over the poet's consciousness. Eliot is a poet in whom consciousness balances unconsciousness. He may be subject to a demon in his moments of inspiration, but he does not want the demon to take over (as Blake, Rimbaud, and surrealists wished it to do) or the angel to take over (as Mallarmé wished it to do). He wants to exorcise both demon and angel. In an earlier essay (on "The Function of Criticism") he wrote of poets in whom "critical discrimination . . . has flashed in the very heat of creation" (*Selected Essays*, p. 30).

Eliot writes poetry out of opposed forces within himself, out of a perpetually maintained struggle of consciousness and unconsciousness. It is a balancing of forces, not a victory of one over the other. Subject matter comes from the conscious mind, psychic material from the unconscious.

The Point of Intersection of the Timeless

●

IX

An aim which Eliot consistently pursued was
the negative one of not expressing his personality in his poetry. The poet must study to become part of the tradition.

Of course, the poetry had roots in the poet's
own experiences: his earliest, almost unconscious memories, the rhythms of body and soul,
his unconscious as well as his conscious mind.
All these are indeed "personal." But there is a
difference between saying that the poetry reveals
a uniquely personal aural, visual, and moral
sensibility and saying that the poet expresses
his personality in it.

Eliot was, as we have seen, much concerned
with the relationship of the subject and poet.
The subject is that of which the poet is aware,
as a structure of ideas or experience, before he
writes the poem. Throughout his criticism Eliot
keeps the subject at a distance, as something to

be considered almost apart from the poetry. It is important not as material to be imposed, but as it can be transformed into poetry.

After his conversion to Christianity, the separation which he had formerly insisted on, between the *emotion* which the poet felt about a philosophy or a religion and his actual belief in it, tended to disappear: the emotion and the belief became the same. The poetic symbols now referred to a further religious symbolism beyond them, in which the symbols related to "final causes." As he wrote in discussing Dante's *Vita Nuova*: "The attitude of Dante to the fundamental experience of the *Vita Nuova* can only be understood by accustoming ourselves to find meaning in *final causes* rather than in origins. . . . The final cause is the attraction towards God" (*Selected Essays*, p. 274). The difference between symbols in poetry and in Christianity is that in poetry they may be regarded as purely aesthetic or symbolist— that is, relating only to the poetry itself—and in religion they refer to things held to be literally true.

When Eliot came to write *Four Quartets*, in which he was summing up experience which "set a crown upon your lifetime's effort," his subject was inevitably religious, since his religion had become his central experience. The gap between the philosophic subject and the poetry was bound to narrow if not entirely to disappear. The religious symbolism and the poetic symbolism tended to coincide, as they do overtly in several passages of the poem. For example, in the third section of "Little Gidding," remembering the dead of the opposing sides of the English Civil War, he reflects:

> *Whatever we inherit from the fortunate*
> *We have taken from the defeated*
> *What they had to leave us—a symbol:*
> *A symbol perfected in death.*

> *And all shall be well and*
> *All manner of thing shall be well*
> *By the purification of the motive*
> *In the ground of our beseeching.*

The poetic symbol here becomes absorbed within the religious.

A difference, which I have been trying to emphasize, between the aesthetic and the religious in art is that the appeal of the aesthetic is to the exceptional reader. You will not like purely aesthetic art unless you like art purely as art, and not on account of the subject or ideas which it expresses. Aesthetic art tends to breed aesthetes. Most people, however, are incapable of aesthetic purism, although perhaps capable of appreciating art by way of their interest in its subject matter. The ground of the appeal of religion is that it is concerned with feelings that we share in common. This does not mean that everyone approaches the fundamentally religious situation of being alone in this world, and of having to die, from the same point of view. For some, the religious situation leads to philosophic questions about the existence (or nonexistence) of God. For others, it arises only when they are confronted with superstitious fears of death or eternity, or when they consult a clairvoyant about the future. While, on the one hand, Eliot makes poetry out of this material in *Four Quartets*, on the other, he approaches readers on levels of their lived experience where "the poetry does not matter."

After his conversion, Eliot became increasingly conscious of the difference in attitude between those who were "humanists" and "aesthetes," and those "ordinary" people who were concerned with ultimate problems but who could not base their whole attitude to life upon consolation obtained by contemplating examples of heroic idealism in the past or the achievements of great art. He draws a distinction between "ordinary" people and individuals capable of some kind of exalted consolatory philosophy in a letter he wrote to his friend Bonamy Dobrée, early in 1929, discussing Irving Babbitt's humanism:

> My point is: I don't object in the least to the position of Babbitt for Babbitts. It is a perfectly possible position for an individual. I only say: this is not a doctrine which can help the world in general. The individual can certainly love order without loving God. The people cannot. And when I say people, don't think I mean any slum or suburb or Belgravian square; I mean any number that can be addressed in print.[1]

Previously, Eliot had considered that the majority of people were little better than automata, "hollow men," scarcely alive. But *Four Quartets*, especially "The Dry Salvages," reflects his recognition that all people, ordinary or extraordinary, are individuals, each of them alone with God.

And yet he did not want to write didactic poetry. Didactic poetry is that in which the subject is already given as an intellectual structure of ideas and in relation to which the poetry is illustrative. Eliot always wished to transform his material into language "rich and strange." But sometimes the poetic statement became inseparable from the religious. This tends to happen throughout *Four Quartets*, as at the end of "The Dry Salvages":

> *For most of us, this is the aim*
> *Never here to be realised;*
> *Who are only undefeated*
> *Because we have gone on trying;*

[1] *T. S. Eliot: The Man and His Work*, Allen Tate, ed., p. 72.

> *We, content at the last*
> *If our temporal reversion nourish*
> *(Not too far from the yew-tree)*
> *The life of significant soil.*

Four Quartets[2] consists of four long poems written in a form analogous to the late quartets of Beethoven. Eliot was not trying to imitate Beethoven or to produce in his verse an effect which Beethoven produces in music. But the so-called "posthumous" quartets provided him with an example of form at once fragmentary and having a unity of feeling and vision. For the late quartets are fragments held together by a mood of suffering which becomes transcended in joy beyond suffering. Out of intense suffering gaiety emerges.

Each of Eliot's quartets has five movements: the first consisting of introduction and statement; the second, the transcendence of the theme of the first in a lyric-like minuet, followed by a sustained meditative passage further developing the thought; the third, illustrative, through the metaphor of journey or pilgrimage, of the theme of exploration; the fourth, a lyric; the fifth, a summary of the whole, and a return to the theme of the opening of the first movement.

"Burnt Norton," published in 1935, was written five years before the other three quartets, which were published within a year of one another: "East Coker" in 1940, "The Dry Salvages" in 1941, and "Little Gidding" in 1942. "Burnt Norton" began with a passage omitted from *Murder in the Cathedral.* Eliot had at the time no

---

[2] For description and commentary I recommend Helen Gardner's *The Art of T. S. Eliot,* advising the reader, however, to begin with the last chapter, "The Approach to the Meaning," in which Dame Helen gives a lucid account of the background and development of each quartet with its several movements.

idea of writing the additional three quartets; and he only did so because production of further plays by him was rendered impossible by the war.

Each quartet is associated with a particular place which has historical associations and is also associated with Eliot's own life. Thus Burnt Norton is an English country house in Gloucestershire.

"Burnt Norton" is different in treatment and as poetry from the other quartets, though Eliot took from it the theme of time which he explores in the other three quartets. This is the intersection of a moment in time with eternity: the incarnation of Christ, accepted dogmatically as a historic event, though outside the logic of history. The theme is stated very clearly in the seventh Chorus from *The Rock* (1934):

Then came, at a predetermined moment, a moment in
*   time and of time,*
A moment not out of time, but in time, in what we call
*   history: transecting, bisecting the world of time, a*
*   moment in time but not like a moment of time,*
A moment in time but time was made through that
*   moment: for without the meaning there is no time,*
*   and that moment of time gave the meaning.*

These lines are an example of the coincidence of religious dogma (by which is meant insistence on the literal truth of the miraculous or incredible) with poetic truth. They are true both as poetic imagination and as dogmatically held belief. They are also *persuasive*. The audience is invited to assent to what is being asserted.

In *Four Quartets* there is poetry in which the subject of the philosophy of experience does not matter, because it has been transformed into objects of language that are independent of their origins; and poetry in which the common ground of religious experience of life matters more than the language-object. In "Burnt Norton" there is more pure poetry than in the other three quartets. In the others, although there is poetry of the highest order—in "Little Gidding" the greatest poetry Eliot ever wrote—the subject matter of religious experience is often at least as important as "the poetry."

In this book I have noted that the center of consciousness changes in different phases of Eliot's poetry. This change is indicated in the different significance, in "Prufrock," *The Waste Land*, and *Ash Wednesday*, conveyed by the pronoun "I." In *Ash Wednesday* the "I" is that of the individual soul alone with God—or perhaps without Him—having to construct the idea of Him if life is to have any meaning.

In *Four Quartets* the multiple situation of the "I" is perhaps best conveyed in the word "humility":

> *The only wisdom we can hope to acquire*
> *Is the wisdom of humility: humility is endless.*

This humility accepts that the poet's ground of experience is the same as that of other men, even though he happens to be a poet and to have had experiences which are—as are those of all men, to themselves—special to himself. The barrier between the aesthetic and the religious consciousness is abolished by the appeal to the shared experience of writer and reader, both voyagers on the earth and within eternity. The writer is not concerned with expressing his personal idiosyncracies and his originality, though they constitute part of his uniqueness. Being someone who calls himself "I," both expresses that which is unique with him, and that which, as an isolated consciousness, he shares with the reader. Like the reader's, his personal history is a sum of moments of time. Among these he has had experience of the intersection of time with timelessness. The experience of timelessness is religious and not aesthetic, though art (as with the Chinese jar moving "perpetually in its stillness") may be the occasion for it. But if the experience of the eternal were advanced as an effect peculiar to art (as it is in some of Yeats's later poems and in the poetry of Wallace Stevens) then it would be special to the poet, and not accessible to "ordinary people" except to the extent to which they were able to enter into such art.

The "I" therefore of Eliot the man, who is growing old, provides the connection between the author of the poem and the reader or, rather, the several readers: for the experience of different kinds of reader is appealed to. The fact that the writer is involved both in his own life, which is the lives of all men, and with writing poetry, is made accessible to the reader by the theme of the poet discussing his own struggle with words, with language. He lays his cards on that table whose carpentry is art, but whose material is religious concern with life.

"Burnt Norton" never deviates into the sententious philosophic self-communings which some readers find disconcerting in passages of the other quartets. It is conducted on levels of incantatory poetry and philosophic argument. It cannot, I think, be taken as symbolist poetry in which experience and subject are treated only as starting points on a journey which leads into a world created purely from language, though there are symbolist passages in it. The poet appeals to the reader on the grounds of shared experience of living within time. This experience of being both bound to time and also outside it, is religious. However set Eliot may be on transforming this time-subject into poetry, he is equally set on persuading the reader—*"hypocrite lecteur"*—that he shares with him the fundamental religious situation of being both inside the particular moment and outside it. The difficult opening of "Burnt Norton" works both as very transparent poetry made out of abstract statements, beautifully contained within the rhythm, and intellectual argument of pressing urgency:

> *Time present and time past*
> *Are both perhaps present in time future,*
> *And time future contained in time past.*
> *If all time is eternally present*
> *All time is unredeemable.*

If everything is predetermined, then is not the future, just as much as the past, part of a fixed pattern? The word "perhaps" has great weight because it casts doubt on the idea that we live in a past-present-future co-existent time, completely predetermined, and suggests that the opposite of the statement "all time is un-redeemable" may be true. The sense of the statement is that since time is redeemable, then predetermined time cannot be true, the truth lies in timelessness experienced within but outside time.

Such thoughts are common ground for whoever has not just thought about philosophical questions but experienced them as part of his life. Eliot, like Proust, appeals to grounds and experience of living in time as well as to thought about it. This is equally true of the lines that follow:

> *What might have been is an abstraction*
> *Remaining a perpetual possibility*
> *Only in a world of speculation.*
> *What might have been and what has been*
> *Point to one end, which is always present.*
> *Footfalls echo in the memory*
> *Down the passage which we did not take*
> *Towards the door we never opened*
> *Into the rose-garden. . . .*

Some people lead an intense interior mental life in which the choice not made remains for them the subject of endless speculation. A crude example of this would be some possibility of leading a life which one has not led which seemed open in childhood and about which one "fantasizes" so intensely that it seems almost an alternative life. The road not taken is one of the most trodden in a lifetime. Here again, despite the abstract language, Eliot is meeting the reader on the ground of shared experience. In the passage which follows it is left in doubt whether what is referred to is an actual childhood memory or the echo in the memory of "a world of speculation."

> *Through the first gate,*
> *Into our first world, shall we follow*
> *The deception of the thrush? Into our first world.*
> *There they were, dignified, invisible,*
> *Moving without pressure, over the dead leaves,*
> *In the autumn heat, through the vibrant air,*
> *And the bird called, in response to*
> *The unheard music hidden in the shrubbery,*
> *And the unseen eyebeam crossed, for the roses*
> *Had the look of flowers that are looked at.*
> *There they were as our guests, accepted and accepting.*
> *So we moved, and they, in a formal pattern,*
> *Along the empty alley, into the box circle,*
> *To look down into the drained pool.*
> *Dry the pool, dry concrete, brown edged,*
> *And the pool was filled with water out of sunlight,*
> *And the lotos rose, quietly, quietly,*
> *The surface glittered out of heart of light,*
> *And they were behind us, reflected in the pool.*
> *Then a cloud passed, and the pool was empty.*
> *Go, said the bird, for the leaves were full of children,*
> *Hidden excitedly, containing laughter.*
> *Go, go, go, said the bird: human kind*
> *Cannot bear very much reality.*

Helen Gardner's comment on this passage is admirable:

> What the purpose of such memories is the poet cannot say; they disturb the "dust on a bowl of rose-leaves," stirring something dead and buried in the present. The garden also is full of echoes, and in the garden what might have been and what has been, for a moment, are.[3]

There is much that is mysterious in the passage, just as there is much that is mysterious in such a moment. "They" are not identified and might be the children in the garden or adults representing authority or even local deities. Yet although they elude definition "they" are seen. There is an almost glassy clarity about the phrase "the roses/Had the look of flowers that are looked at." What is present in the poem is the seen, the unseen, and the see-er.

The contrast between two kinds of reality is suggested in the passage about the garden. Time regained (*le temps retrouvé*) is this moment of past memory and present vision, in which the pool which is in actuality drained and dry concrete (as it was on the day when Eliot visited Burnt Norton), is "filled with water out of sunlight." The whole passage is reminiscent of the hyacinth garden in *The Waste Land*:

> *I could not*
> *Speak, and my eyes failed, I was neither*
> *Living nor dead, and I knew nothing,*
> *Looking into the heart of light, the silence.*

Such were Wordsworth's "spots of time" which opened on to the mystery of the universe, and Proust's moments of dizzying sensation in which the past was regained. Throughout *Four Quartets* Eliot appeals to the reader

[3] *Ibid.*, p. 160.

at various levels of his possible experience for confirmation in his own life of such moments.

> *To be conscious is not to be in time*
> *But only in time can the moment in the rose-garden,*
> *The moment in the arbour where the rain beat,*
> *The moment in the draughty church at smokefall*
> *Be remembered; involved with past and future.*
> *Only through time time is conquered.*

To live in reality, *dans le vrai*, for more than moments,
is almost intolerable. Reality is that moment in time
which, for the person experiencing it, stands outside
time.

"Human kind/Cannot bear very much reality." Our
existence is diurnal, fixed to timetables which are our
bodily and psychological existing. To be outside time
implies stasis, total realization of an unaltering unalterable condition flooding the mind with awareness
which would drown the time-bound illusions of the
body that there is yesterday, today, and tomorrow and
that we must move half-wearily but half with appetency
upon a treadmill of days.

Because total unconditioned consciousness is intolerable, therefore

> *the enchainment of past and future*
> *Woven in the weakness of the changing body,*
> *Protects mankind from heaven and damnation*
> *Which flesh cannot endure.*

Eliot is like Wordsworth and Proust in being a poet
of the moment within time which is outside time—the
moment of envisioning a condition which is significant
and always and fundamentally true: as though a digit
among columns of figures were suddenly to become

aware of the sum of all the figures in all the columns as giving its existence sense and meaning. For the individual this particular moment is the deathbed life-awakening moment in which he sees his own being as a significant measurable moral condition within a pattern of all life.

The third section of "Burnt Norton" treats of life as a journey, employing the metaphor of the London Underground with travelers whose minds are in a state of suspended awareness, neither inside time nor outside it, a kind of no-time or limbo between today and tomorrow, "Distracted from distraction by distraction." Again Eliot appeals to the reader on the level of familiar experience. Better than the unreal meaninglessness of apathy—a kind of modern city *acedia*—the real darkness, solitude, deprivation.

In the fifth section, the separation of the experience of timelessness from that of being enchained in time is reinforced by a figure which extracts the visual image of a pattern from language and music which move in time. The identity as pattern of aural and visual art illustrates that time, in art, can be conceived of as space:

> *Only by the form, the pattern,*
> *Can words or music reach*
> *The stillness, as a Chinese jar still*
> *Moves perpetually in its stillness.*

After the Chinese jar, the stillness of the note of a violin. The theme of the end preceding the beginning, and of the pattern preceding both end and beginning presses toward a metaphysical pattern that lies beyond the patterns of which the poet is capable in language.

This introduces another main theme of the *Four Quartets* which is that of language. At the most superficial level this is the poet discussing with himself his craft and the difficulty of the medium of words. Poetry "purifies the dialect of the tribe" ("Little Gidding") a task, let us say, of superb humility and which for a modern poet means "making it new" as well as preserving the integrity of past language. However, Eliot is also considering the relationship between poetry as being, and poetry as what it says, the subject. As we have seen, in his early criticism he considered that the subject of a poem—even when the poet is writing about his beliefs— is simply material to be transformed into the poetry. However, in a religious poem in which the poet expresses his most profound beliefs, a tension arises between the beliefs existing simply as material to be transformed into poetry and their being the language of the individual alone with God: a language which, in the Bible for example, is poetry. In the following passage about words, a transition takes place which is like a change of key when the music breaks through into a new statement. It is quite unlike the transition earlier in the poem from the discussion about "the world of speculation" to the language of pure poetry (or of symbolism) about the garden. The transition is now from the words in poetry to "the Word in the desert"— the Word of God. Poetry, subject, and words now become transformed in the Incarnation:

> *Words strain,*
> *Crack and sometimes break, under the burden,*
> *Under the tension, slip, slide, perish,*
> *Decay with imprecision, will not stay in place,*
> *Will not stay still. Shrieking voices*
> *Scolding, mocking, or merely chattering,*
> *Always assail them. The Word in the desert*
> *Is most attacked by voices of temptation,*
> *The crying shadow in the funeral dance,*
> *The loud lament of the disconsolate chimera.*

"Burnt Norton" lays down the themes which are extended in the remaining *Quartets*. But whereas in "Burnt Norton" the language seems to hover between the subject matter of the experiencing of the timeless within time, and the language as poetry, in "East Coker," "The Dry Salvages," and "Little Gidding" the religious meaning predominates. What is being said becomes what the poetry is. This equation is not always balanced, and sometimes, as in the lyrics, deliberately evaded or avoided. There is an equal risk felt of the meaning becoming absorbed into the poetry and of the poetry being sacrificed to the meaning. This balancing act between two kinds of meaning provides part of the tensions of *Four Quartets*, the not unselfconscious inner drama of the artist manipulating his art.

The religious ground of experience of time is again that of the first section of "East Coker" which opens with the motto of Mary Stuart: "In my beginning is my end." This works like a phrase in music. It also emphasizes the cyclical view of history which is contained in the first section of the poem:

> *Old stone to new building, old timber to new fires,*
> *Old fires to ashes, and ashes to the earth*
> *Which is already flesh, fur and faeces,*
> *Bone of man and beast, cornstalk and leaf.*

The theme of seasons, years, nature, the world itself revolving, introduces the vision of the village wedding dance which Eliot cites from the work of his sixteenth-century ancestor Sir Thomas Elyot:

> *Round and round the fire*
> *Leaping through the flames, or joined in circles,*
> *Rustically solemn or in rustic laughter*
> *Lifting heavy feet in clumsy shoes,*
> *Earth feet, loam feet, lifted in country mirth*

> *Mirth of those long since under earth*
> *Nourishing the corn.*

There follows a lyric, as brilliant as a Catherine wheel, of the whirling of seasons, of November overtaken by the spring, the constellated wars of the symbolic stars, the end of the world brought to "that destructive fire/ Which burns before the ice-cap reigns." Following a late Beethoven device of introducing a new theme by brusquely dismissing an earlier one, Eliot dismisses this as "A periphrastic study in a worn-out poetical fashion," adding the remark that has puzzled critics: "The poetry does not matter." He then launches out into what may seem a very unpoetic, rather sententious, and hesitating passage of ponderings on old age. This is unlike anything he had written before in being unequivocally personal, though perhaps not quite unembarrassedly so. The first person pronoun is studiedly avoided, at first the impersonal "one" being used, then the editorial "we":

> *There is, it seems to us,*
> *At best, only a limited value*
> *In the knowledge derived from experience.*
> *The knowledge imposes a pattern, and falsifies,*
> *For the pattern is new in every moment*
> *And every moment is a new and shocking*
> *Valuation of all we have been. We are only undeceived*
> *Of that which, deceiving, could no longer harm.*

The passage has a gravity of tone which is moving, and after protesting against the idea that old men have wisdom, and adopting the Yeatsian stance of proclaiming their folly, it ends:

> *The only wisdom we can hope to acquire*
> *Is the wisdom of humility: humility is endless.*

Humility means acceptance of the limitations of knowledge and experience. Its endlessness implies indeed more than this: immersion in the darkness of extinction, the dark side of the moon. The world is that nullity in which everything becomes nothing and humility becomes pride's opposite. Again there is a hint of Yeats's tragic view of life, as expressed in his old age, in that the ultimate reality of life is the terrible—*terribilità.*

Wait without thought, for you are not ready for thought:
So the darkness shall be the light, and the stillness the
    dancing.

These are lines in which poetic statement coincides with the ascetic humility of mystical experience. If it is symbolist, then the symbolism is religious as much as poetic. In the lyric in the fourth section, poetic and religious symbolism coincide in the manner of "metaphysical" poetry:

The wounded surgeon plies the steel
That questions the distempered part;
Beneath the bleeding hands we feel
The sharp compassion of the healer's art
Resolving the enigma of the fever chart.

Our only health is the disease
If we obey the dying nurse
Whose constant care is not to please
But to remind of our, and Adam's curse,
And that, to be restored, our sickness must grow worse.

This is opposite from symbolist poetry, in which the object in the world of actuality to which the symbol refers tends to disappear into the poetry and acquires an independent self-sufficient existence there. For here the poetic symbols point like arrows into the religious ones beyond them. The symbols of the "wounded surgeon" with his "bleeding hands" and his "sharp compassion" do not have a life in the poetry which is independent of the religious beliefs to which they refer. The surgeon symbolizes Christ as healer, and also as wounded, as compassionate, and as bringing a sword of judgment. The nurse symbolizes the Church as healing the sick and accomplishing their death because, being human, they can only find their spiritual cure through dying. This Good Friday lyric is singularly comfortless, the bleakest aspect of Christianity, emphasizing that surgical side of the religion whose ultimate logic discovers that it is the love of God which stokes the furnaces of hell, a theme taken up again in "Little Gidding":

> *Love is the unfamiliar Name*
> *Behind the hands that wove*
> *The intolerable shirt of flame*
> *Which human power cannot remove.*
> *We only live, only suspire*
> *Consumed by either fire or fire.*

As in the other *Quartets* Eliot takes up again the theme of language, language here considered above all, as communication of exact meaning:

> *And so each venture*
> *Is a new beginning, a raid on the inarticulate*
> *With shabby equipment always deteriorating*
> *In the general mess of imprecision of feeling,*
> *Undisciplined squads of emotion. . . .*

But the exploration in loneliness of the old leads to reconcilation through death. The cycle which opens with "In my beginning is my end" is completed by the reversal of the phrase in its conclusion. The music has been brought to a close:

We must be still and still moving
Into another intensity
For a further union, a deeper communion
Through the dark cold and the empty desolation,
The wave cry, the wind cry, the vast waters
Of the petrel and the porpoise. In my end is my begin-
ning.

"The Dry Salvages" opens with a further consideration
of the lived experience of time, by contrasting the time
that is within us—in the unconscious, the life blood—
with the oceanic impersonal time outside. Eliot was
acquainted with Rainer Maria Rilke's *Duino Elegies*
(which, in the translation by Edward and Victoria
Sackville-West, were warmly reviewed in *The Criterion*).
In the Third Elegy, Rilke describes what he calls the
"hidden guilty river-god of the blood." Rilke's elegies are
written in approximative pentameters and there is an
echo of the hexameter in the opening of "The Dry
Salvages"; that is to say, the rhythm is marked by
dactyls and spondees:

I do not know much about gods; but I think that the river
Is a strong brown god—sullen, untamed and intractable,
Patient in some degree, at first recognised as a frontier;
Useful, untrustworthy, as a conveyor of commerce;
Then only a problem confronting the builder of bridges.

Rilke's meter in the German goes:

Eines ist, die Geliebte zu singen. Ein anderes, wehe,
jenen verborgenen schuldigen Fluss-Gott des Blut

This meter is reproduced in English in:

One thing to sing the beloved, another, alas!
That hidden guilty river-god of the blood.[4]

[4] Rainer Maria Rilke, *Poems 1906 to 1926*, J. B. Leishman
and Stephen Spender, trans. (London, 1957), p. 41.

The river in Eliot's opening lines is obviously a metaphor for the blood, though the description is external and may make one thing of the Mississippi at St. Louis. The passage has the force of childhood memory:

> *His rhythm was present in the nursery bedroom,*
> *In the rank ailanthus of the April dooryard,*
> *In the smell of grapes on the autumn table,*
> *And the evening circle in the winter gaslight.*

"The river is within us" is contrasted with a different kind of time "the sea is all about us." Here, Eliot also draws on childhood memories: these are of the Dry Salvages, the "small group of rocks, with a beacon, off the N.E. coast of Cape Ann, Massachusetts," as the poet explains in a note. The imagery of the sea with boats and sailors reasserts itself throughout all but the last section of the poem, the lyric that forms the first part of Section II, being about the fate of fishermen on the sea, and, after a prosy passage about the significance of past experience within the consciousness of increasing age, the river and the ocean become reconciled within the concept of "time the destroyer" as being also "time the preserver."

"The Dry Salvages" is a poem in which the author turns back to his childhood, the preoccupations of his education, to Madame Sosostris "With a wicked pack of cards" (in *The Waste Land*) and to Buddhism. Section V opens with a long passage about palmistry and various other forms of fortunetelling. It also recapitulates, without adding to them, themes which have already been treated of in the earlier quartets. The opening, inspired by memories of the Mississippi and of Massachusetts, is magnificent, but for the rest it reads a bit tired. Like the other *Quartets* it appeals to the experience of the reader, but now the appeal is to materialists, whose moments of corporeal happiness can nevertheless be moments of illumination:

The moments of happiness—not the sense of well-being,
Fruition, fulfilment, security or affection,
Or even a very good dinner, but the sudden illumina-
  tion—

The persuasiveness which Eliot employs here is similar
to that of Baudelaire addressing the reader—*"hypo-*
crite lecteur, mon semblable, mon frère." Baudelaire
persuades the reader that he shares the experience of
boredom: Eliot, that he shares "moments of agony of
others, involved in our own. For our own agony is
'covered by the currents of action' ":

But the torment of others remains an experience
Unqualified, unworn by subsequent attrition.

The abiding quality of agony brings Eliot back to the
imagery of the river and the sea, internal and external
time here joined: "the river with its cargo of dead
Negroes, cows and chicken coops" (an image derived
perhaps from Turner's painting *The Slave Ship*), and
"the ragged rock in the restless waters."
  "The Dry Salvages" is the quartet which Eliot's commentators have found least satisfactory of the four, one
critic even wondering whether it is not an exercise in
self parody. It is true that Eliot relished Henry Reed's
parody of *Four Quartets*, "Chad Whitlow," but I don't
think that he sought to emulate Henry Reed. The first
section about the river and the sea is magnificent but
relies so much on early memories that perhaps this
makes the development of themes from the earlier
quartets rather difficult. Certainly the meditations about
old age in the second and third sections are the most
sententious of the series. The discussion of Buddhism is
a reversion to Eliot's Harvard studies. It has been
pointed out that "The Dry Salvages" discusses time on
the level of the ordinary man. If this is so, it partly fails,

by falling back into that tone of rather tired superior satire which seems glib in certain choruses of *The Rock*, where Eliot attacks "decent godless people: /Their only monument the asphalt road /And a thousand lost golf balls."

The opening of the fifth section of "The Dry Salvages" echoes what Eliot does far more effectively in the passage about the Tarot pack and Madame Sosostris in *The Waste Land*:

> *To communicate with Mars, converse with spirits,*
> *To report the behaviour of the sea monster,*
> *Describe the horoscope . . .*

and so on:

> *. . . all these are usual*
> *Pastimes and drugs, and features of the press:*
> *And always will be, some of them especially*
> *When there is distress of nations and perplexity*
> *Whether on the shores of Asia, or in the Edgware Road.*
> *Men's curiosity searches past and future*
> *And clings to that dimension. But to apprehend*
> *The point of intersection of the timeless*
> *With time, is an occupation for the saint—*
> *No occupation either, but something given*
> *And taken, in a lifetime's death in love,*
> *Ardour and selflessness and self-surrender.*

The tone here is that of Eliot's Harry, Lord Monchensey, in *The Family Reunion*, a character whom Eliot later described as an insufferable prig. Eliot is drawing on old attitudes of satire in his early poetry which seemed justified because they were deeply felt, but which here seem like habitual attitudes unredeemed. They do not go well with the newly discovered humility of the rest of "The Dry Salvages." This partly reasserts itself, however, in the lines that follow which, though a bit patronizing of "us" (among whom the author however includes himself), are commonsensical, emphasizing that ordinary people share the experience of getting outside time:

For most of us, there is only the unattended
Moment, the moment in and out of time,
The distraction fit, lost in a shaft of sunlight,
The wild thyme unseen, or the winter lightning
Or the waterfall, or music heard so deeply
That it is not heard at all, but you are the music
While the music lasts. There are only hints and guesses,
Hints followed by guesses; and the rest
Is prayer, observance, discipline, thought and action.

"Little Gidding" is the darkest, most wintry, most death-saturated of the *Quartets*, and it is also the culminating point of Eliot's oeuvre. "In my end is my beginning." The poem completes the circle of returning by going back to that point in Eliot's early criticism where (in "Tradition and the Individual Talent") he writes that "the progress of an artist is a continual sacrifice, a continual extinction of personality" (*Selected Essays*, p. 17). That extinction is achieved by the artist turning back along the roads of the tradition to place himself, or, rather, to place the life he has created in his work, among the dead. And in this last great quartet that is what the poet is doing.

The setting is midwinter at Little Gidding, "the seat of an Anglican religious community established in 1625 by Nicholas Ferrar, three times visited by King Charles, and subsequently desecrated by the Roundheads." Written in 1942, this midwinter poem was also at the dark cold center of the war, "the intersection of the timeless moment/ Is England and nowhere. Never and always."

The marvelous opening matches "Midwinter spring" against the "electric heat" of the summer in "East Coker." But this "unimaginable/ Zero summer" is the opposite pole of the hallucinatory brightness-within-darkness of midwinter. Here the fire in the dark time of year, is "pentecostal." Everything points to an order of reality beyond the world.

> . . . *Between melting and freezing*
> *The soul's sap quivers. There is no earth smell*
> *Or smell of living thing. This is the spring time*
> *But not in time's convenant. . . .*

The season and occasion is that of the ritual visiting of the ghosts of the dead, like those of Odysseus in *The Odyssey*, and of Aeneas in the *Aeneid.* "You" who come here have come in order to pray and achieve communication with the dead; and it would be the same

> *If you came this way in may time, you would find*
> > *the hedges*
> *White again, in May, with voluptuary sweetness.*

and

> > . . . *You are here to kneel*
> *Where prayer has been valid. And prayer is more*
> *Than an order of words, the conscious occupation*
> *Of the praying mind, or the sound of the voice praying.*
> *And what the dead had no speech for, when living,*
> *They can tell you, being dead: the communication*
> *Of the dead is tongued with fire beyond the language*
> > *of the living.*

The whole movement of the poem is toward the acceptance of death, but, as in Donne's great sonnet, death is dead. The brittle yet somehow debonair lyric which introduces Section II proclaims the death of civilization by the elements:

> *Water and fire shall rot*
> *The marred foundations we forgot,*
> *Of sanctuary and choir.*
> *This is the death of water and fire.*

These rituals of death and immortality introduce a long passage in a meter—and in a typographical setting —which paraphrases the effect of Dante's *terza rima*. This is a triumphant example of paraphrase of the effect of a meter in Italian with an English meter which does not imitate it and yet provides its parallel. In the opening lines the parallel is partly produced by the repetition of endings of the last words (*morning, unending,* and *homing*) of lines 1, 3, and 5, and partly by the "t's" of the monosyllabic words (*night, tongue,* and *tin*) of the alternate lines, 2, 4, and 6. But having hinted at (rather than established) this pattern, Eliot drops all suggestions of rhyme and concentrates simply on ending each line with a monosyllabic, disyllabic, or trisyllabic word which has usually the ultimate but sometimes the penultimate syllable very strongly stressed. Each line is self-contained and almost none runs over onto the following line.

In the *terza rima* passage, the poet meets a Dantesque "familiar compound ghost" with whom he has a grave conversation. This figure, he declares, is "Both intimate and unidentifiable," so there does not seem much point in trying to identify him. Nor need we ask whether the ghost is "real."

The ghost is conjured out of language, like the "spectre of a Rose." Nowhere does Eliot's manipulation of associations work better than here. He sets them up like lights around this figure in the darkness and we know at once from "pointed scrutiny" and "the brown baked features" that this is a meeting of two masters of language, like that of Dante with Brunetto Latini, conjured out of language. There follows a passage which has puzzled commentators:

So I assumed a double part, and cried
And heard another's voice cry: "What! are you *here?"*
Although we were not. I was still the same,
Knowing myself yet being someone other —
And he a face still forming; yet the words sufficed
To compel the recognition they preceded.

Here, I think, the point is not what is said but what is avoided being said, not that the ghost is identifiable but that Eliot has avoided identifying him. Nor do I believe that Eliot means to suggest that he is a split personality, a *Doppelgänger*. What may be indicated is that he is both inside historic time and outside it, double in the sense of being both body and ghost: the fusion being effected by the scene which is an air raid warning in wartime London:

And so, compliant to the common wind,
Too strange to each other for misunderstanding,
In concord at this intersection time
Of meeting nowhere, no before and after,
We trod the pavement in a dead patrol.

The Dantesque ghost also has something of Yeats whose thoughts at the end of his life send ripples through Eliot's communings on old age throughout the *Four Quartets.* His talk provides a freezing finale for two topics of self-communing conversation in the quartets: language and old age.

The Yeatsian voice, indeed, perhaps predominates in Eliot's reflections on decrepitude. One cannot easily imagine Eliot proclaiming the folly of old men without the ghost of Yeats standing behind him. The reveries on old age are partly a murmuring of ghosts of poets.

"Do not let me hear/ Of the wisdom of old men." Wordsworth rashly does just this in *The Excursion*, comparing age to a final eminence

> *. . . a place of power,*
> *A throne that may be likened unto his,*
> *Who, in some placid day of summer, looks*
> *Down from a mountain-top . . .*

Matthew Arnold, who haunted Eliot throughout his life, made a report on old age which is very close to some of the lines of the "compound ghost" in that most haunted poem, "Little Gidding." Arnold writes in "Growing Old":

> *It is to suffer this,*
> *And feel but half, and feebly, what we feel.*
> *Deep in our hidden heart*
> *Festers the dull remembrance of a change,*
> *But no emotion—none.*
>
> *It is—last stage of all—*
> *When we are frozen up within, and quite*
> *The phantom of ourselves,*
> *To hear the world applaud the hollow ghost*
> *Which blamed the living man.*

There is also an echo perhaps of Housman's vision of a meeting with a dead soldier in "Hell's Gate."

I do not mention these for the sake of source-hunting but to emphasize the way in which the dead, with echoes of their voices, crowd in on the scene of war-bombed London in this poem. There is the compound ghost who makes salutation to the living poet, but the living poet has also crossed into the darkness among the dead poets. It is as his living, fire-watching self and his own posthumous voice placed among the living dead of the tradition, that he assumes a double part. The scene resembles Dante meeting some friend in Purgatory who describes the nature of his punishment, with the promise of entry beyond the suffering into the pattern of the *Paradiso*—

"From wrong to wrong the exasperated spirit
Proceeds, unless restored by that refining fire
Where you must move in measure, like a dancer."

All manner of thing shall be well
When the tongues of flame are in-folded
Into the crowned knot of fire
And the fire and the rose are one.

—and "We are born with the dead: /See, they return, and we bring us with them."

After "Little Gidding" Eliot wrote plays, but the best poetry in them draws on themes he had already used in *Four Quartets*. "Little Gidding" is the furthest point in his spiritual and poetic exploration, his meeting with death.

X

In "Prufrock," "Portrait of a Lady," and *The Waste Land*, Eliot tends to see poetic situations as drama: soliloquies, implicit dialogues between characters, or that most Elizabethan of devices, the "aside." He owed much to the Elizabethans and also to Browning, though he saw that Browning's dramatic monologues were written for a voice speaking on that stage which is the reader's mind and imagination, and not for actors in the theater.

Eliot's obsession with poetic drama is apparent not only in his poetry but also in his criticism. After *The Divine Comedy* (the supreme collection of dramatic monologues addressed to each listener in solitude), his next great loves were the Elizabethans and the Greek dramatists. In his early essays he discusses dramatic poetry more than any other apart from Dante's. In his *Selected Essays* (1932), his topics include Shakespeare and the Elizabethan dramatists, Greek tragedy, Seneca, Dryden, Rostand's *Cyrano de Bergerac*. An essay on "Rhetoric and Poetic Drama" is followed by "A Dialogue on Dramatic Poetry," and that is followed by the famous attack on Gilbert Murray's translations of Euripides.

Ezra Pound once argued that a short poem is, in essence, a speech made by a character within a situation which implies a whole drama. Eliot took the view which was the converse to this: that the poem should project its drama. Also, drama tended toward poetry. In "A Dialogue on Dramatic Poetry" one of Eliot's speakers states that prose drama is only a "by-product of verse drama." "The human soul in intense emotion, strives to express itself in verse" (*Selected Essays*, p. 46).

However, Eliot was well aware of the dangers in reviving poetic drama, made very clear by various writers in his youth, of treating it as something hushed and holy, special to poetry lovers. He thought that the first business of the poet writing for the theater was to entertain. The member of the audience whom he should aim to entertain should not be some earnest lady or gentleman who was a declared and dedicated poetry lover, but some complete outsider who bought a ticket for a play of which he knew nothing and who, having recovered from the shock that the people on stage were talking in verse, was unable to tear himself away from an action which enthralled him.

At a time when the possibility of his writing anything that would get onto the stage remained theoretical, Eliot felt that the music hall offered the best mode for a new poetic drama. In his essay on the death of the famous music-hall artist Marie Lloyd (1923), he attacks the upper-middle-class London West End theater, and finds in Marie Lloyd "the expressive figure of the lower classes." He thinks that the middle classes cannot support a performer of such vitality because they are "morally corrupt . . . their own life fails to find a Marie Lloyd to express it; nor have they any independent virtues which might give them as a conscious class any dignity" (*Selected Essays*, p. 453). Thus Eliot made clear his opinion that the future of the English theater could not be created within the conventions of upper-middle-class plays with drawing-room settings.

In 1926 and 1927 Eliot published in *The Criterion* two dramatic sketches in verse: "Fragment of a Prologue" and "Fragment of an Agon," later entitled *Sweeney Agonistes*. These show him experimenting with jazz, the minstrel show, expressionist drama of the 1920s, and the revue sketch. They belong to the ambience of the "Sweeney" poems. The flat of two call-girls, Doris and Dusty, is visited by Sweeney, Wauchope, Horsfall, Klipstein, Krumpacker, Swarts, and Snow. As in jazz songs like the later "St. James Infirmary Blues," the effect is of heart-breaking statements carried in pulsating, unrelenting rhythm. Sweeney invites Doris to accompany him to the cannibal isle where:

> There's no telephones
> There's no gramophones
> There's no motor cars
> No two-seaters, no six-seaters,
> No Citroën, no Rolls-Royce.
> Nothing to eat but the fruit as it grows.
> Nothing to see but the palmtrees one way
> And the sea the other way,
> Nothing to hear but the sound of the surf.
> Nothing at all but three things

DORIS: What things?
SWEENEY: Birth, and copulation, and death.
> That's all, that's all, that's all,
> that's all,

Birth, and copulation, and death. . . .
DORIS: I'd be bored.
SWEENEY: You'd be bored.
Birth, and copulation, and death.
That's all the facts when you come to
    brass tacks:
Birth, and copulation, and death.
I've been born, and once is enough.
You don't remember, but I remember,
Once is enough.

Whatever terrifying thoughts are conveyed by these bone-rattling statements, the jaunty, carefree, and sadistic carrying tone is wonderfully maintained. One feels that if Gilbert and Sullivan had not subdued their gifts to the morals of the late Victorian English upper class, this is the kind of thing they might have done.

The virtue and also the limitation of *Sweeney Agonistes* lie in its being a vision of disgust treated with black humor, without relief. One never feels for a moment, as one does with *Old Possum's Book of Practical Cats* and in Eliot's comedies, that the poet is trying to be funny. This humor is the spontaneous overflow of something darkly sardonic in his nature. One suspects that he never lost this and that at the Garrick Club or at a board meeting of Faber and Faber or at a luncheon for encouraging some young poet, he would suddenly see people in this way, as empty vulgarians acting out an obscene comedy.

In his "Lines for an Old Man" he introspects on his flashes of malicious deadly insight:

> *Reflected from my golden eye*
> *The dullard knows that he is mad.*
> *Tell me if I am not glad!*

Sweeney, Wauchope, Horsfall, and the others, the male characters in *Sweeney Agonistes*, are not objects of the poet's charitable consideration. Nevertheless, there is no doubt that he savors them, enjoys his creations with a certain rich malicious pleasure. They are favorites of his repertoire. Their names convey some toothsome private joke.

Doris, like other women in Eliot's work, is a victim, a murderee. She represents squalor and passivity. Her role is to sit at home, dealing out the cards which are emblems of the fate that will overtake her when she turns up the Hanged Man or the Two of Spades which signifies the Coffin. Her relationship with Sweeney is that of devouree with devourer, the fulfiller of his masculine fantasies which are based on murder reports in newspapers:

> *Any man might do a girl in*
> *Any man has to, needs to, wants to*
> *Once in a lifetime, do a girl in.*

In *Sweeney Agonistes* Eliot does not sentimentalize disgust. He offers no feelings except those of hypnotic chilling horror at his characters.

He introduces into his two last comedies, *The Confidential Clerk* (1953) and *The Elder Statesman* (1958), characters reminiscent of those in *Sweeney Agonistes*. They are, in *The Confidential Clerk*, B. Kaghan (who, entering any room, announces brassily: "Enter B. Kaghan"), and those vengeful figures out of the elder stateman's past, Frederico Gomez and Mrs. Carghill. When these characters first appear in their respective plays there is a rhythmic speeding up of the action, a wave of dark zest, like a blast of air from some Hades not just of Lord Claverton's youth but of the author's poetic past. However, instead of being positive figures of black fun, they turn out to be negative preachers of moral lessons. B. Kaghan has a heart of gold. Frederico Gomez and Mrs. Carghill, though talking the language of blackmail and even prepared to employ its means, are really occupied only in vulgarly claiming a past friendship with the successful Lord Claverton, who in the past was their familiar.

Eliot's conversion to Christianity doubtless inhibited him from putting characters like Sweeney, Mrs. Porter, Klipstein, Krumpacker, Doris, and Dusty into his work. They represent a view of life in which redemption is scarcely on their Tarot cards. If invoked, as in the portraits of Frederico Gomez and Mrs. Carghill, they appear sad and shabby, like pagan gods at a tea party on a vicarage lawn.

In discussing Eliot's last play, *The Elder Statesman*, before those which come between it and the *Sweeney Agonistes* fragments, I am anticipating. I do so because it has several features that emphasize very strikingly and almost with an effect of caricature certain attitudes common to the later plays, so very different from the view of life expressed in *Sweeney Agonistes*.

The Elder Statesman has a very simple plot. Lord Claverton, a successful business man (called Richard Ferry before he attained the peerage and "plain Dick Ferry" when he was an Oxford undergraduate), is declining in years, with a self-importance to match the whole of his distinguished career in the City, when he is visited by two characters from his past: Frederico Gomez (at Oxford, Fred Culverwell), and Mrs. Carghill (formerly the comedienne Maisie Mountjoy). The rhythm and idiom of Gomez' opening speech immediatly indicate that he is a faint echo—a ghost—from the Sweeney repertoire. He says to Lord Claverton:

You've changed your name too, since I knew you.
When we were up at Oxford, you were plain Dick Ferry.
Then, when you married, you took your wife's name
And became Mr. Richard Claverton-Ferry;
And finally, Lord Claverton. I've followed your example,
And done the same, in a modest way.

Mrs. Carghill as obviously is a ghostly echo of Doris and
Dusty:

You attracted me, you know, at the very first meeting—
I can't think why but it's the way things happen.
I said "there's a man I could follow round the world."
But Effie it was—you know, Effie was very shrewd—
Effie it was said you'd be throwing yourself away.
"Mark my words" Effie said, "if you choose to follow that
*   man*
He'd give you the slip: he's not to be trusted.
That man is hollow." That's what she said.

Although the rhythms here do not have the barbaric
throb of *Sweeney Agonistes* they raise expectations that
we are to be transported back to some cannibal isle in
a bed-sitter. But this is not to be. Gomez and Mrs.
Carghill have, like Lord Claverton, gone up in the world.
It is true that in the past they have lived criminal lives,
but they no longer need to indulge in forgery or prostitu-
tion. They have made their fortunes. They are black-
mailing Lord Claverton not for money but for love:
through him they wish to experience again some spunk
and spark of those early days.

Their effect on Lord Claverton is to bring into full
consciousness a past that he has attempted to bury
under his worldly success. The lesson he learns from
meeting them is that he must confess to his daughter
the truth about his past which he has concealed from

her, as he had from his wife. By facing this truth, he achieves a state of peace and happiness which we are supposed to think analogous with that of Oedipus at Colonus. In view of the comparison with Sophocles, we have to believe that Lord Claverton's state of mind is sincere when he says to his daughter, Monica:

This may surprise you: I feel at peace now.
It is the peace that ensues upon contrition
When contrition ensues upon knowledge of the truth.
Why did I always want to dominate my children?
Why did I mark out a narrow path for Michael?
Because I wanted to perpetuate myself in him.
Why did I want to keep you to myself, Monica?
Because I wanted you to give your life to adoring
The man that I pretended to myself that I was,
So that I could believe in my own pretences.
I've only just now had the illumination
Of knowing what love is.

Just before he makes this speech, full of contrition, Gomez and Mrs. Carghill, who have now met, have formed a very unpleasant conspiracy for the purpose of taking revenge on Lord Claverton. They have arranged that his son, Michael, a bright young unscrupulous member of the new brash generation, shall enter Gomez' business in San Marco, a fictitious South American republic, where Gomez has made a fortune that could buy out Lord Claverton several times over, and where business morals are minimal. In view of the fact that Gomez, abetted by Mrs. Carghill, is about to make Michael a scoundrel as great as the former Fred Culverwell and Maisie Mountjoy, Lord Claverton's calm and happiness after receiving this news seem remarkable, especially when he goes on to observe (a few minutes before his peaceful death under a large tree on the lawn):

And now that I love Michael,
I think, for the first time—remember, my dear,
I am only a beginner in the practice of loving—
Well, that is something.

Lord Claverton's own explanation of his acquired in-difference to Gomez and Mrs. Carghill and their threats is that he has realized that they are "ghosts" from his past. They are not real. He says of Maisie Carghill, with whom he was deeply involved:

. . . she knows that the ghost of the man I was
Still clings to the ghost of the woman who was Maisie.
We should have been poor, we should certainly have
*   quarrelled,*
We should have been unhappy, might have come to
*   divorce;*
But she hasn't forgotten or forgiven me.

The use of the ghosts, from Lord Claverton's point of view, is that they enable him to face up to his own past, make his confession, experience contrition. (In this respect they are like the Furies who pursue Harry in *The Family Reunion*.) Yet there is a plane of reality on which Gomez and Mrs. Carghill are not unreal. They have quite realistically come to ask Lord Claverton to remember the past and with some part of his mind acknowledge their existence. Even if they are ghosts, they still might have implored such recognition. One reading of this play might be, then, that from their point of view Gomez and Mrs. Carghill are quite justi-fied in the revenge they attempt to take on that old humbug their ex-lover and friend Lord Claverton, who refuses to speak to them directly about a relationship they once shared.

The Elder Statesman provides the most extreme in-stance of a kind of juggling of values between two planes of reality, or, to put it more in Eliot's terms, of two different time-scales—the temporal and the eternal. Lord Claverton has purged his soul, by contrition, of crimes in which he participated with cherished companions when he was young. He lives (or dies, rather) on a plane of reality viewed from which those companions (who have now enlisted his own son to join their company) are "ghosts" in a shadow world of unrealities. In *The Family Reunion*, the wife of Harry, Lord Monchensey, whom Harry thinks he has pushed overboard (and whom Harry's mother describes as "A restless shivering painted shadow"), is a ghost whose function in the life of her husband is to produce in him that contrition which will lead to his living on the plane of reality which is outside the process of historic time. It is remarkable that in the whole of *The Family Reunion* not one kind word is said about Harry's wife, or even one word which makes her life vivid. There are guilt and contrition but no regrets.

Sometimes it is useful to contrast the work of one poet with that of another when both are writing about a similar situation. Shelley's first wife, Harriet, did drown herself, and when she had done so, Shelley, Mary Shelley, his second wife, and all the Shelley family did everything they could to blackguard her. Nevertheless, Shelley's real feelings sprang forth occasionally in poetry that expressed a sense of a real person—even if a ghost —which is entirely lacking in Harry when he is feeling guilty about his wife:

> *The moon made thy lips pale, beloved—*
> *The wind made thy bosom chill—*
> *The night did shed on thy dear head*
> *Its frozen dew, and thou didst lie*
> *Where the bitter breath of the naked sky*
> *Might visit thee at will.*

This sense of the reality of the sacrificed person is curiously lacking in the accounts of women who meet terrible ends in Eliot's plays—even in the account of the death of Celia Coplestone in *The Cocktail Party*. In these deaths a mocking voice offstage seems to say "Any man might do a girl in." The criticism I am making points to weaknesses in the actual structure of *The Elder Statesman*. It explains why there is a certain tepidity about it and a feeling of unaccountable silences. There are confrontations between Lord Claverton and his former friends on the basis of Gomez and Mrs. Carghill claiming his friendship, of their mildly attempting to blackmail him, and of their being punishingly vindictive, but there is none in which Lord Claverton admits their right to talk about the past. In real life it is of course likely that he would have avoided this subject, but the imaginative life of the play is starved by his avoiding it. If there were a scene in which he admitted to Gomez the depth of their Oxford friendship, or to Mrs. Carghill that he had been deeply in love with her, and if he had spoken about the present out of that recognition between them of the past, then the two planes of reality—that of human love and that of his perfecting his will to meet his God—would have been brought into vital relation or, at any rate, significant collision.

It is perhaps unfortunate that the change of tone that occurs in Eliot's dramatic writing when he shifts from the nihilism of Sweeney to the Christianity of his domestic dramas is accompanied by such a marked change of social environment from the bohemian "bed-sitter" world of Sweeney to the upper-middle-class drawing-room one of Lord Claverton and the Dowager Marchioness of Monchensey. One has an awkward feeling that respectability is being maintained. Young lords, although they may wish to push their wives overboard, don't actually do so. In *The Elder Statesman* it is significant that Lord Claverton, like Harry in *The Family Reunion*, reproaches himself for a crime which he hasn't actually committed. He thinks that when he was an undergraduate he had run over a man, but in fact he has not done so, he had only run over a corpse, already dead, which happened to be lying in the road (afterward it is run over by someone else). Gomez, however, who is not a gentleman and is, indeed, one of nature's dagos, has actually forged a check and served time for doing so. The play would have been strengthened, surely, if the crimes of Claverton and Gomez had been legally as well as (in Eliot's view) morally equivalent. The point Eliot is trying to make is of course that "sin" is worse than "crime." As Lord Claverton, when contrite, himself explains:

> *It's harder to confess the sin that no one believes in*
> *Than the crime that everyone can appreciate.*
> *For the crime is in relation to the law*
> *And the sin is in relation to the sinner.*

It may be harder, but the complacency of an upper-middle-class audience is likely to be shocked more by the idea of an English lord having committed a real crime (run over a living child, failed to report the matter to the police, and been found out, for example), than by learning that he has committed a driving misdemeanour which he has failed to report to the police and on account of which he feels irrationally sinful.

The difference between legal crime and "sin" in Eliot's mind is that legal crime happens on the temporal plane of reality, whereas sin happens within the conscience of the individual alone with God. However, a crime may be not only legally wrong but also a sin. The distinction that makes crime and sin belong to two different orders of reality is a more suitable subject, perhaps, for a novel than for a play. In any case, it undermines Eliot's attempt to establish a parallel between his plays and Greek tragedies. For Oedipus and Orestes have certainly committed crimes as well as the sin of pride. The idea of an Orestes who has sinned by wishing that someone might die but who does not realize this wish as action is undramatic.

Although in the course of his development as a poetic dramatist Eliot became more tolerant of ordinary human beings and their activities, including the love life of "average sensual man," he probably had too great a distaste for the modern world to regard most contemporaries as anything but reflections of its values. In *The Rock* (1934), a pageant play written with the purpose of promoting the building of churches in newly developed areas of London, he emphasizes that without the spiritual aims set by the Church, modern life is meaningless and empty. Eliot provides many examples from modern society to show that life only acquires significance within the context of the Church's teaching. Since most contemporaries ignore this teaching, it and they are meaningless, dead.

The true theme of Eliot's plays written after his conversion is the discovery by heroes, and one heroine, of their religious vocation. It is required of the hero that he perfect his will so as to make it conform completely with the will of God. The play in which these aims are revealed in a very pure state—*naturaliter*—is *Murder in the Cathedral*. The problem of Thomas Becket is not to attain the courage necessary for him to undergo martyrdom—from his first entrance on the stage he is set on being martyred—but to purify himself of all self-regarding motives for martyrdom. His conversations with the Tempters reveal this aim.

The dramatic purpose of the First and Third Tempters is not really to tempt, since they offer Thomas choices of pleasure and political partisanship which he has already clearly rejected. Their purpose is to set before the audience images of Thomas's past—the life of personal enjoyment, friendship with the king, and temporal power. These Tempsters are ghosts from that past. The Second Tempter also offers Thomas a choice he has rejected. However, this choice is not just evocative of the past, but needs to be defined and explained in order that the spectator may clearly understand Thomas's present position. It is the choice of doing material good in the temporal world, an action which Thomas, as a spiritual leader in command of temporal power, might well undertake. The Second Tempter asks him to become Chancellor again in order that he may save the people from misgovernment. Thomas has no difficulty in rejecting the part of this temptation which concerns covering himself in worldly glory. But a further temptation involves him in exacter definition of his aims: the temptation to use a power in order to achieve good:

> *Temporal power, to build a good world,*
> *To keep order, as the world knows order.*

Thomas rejects this on the grounds that he has made a choice beyond that of doing good in the world through power. It is that of spiritual power and carrying out the will of God.

The Third Tempter, like the first, offers a temptation which can scarcely be expected to tempt. This is for Thomas to ally himself with the English barons against the King with whom his friendship has been broken. As a temptation this is meaningless. In the terms of temporal power Thomas is on the side of the King against the barons.

Finally there is the Fourth Tempter—the only one who really tempts Thomas because he echoes what are his own thoughts, the prospects of the "enduring crown to be won" through martyrdom:

What can compare with glory of Saints
Dwelling forever in presence of God? . . .
Seek the way of martyrdom, make yourself the lowest
On earth, to be high in heaven.
And see far off below you, where the gulf is fixed,
Your persecutors, in timeless torment,
Parched passion, beyond expiation.

Thomas recognizes this voice as the echo of his own and knowing this he cries:

Can sinful pride be driven out
Only by more sinful? Can I neither act nor suffer
Without perdition?

The hero or the martyr may be acting out of pride and the desire for glory. Glory is indeed the crown of martyrdom, but for the martyr to act on this knowledge corrupts his action and puts him on the level of those concerned with their own power and glory. The will of the individual has to be absorbed within the objective will which is the love of God so disinterestedly that action becomes passive suffering, subjectively motiveless. There are, of course, theological arguments, going back to Aristotle, and resumed by Thomas Aquinas and Dante, which discuss this. But drama concretizes abstractions as living situations, and the situation of Thomas Becket, with his tormenting doubt as to his motives, is real. We can see this for ourselves by taking the example of the Agony of Christ in the Garden of Gethsemane. If any thought had entered his mind that his crucifixion would be the most successful advertising operation in the history of Western civilization, and if this thought were any element of a motive in his action, then the pure act of submission to his enemies, in order that his will might become perfect within the love that is God, would have been corrupted, and the crucifixion would have been a kind of betrayal. It is because people see the crucifixion in the light of success and triumph that we end up with Jesus Christ Superstar (a transformation of the original Christian myth into terms of the modern world of business which corresponds perhaps to James Joyce's ironic transformation of Odysseus into Leopold Bloom).

The Fourth Tempter, having echoed and clarified for him Thomas's aspirations for the glory of martyrdom, now echoes his rejection of his own self-regard, his dedication to the aim of submerging every element of his own will within the will of God. The Fourth Tempter takes up indeed the very words that Thomas has himself spoken to the Chorus:

You know and do not know, what it is to act or suffer.
You know and do not know, that action is suffering,
And suffering action. Neither does the agent suffer
Nor the patient act. But both are fixed
In an eternal action, an eternal patience
To which all must consent that it may be willed
And which all must suffer that they may will it,
That the pattern may subsist, that the wheel may turn and still
Be forever still.

This is a moment when Eliot merges his own poetry in what was for him the supreme moment of Dante—"in his will is our peace."

In his concluding speech of the first act, Becket moves forward spiritually into an area of lucid consciousness. The Fourth Tempter, echo of his own wishes (and perhaps his angel in the same way that Satan is the angel sent forth by God to tempt Job), has shown him his own heart's way to purge his soul of impure motivation:

Now is my way clear, now is the meaning plain:
Temptation shall not come in this kind again.
The last temptation is the greatest treason:
To do the right deed for the wrong reason.

The first three Tempters are now seen as visitations from the past, "ghosts" (like Gomez and Mrs. Carghill in *The Elder Statesman*). They are the occasion for a review of his past as friend of the King, and for confrontation with the fact that spiritual authority puts the soul in even deadlier danger than temporal power:

For those who serve the greater cause may make the
cause serve them,
Still doing right: and striving with political men
May make that cause political, not by what they do
But by what they are. . . .

Thomas, addressing out of his past a "modern" audience, knows that his history will seem futile to most of these onlookers, the lunatic self-slaughter of a fanatic. His aim is further elucidated in the sermon which he preaches in the cathedral on Christmas morning, 1170:

A Christian martyrdom is no accident. Saints are not made by accident. . . . A martyr, a saint, is always made by the design of God, for His love of men, to warn them and to lead them, to bring them back to His ways. A martyrdom is never the design of man; for the true martyr is he who has become the instrument of God, who has lost his will in the will of God. . . . The martyr no longer desires anything for himself, not even the glory of martyrdom.

This way of thinking, culminating in his religion, had fundamentally been Eliot's since the discussion of the relation of the living poet to the whole past tradition in the essay on "Tradition and the Individual Talent." The poet is seen not as expressing his own personality but as surrendering and even extinguishing it within the objective life which is the tradition. The relation of the subjective individual who has found his vocation to an impersonal objective life is sacrificial. Eliot has found beyond literature, beyond the tradition, that further life which, in his view, creates living values.

The Four Knights, agents of the King, who come to murder Thomas and who explain at considerable length, in a style that owes something to Shaw's *St. Joan*, their reasons for doing so, correspond to the Four Tempters. In a sense they are indeed Tempters, not of Thomas but of the Chorus in seeking their approbation of the murder. They are also, just as much as Thomas, instruments whereby Thomas perfects his own will within that of God. Although agents of ultimate good, they are, nevertheless, wicked not only before God but in the temporal world. As Archbishop of Canterbury, Thomas Becket, their opponent, is a doughty champion of the war of the spiritual authority against the temporal powers, whether of the King or of the barons, in his time.

It is a very fine stroke whereby Eliot makes Thomas, a few seconds before his assassination, recover his sense of his real authority in the world, which derives from his office and from Rome, and rebuke one of the Knights who calls him traitor. He cries:

> *You, Reginald, three times traitor you:*
> *Traitor to me as my temporal vassal,*
> *Traitor to me as your spiritual lord,*
> *Traitor to God in desecrating His Church.*

The Women of Canterbury are not wicked but vacillating, concerned with their own interest but capable of accepting the burden of participating in a drama which can offer them nothing but the worsening of their own material conditions. Their poetry is perhaps the greatest triumph of *Murder in the Cathedral*. It is unparalleled in Eliot's work.

The choruses of *The Rock* are preparatory exercises for it, but tend to provide examples either of spiritual exhortation (which does not fit well in the mouths of a chorus of common folk who are being exhorted) or of Eliot's mysticism. In *The Rock* Eliot is incapable of giving expression to the feelings of ordinary modern men and women, because he cannot see them except as corrupted by the time. It is only when, in *The Family Reunion*, he enters into the feelings of the English upper middle class that he can to some extent voice them because they appertain to the unnerved, divided, guilt-ridden, past-conscious English culture by which he himself has been adopted.

The Women of Canterbury are another matter. Eliot can see them as rooted in rituals of toil—rituals of the seasons—as sharing the dignity of their domestic and agricultural labor, as having their place within a hierarchy whose temporal head is the King and whose spiritual head is the Archbishop, representative of the Pope in Rome. Eliot's picture of the people of Canterbury may not be historically exact but it is imaginatively moving. He is able to visualize their lives within the context of values and conflicts which the play is about. They obey the King. They go to Church. They work. They are afraid of the barons. They are therefore capable of commenting on the action which they first obscurely, and later luminously, understand. They are in a relation to Thomas which is that both of chorus and of a generalized protagonist capable of entering into a dialogue with him.

In the magnificent series of choruses which follow on the declaration by the Knights of their intent to kill the Archbishop, Eliot, through these voices of the past, focuses his feelings of horror in a universal vision which includes the present as well as the past:

Clear the air! clean the sky! wash the wind! take stone from stone and wash them.
The land is foul, the water is foul, our beasts and our-selves defiled with blood.
A rain of blood has blinded my eyes. Where is England? where is Kent? where is Canterbury?
O far far far far in the past; and I wander in a land of barren boughs: if I break them, they bleed; I wander in a land of dry stones: if I touch them they bleed.

Eliot here touches the utmost depths of horror that he knows, which we find in "Prufrock," *The Waste Land, Sweeney Agonistes*—indeed, throughout his work. But whereas in the earlier poetry the horror seems cut off, unrelated, an individual's nightmare, here is seems brought up into a light capable ultimately indeed of cleaning the sky and washing the wind.

No one knows better than Eliot the horror of waking in the uncertain hour between darkness and the first dawn of an icy gritty day in Paris or London; of un-swept corners of attics; of funguses that grow behind dark wainscoting; of a cat in an alley gutter licking the inside of a sardine tin; of the war between clawed enemies that takes place under rocks fathoms down on the sea floor. There is a remarkable list of the in-finitesimal glimpsed terrors that surround us throughout our lives and which burrow through our flesh in these choruses:

. . . I have tasted
The living lobster, the crab, the oyster, the whelk and the
prawn; and they live and spawn in my bowels, and my
bowels dissolve in the light of dawn. I have smelt
Death in the rose, death in the hollyhock, sweet pea,
hyacinth, primrose and cowslip. I have seen
Trunk and horn, tusk and hoof, in odd places;
I have lain on the floor of the sea and breathed with the
breathing of the sea-anemone, swallowed with in-
gurgitation of the sponge. I have lain in the soil and
criticised the worm. In the air
Flirted with the passage of the kite, I have plunged with
the kite and cowered with the wren. I have felt
The horn of the beetle, the scale of the viper, the mobile
hard insensitive skin of the elephant, the evasive
flank of the fish. . . .

This is to make the whole animal world and all its
processes corrupt, whether they operate outside us or
within our bodies, in the elements or in the intestines, a
vast psalm of life metabolistically changing into death
surrounding human beings and happening inside them.

Nietzsche thought that the genius of Wagner was
as a miniaturist, an observer of minutiae which make
the spirit most uneasy, with the gifts of a painter of
Dutch interiors; and that his mistake was to compose
on the scale of epic grandeur. The most real horror that
Eliot conveys in his work is also in the isolated phrase
suspended between commas, as in the early "Preludes"
and "Rhapsody on a Windy Night." Eliot, a poet of
fragments skilfully dovetailed into wholes, is a miniaturist. He is more immediately convincing when conveying the terror inspired by a spider in its web in the
corner of an attic, by cigarette butts on the unswept
floor of a bar at dawn, than at comparing the case of
bad conscience of a retired businessman with that of

Oedipus at Colonus, or the sense of guilt of a young man who thinks he has pushed his wife overboard an ocean liner, with that of Orestes pursued by the Eumenides.

There is indeed some affinity between Eliot and Wagner. Once, after having followed a radio performance of *Das Rheingold* with the score, I asked him whether, when he wrote *The Waste Land*, he had been studying this libretto. He looked at me slyly and said: "Not just *Rheingold*—the whole of the Ring."

Die Meistersinger is probably Wagner's opera which is most successful as a work of art, precisely because it is woven out of scenes like paintings by some Dutch master. Wagner's vision of medieval Nuremberg is of a society which forms an organic unity. Eliot can enter into the conflicts of Canterbury in the year 1170 because the struggle between the temporal and the spiritual powers—within the context of a society in which heaven and hell were regarded as real places—is one that he can imagine. In *Murder in the Cathedral* he does not have to resort to the Joycean device of the parallel myth taken from antiquity which he applies to *The Waste Land* and which can with some effort be interpreted as parallels from Greek tragedy in his later dramas.

The Family Reunion is a play about the hero's discovery of his religious vocation as the result of his sense of guilt and contrition about the death of his wife, whom he believes himself to have pushed overboard from a liner in mid-Atlantic. It is characteristic of Eliot's way of setting up his plots (a) that no one in the play expresses the slightest sympathy for the wife (and, in fact, the more robust members of the Monchensey family are agreed that to push her over was a jolly good thing), and (b) that Harry's chauffeur provides his master with an alibi which makes it improbable that he did away with his wife (Eliot was a reader of crime stories and it may have occurred to him that this alibi would scarcely hold water in a court of law). At any rate, Harry is guilty of having wished his wife's death. Whether he actually killed her is immaterial in the world of Eliot's values.

The play opens with a family party at Wishwood, a country house in the north of England, to celebrate the birthday of its owner, the head of the family, Amy, Dowager Lady Monchensey. In the course of the development of the drama, Harry's Aunt Agatha reveals to her nephew that his dead father also wished to "get rid" of his mother. Agatha (his mother's sister), besides being head of a woman's college, has a spiritual vocation almost as intense as that of Harry, to whom she is spiritually attuned. After describing the domination which Amy obtained over Harry's father, Agatha goes on:

> *The autumn came too soon, not soon enough.*
> *The rain and wind had not shaken your father*
> *Awake yet. I found him thinking*
> *How to get rid of your mother. What simple plots!*
> *He was not suited to the rôle of murderer.*

A passion for uxoricide seems part of the heredity of eldest sons of the Monchensey family. And every one except Harry seems to agree that the fact that it is frustrated is rather a pity, something like *coitus interruptus*. Amy, Dowager Lady Monchensey, is certainly a matriarch. Her death at the end of the play is received by Agatha and her younger relation Mary as a kind of consummation devoutly to be wished. The rather macabre circumstance of members of a family wishing to murder one another—which resembles some situation in a novel by Ivy Compton-Burnett—is muted. It becomes a kind of subplot underlying the main plot which is—quite the opposite of this—about redemption.

The story is of Harry's discovery of his vocation, in which he is aided by Agatha and hindered by other members of his family. They wish him to remain in "the world" in order that he may assume the responsibilities consequent on his inheriting Wishwood. Parallel with this there is the story of the death of his mother, the matriarchal Amy, defeated by her son's refusal to take over Wishwood.

Eliot himself wrote that he considered *The Family Reunion* defective, first, because the device of introducing into the play the Furies (the Eumenides) does not work, and, second, because his hero, Harry, is "an insufferable prig." (Eliot adds rather interestingly that his "sympathies have now come to be all with the mother"—Amy—a judgment with which I would concur, but which suggests that a good word might also have been put in for Harry's wife.) Harry is certainly a prig in the sense that he feels spiritually superior to all other members of his family, excepting Agatha. He wears the hallmark—or plays the signature tune—of the prig, which is to tell other people that they are incapable of understanding him. But Thomas Becket and Sir Henry Harcourt-Reilly in *The Cocktail Party* also live out fantasy roles of moral superiority which enable them to spend much time putting other characters in their place. Being a prig is a vocational risk of an Eliot hero. Thomas Becket's first remark on his first entry in *Murder in the Cathedral* is to snub his priests—who have already been snubbing the chorus of Canterbury Women—by announcing:

Peace. And let them be, in their exaltation.
They speak better than they know, and beyond your
   understanding.

This spiritual one-upmanship is a fault which Eliot attempts to correct in *The Confidential Clerk* and *The*

Elder Statesman by bringing his main characters more nearly to the level of the other protagonists. But something is gained by Harry's overt and conscious superiority, closely related to, and perhaps a result of, his sense of guilt. His isolation releases very deep springs in Eliot's poetry. He and his Aunt Agatha communicate in the language of the Arnoldian "buried Life," which in Eliot's poetry seems situated in childhood (in this case, Harry's childhood, remembered by Agatha, who is older than he) and in the setting of a garden. Agatha says:

> *I only looked through the little door*
> *When the sun was shining on the rose-garden:*
> *And heard in the distance tiny voices*
> *And then a black raven flew over.*
> *And then I was only my own feet walking*
> *Away, down a concrete corridor*
> *In a dead air. . . .*

Harry and Agatha are in a relation in which the most direct way they can communicate with one another is poetry. Poetry seems a clearer and more direct language for them than prose. The center of the play is Agatha's speech, just after Harry has admitted to her that perhaps it was only in a dream that he pushed his wife overboard. She answers:

> *So I had supposed. What of it?*
> *What we have written is not a story of detection,*
> *Of crime and punishment, but of sin and expiation.*
> *It is possible that you have not known what sin*
> *You shall expiate, or whose, or why. It is certain*
> *That the knowledge of it must precede the expiation.*
> *It is possible that sin may strain and struggle*
> *In its dark instinctive birth, to come to consciousness*
> *And so find expurgation. It is possible*
> *You are the consciousness of your unhappy family,*

Its bird sent flying through the purgatorial flame.
Indeed it is possible. You may learn hereafter,
Moving alone through flames of ice, chosen
To resolve the enchantment under which we suffer.

Agatha here provides some of the play's best poetry and also its justification as the correct language for the drama. The detective-story plot is only a pretext for introducing the poetry. In *The Family Reunion* the pretext is flimsier and the poetry better than in the subsequent plays. Eliot evidently felt that the dosage of poetry in relation to naturalistic presentation in this play was too strong for his West End audience, and his subsequent development was toward increasing the quantity of prose naturalism and reducing the poetry. However, there are those who may regret this and feel that Harry's priggishness is not too high a price to pay for the poetry of the guilt-ridden soul and of the seeking of spiritual vocation. It is a play which contains echoes of the literature that struck the deepest chords in Eliot's sensibility: echoes which become transformed and transcended within it. For example, here are lines from Middleton's *The Changeling* which haunted Eliot all his life. The heroine says these lines when it is revealed that she is the mistress of the villain, de Flores, who has murdered her betrothed in order that she may marry the insipid young man of her choice. The murder having been accomplished, she is compelled to accept de Flores as lover. She sums up her life in these words:

I that am of your blood was taken from you
For your better health; look no more upon't,
But cast it to the ground regardlessly,
Let the common sewer take it from distinction.
Beneath the stars, upon yon meteor
Ever hung my fate, 'mongst things corruptible;

I ne'er could pluck it from him; my loathing,
Was prophet to the rest, but ne'er believed.[1]

Something of the strange, tragic decisive solemnity of
this speech is recalled in the speech in which Harry
pronounces the choice of his vocation, a transformed
transcendent echo:

> *. . . Why I have this election*
> *I do not understand. It must have been preparing always,*
> *And I see it was what I always wanted. Strength de-*
> *manded*
> *That seems too much, is just strength enough given.*
> *I must follow the bright angels.*

The detective-story plot and the plot of pursuit by the
Eumenides seem imposed on this story of sin and expiation and discovery of vocation, adding to it voices
which appeal to both the lowest and the highest de-
nominators of the West End audience: on the one
hand, to those who think that they are going to see a
play like Agatha Christie's *The Mousetrap* and, on the
other, to men of learning who know that Mr. T. S. Eliot
is interested in Greek tragedy. These devices do, however, intermittently, pay off. Even the sense of pursuit
by agents derived from Greek antiquity and visible to
Harry alone, pays off at the end, when the Eumenides
appear in the double aspect which they have in
Aeschylus: of being accusers which the guilt-ridden
hero flees from when he has not become reconciled to
his guilt, and friends when he has accepted it so
absolutely that he sees it as the path to his salvation:

> *Now I know that all my life has been a flight*
> *And phantoms fed upon me while I fled. Now I know*

[1] Quoted in T. S. Eliot, *Selected Essays*, p. 169. The first line
should probably read, "I am that . . ."

That the last apparent refuge, the safe shelter,
That is where one meets them. That is the way of spec-
tres . . .

The Cocktail Party is another study of the search for
religious vocation. Celia Coplestone is the mistress of
Edward Chamberlayne who, at the opening of the play,
has been left by his wife, Lavinia. With Lavinia away,
Celia believes that all problems between her and Edward
are solved and that they will live openly together. However, Edward does not see it in this way: his wife's disappearance makes him realize that he wants her back.
Celia has to face the unpleasant truth that from
Edward's point of view his relationship with her depends
on his being respectably married, with a wife in evidence whom he does not love. Her disillusionment at
the lack of passion which is the hollow reality of
Edward's character has a positive aspect. It makes her
realize that this love, which she thought she believed
in, is not what she really seeks. This transforms her
into one of Eliot's characters whose problem is to ful-
fill a religious vocation. In realizing this she is greatly
assisted by an *éminence grise* of the psychoanalytical
world, the mysterious Sir Henry Harcourt-Reilly. Harcourt-Reilly has been identified by Eliot exegetes with
various mythical figures from Greek tragedy and anthropological mythology. Eliot may well have had
associations of this sort in mind. As player of a role in
other people's lives the character to whom he most obviously approximates is the Duke in Shakespeare's
Measure for Measure.

In the early scenes of *The Cocktail Party* Harcourt-
Reilly does not reveal his name but nevertheless, by wire-
pulling from Harley Street, affects a reconciliation between Edward and Lavinia who are reunited on the
basis of *faute de mieux* on both sides and, ultimately,

by the death by martyrdom of Celia Coplestone: a result which he reviews with self-congratulatory complacency. Despite his attempts to render himself convivially human by gin-drinking and singing the very bawdy song of which *The Cocktail Party* presents a bowdlerized version, Harcourt-Reilly is best described by a phrase from American juvenile slang. He is a high-class "creep."

Harcourt-Reilly is assisted in his administrations by two of the guests at Edward's cocktail party, on which the first scene of the play opens. These are Julia, an elderly indefatigable cocktail-party frequenter (modeled scrupulously on certain London specimens), and a bright young man called Alex. These are called Guardians, and at the end of the second act, together with Harcourt-Reilly, they perform a ritualistic libation to celebrate the fact that Celia has set forth on her spiritual journey. (One person who proves resistant to salvation is Peter Quilpe, a young guest at the original cocktail party who is head-over-heels in love with Celia.)

The religious activities of Julia and Alex, though perfectly consistent with the mixture of frivolity and seriousness which often enters into English upper-class life, seem not intensely imagined. A well-meaning young man like Alex who, when one has been deserted by one's wife, interrupts one's solitude in order to make one an omelet according to some recipe he has learned in Tibet, is not by any law of his nature also a Guardian (or Christian missionary among the upper classes), without something further being explained about his motives. According to the eccentricities of high society he well might be, but according to those of creative art his case deserves more analysis than that which Eliot provides.

In his role of priest Harcourt-Reilly interviews Celia and prescribes for her a sanatorium, evidently some kind of curative ecclesiastical establishment. He explains that she need take nothing with her to this institution (not even a toothbrush?) and that there will be no expenses, which makes it one up on professionally conducted psychoanalytical therapeutic sanatoria. Yet upon this shaky structure of suspect spiritual institutionalism Celia's spirit does spread wings. She obeys Harcourt-Reilly's injunction to "work out her salvation diligently." She feels the love which is beyond that of human creatures, the call to sainthood, which is also a return to some past vision. As she explains to Reilly:

You see, I think I really had a vision of something
Though I don't know what it is. I don't want to forget it.
I want to live with it. I could do without everything,
Put up with anything, if I might cherish it.
In fact, I think it would really be dishonest
For me, now, to try to make a life with anybody!
I couldn't give anyone the kind of love—
I wish I could—which belongs to that life.
Oh, I'm afraid this sounds like raving!
Or just cantankerousness . . . still,
If there's no other way . . . then I feel just hopeless.

This is not the ecstatic communication of those who share with one another the knowledge of the Buried Life—Harry and Agatha—or who seek a burning solitude—Harry departing on his journey across deserts. But it is authentic—extraordinarily touching—the voice of a lost girl like that in Blake's poem.

The Cocktail Party ends with a second party, balancing the one with which the play opens, and with the same uninvited guests present. Peter Quilpe comes in to inquire of news of Celia, because he is in a position to recommend her to a director for a role in a film. Alex tells him that Celia is dead, having gone to Africa as a missionary and been "crucified . . . near an ant-hill" by some "heathens" who were making an insurrection.

Peter speaks with feeling about his love for Celia. Harcourt-Reilly then explains that when she came to his office for her interview with him:

I saw the image, standing behind her chair,
Of a Celia Coplestone whose face showed the astonish-
*   ment*
Of the first five minutes after a violent death. . . .
*   . . . So it was obvious*
That here was a woman under sentence of death.

He explains that he did not know what form her death would take but that he directed her "in the way of preparation":

That way, which she accepted, led to this death.
And if that is not a happy death, what death is happy?

Part of the happiness, he goes on to explain, is that Celia suffered far more than any one of them would ever be able to suffer, being more conscious.

*   . . . She paid the highest price*
In suffering. That is part of the design.

No one, not even Peter Quilpe, who was in love with Celia and who is not a Guardian, challenges the assumptions behind Harcourt-Reilly's statement. The most striking of these is that her death was not defensible as a risk undergone for the sake of doing real good to ignorant people (she was, it seems, one of the three Sisters of some religious order working in that area), but triumphant because it was the means whereby she perfected her will, bringing it into conformity with the will of God and thus achieving her martyrdom. Julia interrupts to point out that Celia has made her choice, that Peter Quilpe now also has to make his choice—which is to go and make the film he is working on—that the

Chamberlaynes in becoming reconciled have also made their choice, and that they must all now make their choice which is to entertain guests who are arriving for the cocktail party. Lavinia says: "But all the same . . . I don't want to see these people." To which Harcourt-Reilly characteristically replies: "It is your appointed burden. And as for the party, / I am sure it will be a success." Soon after this the doorbell rings and the curtain falls before the party begins.

There is doubtless something of the parable of the talents in Eliot's idea of choices which are made, the duty of each person being to follow his calling. Edward's and Lavinia's choice is to become reconciled and carry on with their lackluster marriage. A problem for Eliot as a playwright is that for him the choice of eternity is so obviously preferable to that of life on this earth that it is difficult for him not to make actual living seem second-rate.

The Confidential Clerk, like *The Elder Statesman*, is a play in which the poet comes at least halfway down to earth and takes a long look at the consolations of second-rateness. The plot is of that wearisome kind which concerns itself with questions of parenthood. The eminent businessman Sir Claude Mulhammer has, without either of them realizing the other's existence, an illegitimate son who goes under the name Colby Simpkins, an illegitimate daughter called Lucasta Angel—or so it seems at the opening of the play. (As the tangled plot unfolds it appears that after all Colby may not be the son of Sir Claude. Lady Mulhammer believes that he is *her* son by a previous marriage.)

The Fairy Godfather who, through his good sense and innate decency, presides over this pavan of interillegitimacy is Eggerson, the elderly confidential clerk from whom Colby takes over at the beginning of the play. It is he to whom Sir Claude's business, domestic and extra-domestic affairs have been confided, who has quietly made all the arrangements about them, and who finally knows who is the mother or father of whom. His chief interest is his garden, but he is a good husband to Mrs. Eggerson, and he is a church warden. It is to him that Colby turns at the end of the play when, pursuing on a more lowly level an escape parallel with that of Harry, Lord Monchensey, he leaves the Mulhammers to disentangle their problems of paternity and maternity and goes off to live in the Eggersons' simple suburban house, accepting the vacant post of organist at their parish church, while—as Eggerson confidently expects—training to take Holy Orders.

It may have struck some members of Eliot's audiences and some readers that there is an element of wishful fantasy about the departures of heroes and heroines at the ends of his plays from their claustrophobic surroundings to distant places. Withdrawal is made acceptable by being built up to appear as disagreeable as possible: but perhaps some young heir of an English country house ruled over by a formidable mother and several aunts may have felt a twinge of envy at the spectacle of the young Lord Monchensey, whose understanding chauffeur keeps his motor car sleekly purring in the garage, ready to drive his Lordship away from all this to foreign parts. Before leaving, Harry loftily tells his relatives that if they wish to correspond with him they can address letters care of his bank; and after his departure, his chauffeur returns to retrieve a cigarette case which his master has left on the drawing-room table. Of course, none of this detracts from the certainty that Harry will suffer immensely. But the suffering, like the motor car, the title, and Wishwood, is on a glamorous scale. Who would not wish to get away from Sir Claude and Lady Mulhammer, even at the price of living with Mr. and Mrs. Eggerson?

These remarks are more in the nature of irreverent but persistent demurrings on the edge of my mind than criticisms. But just because it is difficult to bring them up into the light of critical consciousness, perhaps they should not be altogether repressed. It would be an exaggeration to say that the "escape" motif in Eliot's plays is the expression of a wish which can only be realized in the form of its opposite, punishment. The fact remains, however, that Eliot was himself someone who had escaped from his family, and that his father thought he had gone astray by his life in England and his marriage to Vivien. Valerie Eliot tells me that to say that Eliot's father blamed his son would be to put the matter too strongly. She notes that Henry Ware Eliot "felt that his son had missed his way, but he was not severe with him. To the end of his days Tom was hurt by the fact that his father did not live to see his achievement."

The way Eliot chose was arduous, unpleasant, and self-punishing, but, nevertheless, it was what he wanted. There is, then, perhaps some painful, romantic self-justification projected into these "escapes" of Eliot's protagonists. Artistically speaking they are open to the objection which Eliot himself makes to *Hamlet*: that biographical material enters into the work which has not been resolved as an "objective correlative" in it. The death of Celia Coplestone does not strike one as aesthetically inevitable. Much of the fascination of these plays is that they make one think about the author; but that betokens some measure of failure. It was no part of his intention.

One criticism of the plays, not based on speculation about the hidden motives of the writer, concerns the form which Eliot arrived at. The two fragments of *Sweeney Agonistes* are experimental in a way which makes it impossible to envisage Eliot's writing a full-length play in this manner, quite apart from the incompatibility of style and treatment with his Christianization. *Murder in the Cathedral*, a triumphant success in its way, was written for a special occasion. Even if the captive audience of the devout remained to be captivated, the association of religious with poetic "sacredness" was quite rightly something that Eliot distrusted. He wanted to take the ordinary paying playgoer by storm, and he wanted to write plays about modern men and women.

In adopting (with a view to undermining) the conventions of the drawing-room drama he put himself into a position in which he was as likely to be taken over by his public, and the ideas of West End managements, as to revolutionize the theater the way he had revolutionized English poetry earlier in the century. In the event, Eliot's plays after *Murder in the Cathedral* represent an uneasy compromise between the Anglican Church, Shaftesbury Avenue, and Eliot himself. The producer who effected this compromise was Martin Browne, who as Director of Religious Drama in the Diocese of Chichester produced *The Rock* at Sadler's Wells Theatre in 1930. In an interesting essay in which he recalls working with Eliot in the theater, Mr. Browne remarks of *Sweeney Agonistes*: "To the theatre-folk of the day, dominated by naturalism, such a work was incomprehensible; its verse was too off-beat for the playwriting poets; and for my church audiences, just emerging from a puritan night, it would have been an unbearable shock."[2] Mr. Browne produced not only *The Rock* but (for the Canterbury Festival of 1935,

2 *T. S. Eliot: The Man and His Work*, Allen Tate, ed., p. 120.

written at the suggestion of the Bishop of Chichester)
Murder in the Cathedral and, at Eliot's insistence, all
the subsequent plays which appeared in the West End
during Eliot's lifetime. Eliot was grateful and loyal to
the friend and producer who had staged his first
theatrical successes. While writing his plays he sub-
mitted them to Mr. Browne for advice and often
omitted, wrote, and rewrote passages as a result. The
change from editing *The Waste Land* with Ezra Pound
at his elbow to having his plays edited and produced by
Mr. Browne, who thought that a Church or a West End
audience should not be shocked by a work as "advanced"
as *Sweeney Agonistes*, is rather striking. In the early
1920s Eliot had thought of exploiting that part of the
English theatrical tradition which was liveliest and
most natural and closest to the people—the music hall—
in order to inject poetry into it. After 1945 he worked
within the conventions of what Mr. Browne in his essay
calls "the upper-middle-class play"—that genre which
Eliot had attacked so bitterly in his essay on Marie Lloyd.

Eliot succeeded in molding the genre to some of his
poetic and visionary purposes, but not in transforming
it. In fact, his tendency was more and more to adapt his
dramatic writing to *its* needs—and to those of the audience—rather than the genre's to *his* needs. Thus after
The Family Reunion he reduced what he called the
"dosage" of the poetry in his later plays. After *The
Cocktail Party* the theme of religious vocation, which
must have seemed to the audience of that play excessive, was toned down in *The Confidential Clerk* and
The Elder Statesman.

Eliot has been praised for his "realism" in these plays
but he lacks that intense interest in human behavior in
everyday living which makes realism interesting in a
playwright like Ibsen. What he does have is a rather
surprising grasp of the worldiness that goes with "upper-

middle-class" values. In the case of Lord Claverton, for example, the title, as a seal of success, really applies— Lord Claverton himself is a shrewd measurer of successes. There is a strong feeling for different shades of upper- and middle-class and lower-middle-class social standing in English life in *The Elder Statesman*. Eliot's richest social comedy comes from his grasp of this. However, to handle such material in a way that produces a vision of reality, a writer has to believe, as Balzac believed, that money is an expression of vital genius, that material standards are a measure of something real and true about the characters of people. Eliot takes a mild, ironic, faintly snobbish interest in social status but, even if he enjoys his own success, for him this is not real. It is a kind of game, a way of whiling away a lifetime. His sense of reality is attached to an entirely different order of events. Reality is for him the realization of consciousness. And by consciousness he means the individual's awareness of having an objective place within a hierarchy of moral values, or degrees of states of being. He realizes what he himself, as a result of the way he has lived his life, is within that hierarchy of values that are supernatural. Not to be conscious in this way is, from Eliot's point of view, to be dead. But consciousness of the kind that is the only significant kind for Eliot is only attainable within extreme situations in which a person sees the meaning of his life not as subjective to him but as the objective truth realized through him: and they can only happen at extremes of wickedness, which mean damnation, or of deprivation, which offer the possibility of salvation. Consciousness is not self-consciousness. It is the consciousness that happens when you stand outside yourself. Such consciousness scarcely occurs within the routine semblances of upper-middle-class living.

The success of *Murder in the Cathedral, The Family*

Reunion, and *The Cocktail Party* is that each deals with people who attain the kind of consciousness which consists of standing outside themselves, and that they do this by living through extreme situations for which the only language is poetry. Two assumptions of the West End theater were that people should not be presented as living through situations which shatter the framework of the social environment, nor should they be presented in situations only expressible in poetry. In his last two plays Eliot learned this lesson, toned down the situations, and further reduced the poetry. The result is that whereas characters like Thomas Becket, Harry, Lord Monchensey, and Celia Coplestone had an ecstatic supernatural vitality about them, the characters in the last two plays seem not really alive: not being fully conscious, they don't, in Eliot's imagination, really come to life.

The plays throw light on his whole work. His poetry with all its wonderful qualities is an instrument which has very strong and deep low notes and very beautiful and transcendental high ones, but which is weak in the middle register. He seems always to have had a vision of hell, and he attained, perhaps, a vision of heaven. By the middle register between heaven and hell, I mean ordinary living. Most people's lives are spent preoccupied with this, and for them it means reality. If they have ideas of hell or heaven they form them from their everyday experiences. Most of the novels they read and the theater they see do the same thing. Eliot does just the opposite. Ordinary life for him is measured by the experience of heaven and hell and ordinary living denies those conditions which are to him the real life, and without which, so-called life is merely a kind of death.

Toward the end of his life, particularly after his marriage in January 1957 to his ex-secretary, Valerie Fletcher, Eliot's attitude toward the values of ordinary life changed. His marriage was radiantly and obviously happy. It also had the effect of making him enjoy the great successes that had been pouring in on him for several years, without much affecting his solitary existence, but that now became gratifying because they could be shared. The Nobel Prize, the Order of Merit, extremely well-paid lectures at American universities, and the acclaim with which his plays were received— all these, whether gained before or after his marriage, became signal tributes which he could dedicate to his wife.

Some of this gratitude for sensuous living does get into his last two comedies, but in the development of his poetry it was clearly too late for Eliot to enter on a great new last period parallel with that of Yeats at the end of his life. His health was too precarious for him to do more than register the change of heart, which is recorded in the lines to his wife in the dedication of *The Elder Statesman.*

Politics

XI

Eliot's political views were to a remarkable extent the expression of his temperament. Although after he was received into the Anglican Church they were modified somewhat by the influence of his coreligionists, they remained essentially those of a man who thought that political activity should derive from abstract principles, that principles should be based on dogma, that dogma should be based on supernatural authority. Supernatural authority should be guaranteed by institutions of Church and monarchy. Long before he became sacramentally a Christian, Eliot believed that human standards had to refer to the hypothesis of the supernatural.

Eliot was, in the strictest sense of the term, a "reactionary." He reacted against nonconformism, liberalism, ideas of progress and of the perfectibility of man. Better regard man as wicked and fallen than have him listen to the inner voice of his own conscience and judge himself by his own human standards.

He was reactionary also in preferring his idea of the Europe of the Middle Ages, in which there was unity of belief in shared values throughout the whole society, to the modern West of fragmented aims and values. Yet, while having religious and moral views that were medievalist, he was not nostalgic about that past. He lived no shadow aesthetic life haunting fifth-century Athens or pre-Raphaelite or Renaissance Italy, as, following the example of the 1890s, did Ruskin and Pater and Wilde and Yeats and Pound.

When Eliot was at Harvard, Irving Babbitt expressed in the language of caricature ideas that for Eliot were almost instinctual. No one illustrated better than Eliot the saying:

> *Every little boy or girl born into the world alive*
> *Is either born a liberal or a conservative.*

Sometimes one has the impression that Eliot was born twin with a liberal for whom he retained a lifelong hatred.

When he went to Paris in 1910–11, Charles Maurras reaffirmed for him his own deeply innate conservative traits—as it were to the sounds of drums and trumpets. This royalist and his followers in the Action Française made classicism and reaction romantic. The romantic feeling which he had for Maurras was reawakened in him in 1923 when he read *The Daily Mail* correspondent's account of Mussolini's March on Rome. In a poem entitled "Triumphal March," he wrote:

And the eyes watchful, waiting, perceiving, indifferent.
O hidden under the dove's wing, hidden in the turtle's
* breast,*

Under the palmtree at noon, under the running water
At the still point of the turning world. O hidden.

The achievement of a private peace culminates in the mob-call: "RESIGN RESIGN RESIGN." This Coriolanus is the fusion of two of Eliot's archetypes, the leader of men and the martyr: Charles Maurras and Saint Sebastian. External power is considered not as a social panacea but as a means of attaining inner peace.

To Eliot, Maurras and his *"camelots du roi"* were unique as a movement animated by intelligence, the released energy of the intellect. Though he grew to have reservations about political actions (rather than about his politics), he continued to express admiration for Maurras as a philosopher who had the feelings of a poet and who expressed in excellent prose ideas of order and opposition to democracy, liberalism, and "the mob," ideas that Eliot himself shared. Roger Kojecký quotes a lecture given by Eliot in French entitled "Aspects de la France et du monde" in which Eliot said of Maurras: "Sa conception de la monarchie et de la hiérarchie, plus qu'à beaucoup d'autres m'est proche, comme à ces conservateurs anglais dont les idées demeurent intacte malgré le monde moderne."[1]

In 1928, when the Vatican had condemned the Action Française (described by Eliot as "an important intellectual movement"), he wrote in *The Criterion*,[2] emphasizing that Maurras had written "as fine prose as any French author living":

The work of M. Maurras is little known in England. . . .
The majority of those who are in a position to ad-

[1] Roger Kojecký, *T. S. Eliot's Social Criticism*, p. 63.
[2] Published in 18 vols. (London, 1967). References are to volume number and page.

vertise contemporary French literature are Liberals, horrified by such a word as Reaction, and by no means friendly to Catholicism; or Conservatives, indifferent to foreign thought and equally unfriendly to Catholicism; or Socialists, who can have no use for M. Maurras at all. The fact that he is also an important literary critic, and has written as fine prose as any French author living, makes no difference to his reputation. But if anything, in another generation or so, is to preserve us from a sentimental Anglo-Fascism, it will be some system of ideas which will have gained much from the study of Maurras. His influence in England has not yet begun. (VII, 196)

The situation would indeed have been serious if, as Eliot writes, the English could only have been saved from "sentimental" Anglo-Fascism (what would unsentimental Anglo-Fascism have been like?) by a French writer about French politics whom they showed no inclination to read. Eliot always overlooks the fact that Maurras had been anti-Dreyfusard, that is, on the side of racial hatred and injustice in that great case in which French intellectuals were so passionately involved. It was the writers and intellectuals like Emile Zola who supported this Jewish officer in the French Army until the injustice done to him was rectified. But it was Maurras who represented that intellectual obscurantism which consists of defending contemporary injustice in the name of the historic past.

One explanation of Eliot's support of Maurras is provided later in the same article. Defending Maurras from the charge of being anti-Christian, he maintains, with evident sincerity, that on the contrary, though not a Catholic, Maurras led his readers toward Christianity. Maurras "recognizes that he has much more in common, in the temporal sphere, with Catholics than with Protestants and atheists." Eliot here discovers in Maurras an attitude which readers of his prose written before he became a Christian can hardly fail to discover in Eliot himself: "His attitude is that of an unbeliever who cannot believe, and who is too honest to pretend to himself or to others that he does believe; if others can believe, so much the better not only for them but for the world at large" (VII, 200).

Eliot's religious development seems to have passed through three stages, all deriving from a logic implanted in his mind by Maurras, whom he referred to as "a kind of Virgil who led us to the doors of the temple." These were, first, the idea of a civilization in which classicism was inseparable from faith; second, the hypothesis ("Having to construct something/Upon which to rejoice") of accepting values of religion, though not being able to believe; third, being driven, out of a sense of the necessity of dogma and out of a Dantesque vision of eternity, to believe.

As such, Eliot's political attitudes had a good deal in common with those which compelled some of his contemporaries, notably Ezra Pound, not to Christianity but to fascism. That he never became, or could have become, a Fascist is due to a side of his temperament more deeply Christian, I think, than dogmas, a side which scarcely shows in his polemical criticism but which did show in his relations not only with friends and colleagues but with everyone with whom he had dealings: his tolerance, genuine humility, sympathy, and considerateness, his being, in some very rare sense, a gentleman.

His severe discipline was largely directed against himself. When Eliot made public statements which shocked his friends, he had the kindness and considerateness—so tragically lacking in Pound—to feel it an obligation to explain his position to them. The explanation often enclosed rather than contradicted their point of view. For example, in 1936 Bonamy Dobrée wrote to him expressing his revulsion at the epigraph from Saint John of the Cross which Eliot has placed in front of the text of *Sweeney Agonistes*: "Hence the soul cannot be possessed of the divine union, until it has divested itself of the love of created beings." Eliot sent a reply which establishes the link between the love that is supernatural and his essential humanity. The passage is exemplary and bears quotation in full:

> The doctrine that in order to arrive at the love of God one must divest oneself of the love of created beings was thus expressed by St. John of the Cross, you know: i.e. a man who was writing primarily not for you and me, but for people seriously engaged in pursuing the Way of Contemplation. It is only to be read in relation to that Way: i.e. merely to kill one's human affections will get one nowhere, it would be only to become rather more a completely living corpse than most people are. But the doctrine is fundamentally true, I believe. Or to put your belief in your own way, that only through the love of created beings can we approach the love of God, that I believe to be UNTRUE. Whether we mean by that domestic and friendly affections, or a more comprehensive love of the "neighbour," of humanity in general, I don't think that ordinary human affections are capable of leading us to the love of God, but rather that the love of God is capable of informing, intensifying and elevating our human affections, which otherwise have little to distinguish them from the "natural" affections of animals. Try looking at it from that end of the glass![3]

[3] *T. S. Eliot: The Man and His Work*, Allen Tate, ed., p. 84.

Eliot's idea that most people are living corpses (he knew very little about most people) may stick in the gullet of some readers. What concerned Eliot, however, was the concept of unalterable Truth as "an immutable object or Reality" outside time, and against which opinions held within time, such as the shifting, relativist values of modern science and of liberalism, are measured.

The nearest he came to expressing views which, with hindsight, can be identified with twentieth-century political wickedness, was in the notorious anti-Semitism of "Burbank with a Baedeker: Bleistein with a Cigar." In this poem, the Jew Bleistein is a symbol of a certain type of tourist who concentrates all the vulgarity of the barbarian invader who has accumulated the wealth of the civilization he ignorantly surveys. Matthew Arnold divided the English into barbarian, philistine, and populace—Eliot is here postulating the American version of barbarian-populace into "Chicago Semite Viennese."

In 1922 Eliot became editor of *The Criterion* (at first a quarterly magazine, but later a monthly, and later still reverting to being a quarterly), the first number of which appeared in October of that year. It was sponsored by Lady Rothermere. He received no salary, and continued for some years to work in Lloyds Band. Until he left the bank in 1927, his name did not appear as editor on the cover of the magazine. He contributed editorial notes called "Commentaries" and also wrote occasional articles and book reviews for it. The "Commentaries" reveal his views over the seventeen years of *The Criterion*'s existence about a great many topics— religious, cultural, and personal as well as political.

In the fourth number he published a statement entitled "The Function of a Literary Review":

A literary review should maintain the application in literature, of principles which have their consequences also in politics and private conduct; and it should maintain them without tolerating any confusion of the purposes of pure literature with the politics or ethics. . . . To maintain the autonomy, and the disinterestedness, of every human activity, and to perceive it in relation to every other, require a considerable discipline.

This is a very clear example of Eliot's thinking. Each activity is conceived of as being separate and apart, boxed off in order to maintain its integrity, governed by rules internal to it which are not those of any other activity. Above all, the literary activity is not allowed to become a substitute for the ethical one. At the same time each activity is subject to principles which are ultimately religious and moral.

In January 1926 Eliot further qualified the aims of the magazine by stating that it had a "tendency towards classicism" (a higher and clearer conception of "Reason"). He cited six books that exemplified the tendency: *L'Avenir de l'intelligence* by Charles Maurras, *Democracy and Leadership* by Irving Babbitt, *Belphégor* by Julien Benda, *Réflexions sur la violence* by Georges Sorel, *Speculations* by T. E. Hulme, and *Réflexions sur l'intelligence* by Jacques Maritain. Later, Wyndham Lewis was added to the list (IV, 1–6). These books have it in common that their authors take the stand of pure intelligence from which to attack the society, which they consider decadent, romantic, and without dicipline or objective standards. All these writers feel themselves to be representative of the true civilization, which is in process of being betrayed by literary romantics and political liberals.

Eliot had praised Benda's *Belphégor*, which attacked romanticism, sensationalism, self-expression, weakness of intellect, and confusion of thought in contemporary French literature—all, of course, from the point of view of "classicism." However, he was critical of Benda's most famous book, *La Trahison des clercs*, published in 1927, which he reviewed in *The New Republic* (December 12, 1928). Benda attacked contemporary intellectuals for being partisan in politics, thus betraying the tradition whereby "*clercs* remained strangers to political passions." Eliot argued that there could be no hard-and-fast rule as to "what interests, the *clerc*, the intellectual, should or should not have." He suggested that the only way to judge the author who "ventured into a new field, whether it be that of political controversy or some other, is to trace, if we can, the growth of his interests and their relations among each other."

Eliot did not, in fact, agree with Benda that the artist should be detached from politics. In June 1926, he had noted in *The Criterion* that

> the artist in the modern world . . . finds himself, if he is a man of intellect, unable to realise his art to his own satisfaction, and he may be driven to examine the elements in the situation—political, social, philosophical or religious—which frustrate his labour. In this uncomfortable pursuit, he is accused of 'neglecting his art.' But it is likely that some of the strongest influences in the thought of the next generation may be those of the dispossessed artists. (IV, 420)

Politics meant to Eliot the defense of the forces of tradition within the society. He had a tendency in his political writings (perhaps by extension of his view that modern poetry should invest the pastness of the tradition in the newness of the modern) to hail as new in politics attitudes which most observers of the time would have regarded as atavistic. For example in his *Criterion* "Commentary" of October 1924 he writes of a magazine called *Youth*—after noting several absurdities—as follows:

> In the most boisterous storm, the ear of the practised sailor can distinguish, and at a surprising distance, the peculiar note of breakers on a reef. This note is not "the great middle-class liberalism," or the great lower-middle-class socialism; it is of authority not democracy, of dogmatism not tolerance, of the extremity and never of the mean. (III, 4)

Well, perhaps this was prophetic.

He was spared from identifying with any existing English political party by the fact that he looked to politics for ideas and in England never found any. Liberals, Conservatives, and Labour were all innocent of thought, and even the extreme parties, of Fascists and Communists, failed to "make it new." Thus in January 1925 commenting on Trotsky's *Problems of Life*, he opines that "a revolution staged on such a vast scale . . . involving such disorder, rapine, assassination, starvation, and plague should have something to show for the expense: a new culture horrible at the worst, but in any event fascinating. Such a cataclysm is justified if it produces something really *new*:

> *Un oasis d'horreur dans un désert d'ennui.*"

He complains that all that Trotsky has to show is a picture of "Montessori schools, playing fields, plasticene, club-houses, communal kitchens, crêches, abstinence from swearing and alcohol, a population warmly clad (or soon to be warmly clad), and with its mind filled (or in process of being filled) with nineteenth-century superstitions about Nature and her forces."

So he despises Trotsky for regarding welfare as "culture." Yet Eliot, working at the foreign desk of the bank at this time, was in a position (as indeed his remarks show) to know very well that in 1925 Russians and central Europeans were only just beginning to recover from a fearful period of starvation.

Eliot rejected fascism because he found that in practice, like Trotsky's communism, the ideas it offered were inferior. Reviewing "The Literature of Fascism" in *The Criterion* (December 1928), he reports that most of the concepts which "might have attracted me in fascism I seem already to have found, in a more digestible form, in the work of Charles Maurras. I say a more digestible form, because I think they have a closer applicability to England than those of fascism" (VIII, 283). William M. Chace argues that Eliot dismisses both communism and fascism because they seem to him to have died as political ideas, in becoming political facts.[4]

In his "Commentary" of April 1933 (a few weeks after Hitler had seized power in Germany) Eliot observes:

> Communism—I mean the ideas of communism, not the reality, which would be of no use in this way— has come as a godsend (so to speak) to these young people who would like to grow up and believe in something . . . stupidity, for the majority of people, is no doubt the best solution of the difficulty of thinking; it is far better to be stupid in a faith, even in stupid faith, than to be stupid and believe nothing. . . . I would even say that, as it is the faith of the day, there are only a small number of people living who have achieved the right *not* to be communists. My only objection to it is the same as my objection to the cult of the Golden Calf. (XII, 472–73)

[4] William M. Chace, *The Political Identities of Ezra Pound and T. S. Eliot* (Stanford, Cal., 1973).

As Chace points out, "This is to make communism relevant not to any corporate social fact, but to personal psychology."

Although Eliot had fixed principles, his day-to-day— or month-to-month or quarter-to-quarter—political opinions in *The Criterion* are largely improvised. He thinks about the principles but not about politics in terms of political realities, nor does he even think that it is anything but a sign of intellectual inferiority to do so. His improvised views are inconsistent and sometimes whimsical. When political realities, close to him in London, force themselves upon his attention, he can suddenly become aware of the dangers of extremism, as when in July 1930 he warns that the English policy of compromise produces its opposite "rather than compromise everyone who believes in principles will be driven in spite of himself into extremity, either of Toryism or Communism" (IV, 590). But when he is thinking in literary, or religious, or moralistic terms extremes appear to be exactly what he wants.

Today many research workers seem to think that the fact that *The Criterion* never had more than a few hundred readers shows how serious it was, how unserious the reading public: of which no proof was needed. The truth surely is that its readership was limited to the not very great number of Eliot-watchers, who were fascinated by the poet whose masterpiece, *The Waste Land*, had been published in the first number and by the critic who endlessly discussed with himself what he thought about Matthew Arnold, Irving Babbitt, and Charles Maurras: matters which had already preoccupied him while he was at Harvard. But what he has to say about the theater is always interesting, and his views about censorship were courageous at the time. It is true that the work of distinguished writers was published in *The Criterion*: on rare occasions there were pieces by Joyce, Lawrence, Yeats, Forster, Virginia Woolf, Adrian Stokes, Auden. But although Eliot admires these writers the magazine gives no feeling that they are the very substance of its life, in the way that Joyce was for *The Egoist* and *transition*, Lawrence for *The Adelphi*, and all the best talent of the time for *The Dial*. The Criterion resembles thick slices of bread with a little nutritious butter very thinly spread over it. There is much editorial conscience but remarkably little passion. In its articles and reviews it gives the impression of being run not so much by a clique as by a bunch of cronies who have formed their own dining club and whose opinions have little reverberation outside its pages. Current politics are discussed on the level of theory by theoreticians without influence or realism and there is practically no sense of the tyrannies, revolutions, murders, tortures, and concentration camps going on in the world outside. Nor is there very much sense of the extraordinary vitality of literature in Europe and America during the 1920s and 1930s.

In the remarks addressed to readers when he closed down *The Criterion* in 1939, Eliot writes of "the state of public affairs—which has induced in myself a depression of spirits so different from any other experience of fifty years as to be a new emotion—" with the result that he no longer "felt the enthusiasm necessary to make a literary review what it should be."

However, the last years and the end of *The Criterion* were the beginning of a period of cooperation with members of various Christian activist committees and conferences. The earliest of these was the Lambeth Conference of the Church of England in 1930, on which Eliot wrote, in the form of a critique of its Report, a pamphlet entitled "Thoughts after Lambeth." It is characteristic of his approach to the Church as an ideally

serious and responsible organization that he takes up a
suggestion which he had already put forward in *The
Criterion*: that if there were to be a censorship of literature it should be directed from Lambeth Palace. He
optimistically supposes that the Archbishop of Canterbury would understand the deep seriousness of D. H.
Lawrence and James Joyce and permit works like
Ulysses (and presumably, though it was subsequent to
this, *Lady Chatterley's Lover*), which were banned by
a succession of Home Secretaries, to be published on
account of their religious seriousness. In this pamphlet
he enjoys himself flogging—the more vigorously by
benefit of his newly acquired Christianity—some of the
tired horses whose flanks he had already whipped over a
great many years—some of them while he was still at
Harvard: Bertrand Russell, with whom he now associated another freethinker, Aldous Huxley; that endlessly
chastised old warhorse Middleton Murry; and the humanist Norman Foerster, presumably a stand-in for
Irving Babbitt whom Eliot did not care to attack. He
supposes some of these adversaries to be, if not
penitent, at least wearied from prolonged attrition of
their moral musculature:

> Emancipation loses some of its charm in becoming
> respectable. Indeed, the gospel of happiness in the
> form preached by Mr. Russell in middle age is such
> as I cannot conceive as capable of making any appeal
> to Mr. Russell in youth, so mediocre and respectable
> is it. It has nothing to offer to those born into the
> world which Mr. Russell and others helped to create.
> (*Selected Essays*, p. 307)

This was written in 1931. In the first flush of conversion Eliot leaped to his religion aggressively, as

Catholic converts rather than Anglicans are wont to do. He sees himself as a defender of the faith and is scornful of watered-down liberal or rationalistic religionists:

> However low an opinion I hold of Youth, I could not believe that it can long be deceived by that vacuous word "religion." The Press may continue for a time, for the Press is always behind the times, to organize battues of popular notables, with the religion of a this and of a that; and to excite such persons to talk nonsense about the revival or decay of "religion." Religion can hardly revive, because it cannot decay. . . . Without religion the whole human race would die, as according to W. H. R. Rivers, some Melanesian tribes have died, solely of boredom. Everyone would be affected: the man who regularly has a run in his car and a round of golf on Sunday, quite as much as the punctilious churchgoer. Dr. Sigmund Freud, with characteristic delicacy of feeling, has reminded us that we should "leave Heaven to the angels and the sparrows"; following his hint, we may safely leave "religion" to Mr. Julian Huxley and Dr. Freud. (*Selected Essays*, p. 37)

Evidently Eliot would, at this stage, have liked to see the Church become the Church militant in a battle between the forces of the false religions with their false sacraments (the car, the golf clubs, and whatever the press thinks up) and the true sacraments of the Catholic faith. He proceeds to attack men of science, such as Einstein, Schroedinger, and Planck, to air his views on contraception (the Church should give couples their instructions about this), youth (recommending "thought, study, mortification, sacrifice") and the supremacy of the Church of England as the Catholic Church in England. In his concluding remarks he strikes the heroic stance that the Universal Church is today set against the world as it has never been at any time since pagan Rome:

> The World is trying the experiment of attempting to form a civilized but non-Christian mentality. The experiment will fail; but we must be very patient in awaiting its collapse; meanwhile redeeming the time: so that the Faith may be preserved alive through the dark ages before us; to renew and rebuild civilization, and save the World from suicide. (*Selected Essays*, p. 387)

At the conclusion of *The Idea of a Christian Society* (1939), Eliot takes up again the theme of depression resultant for him from the events leading to war. Eliot describes September 1938 (the Munich Settlement) as seeming "to demand an act of personal contrition, of humility, repentance and amendment; what had happened was something in which one was deeply implicated and responsible. It was not, I repeat, a criticism of the government, but the doubt of the validity of a civilization." In a postscript added after the outbreak of war, he emphasizes that "the alignment of forces which has now revealed itself should bring more clearly to our consciousness the alternative of Christianity or paganism" (*The Idea of a Christian Society*, p. 64).

The assumption that civilization is at a stage of crisis leading to dread alternatives is fundamental to this book. People will have to choose between paganism (Fascists and Communists) and Christendom. Only liberalism prevents them from seeing that these are the real issues.

The book consists of lectures which were given at Cambridge in March 1939, at Corpus Christi College. Their theme is the role that Christians and the Church should play in the world; Eliot had been discussing this for several years with fellow Christians, particularly with the members of a group belonging to an informal organization called "The Moot." This itself originated in the Oxford Conference on "Church, Community and State," which met for a fortnight in Oxford in July 1937, and the Council on the Christian Faith and the Common life.

To many people the 1930s appeared as a struggle between the immensely powerful forces of authoritarian, Fascist, and Communist states, in which the democratic powers were confronted by the choice either of having to side with one of these extremes (perhaps becoming themselves authoritarian in the process) or of fighting a desperate war of survival. To a few groups it seemed also important that in the transformed world which would emerge from this struggle, new systems of society with new philosophies—or reconstructed old ones— might emerge. Essentially the members of The Moot felt that, drawing dire lessons about the effects of materialism, men would turn back to the truths of Christendom. In *The Idea of a Christian Society* this prospect or possibility is seen not so much as that of the Church of England taking over power as of statesmen and influential leaders of public opinion accepting the idea that the basic values of their society were still Christian. Therefore in forming their policies they must turn to the Church for advice. The only serious enemies to such a turn of events appear to Eliot to be the liberals.

The Idea of a Christian Society provides a very clear example of the way in which Eliot's mind works when he is applying his Christian views to society. He presents the reader with an either/or. Either there is a Christian state or there is a pagan one. He then brings to bear on the situation his ideas of how if the Christian State were put into practice, it would function, assuming that even non-Christians will agree to this (unless they were pagans or completely worm-eaten with liberalism).

But to an open-minded reader it might seem that an argument put forward with so little apparent sense of the difficulties involved or of the opposition which Christian rule would provoke is self-defeating. One can very well read *The Idea of a Christian Society* and find oneself merely persuaded by it that such a society is not practicable. Even if there were a Christian revolution it seems unlikely that it would be under the aegis of the Church of England. On the whole, Eliot's social-religious activities make one reflect on how extraordinarily ineffective the Church of England has been in bringing Christian principles to bear on political life.

Eliot confines himself in this book to discussing the idea of the Christian State in England, which seems the last country in Europe where it would be likely to be adopted—the English being averse to the idea of being governed by the Church. It is surprising that he at no time turns his attention to Europe, where, at the time when he was giving these lectures, there were several countries with parties calling themselves Christian Democrats or Christian Socialists, one of which at least was in power. The Catholic Church had given its Christian blessing to Chancellor Dollfuss in Austria and to Generalissimo Franco in Spain. Chancellor Brüning, the Catholic German Chancellor who was head of the Catholic Zentrum Partei had, in the early 1930s, failed in a desperate struggle against the fascism which Eliot labels pagan. He had, in the course of this struggle, abandoned many of the principles of liberalism and democracy and given his support to the senile Hindenburg, in a presidential election, thus laying open the path on which the pagan Hitler came to power. The Catholic Generalissimo Franco, aided by bombs blessed by the Church, had imposed a Fascist government on Spain, thus, according to Eliot's criteria, converting his country to paganism. Different from these, Gandhi in

India was putting into effect methods of passive resistance to the British Raj, which derived from Tolstoi's interpretation of the preaching of Jesus in the gospels.

Thus at the time when Eliot was lecturing on the idea of a Christian society, prelates and politicians who considered themselves representatives of the Universal Church on this earth, were, usually with disastrous results, putting into practice what they considered to be exactly these principles. It may be that Eliot did not consider the governments of Dollfuss or Brüning or von Papen to be examples of what he meant by the Christian State. But, he should have taken them into consideration, if only to examine the ways in which people professing Christianity can produce a kind of pagan counterpaganism. This gap is all the odder on account of the interest which Eliot showed in European intellectual life in *The Criterion*.

Notes Towards the Definition of Culture (1948) presents us again with an either/or. Either we have a Christian culture or we have nothing. Eliot here surveys culture within existing social structures during a time of change when classes seem on the verge of being abolished and succeeded by "élites"; when, in fact, in some countries class distinctions do no longer exist, though there are great differences between the privileged and the unprivileged. Coming from America where in many parts of the country there are distinctions of wealth rather than of class, Eliot is in a very good position to consider the relation of class to culture. Here he has a completely open mind and is writing as a social observer and not as a Christian dogmatist.

Essentially, Eliot's view is that there is an amalgam of cultural activities, a harmony of diversities, within the unity which is culture. Thus the arts, philosophy, scholarship, and the civility of manners which Matthew Arnold and Henry James thought of as culture—and reproached America for not having—are only aspects of culture. You can very well be specialized in any of these and yet be uncultivated.

In primitive societies everyone shares all the activities of the culture. But in more complex societies, there are different levels of culture. The upper class tends to become representative of the literary, artistic, and higher levels of the culture, because members of it have the time and leisure and money to pay attention to these things. However, the levels of culture in the whole society may become entirely separated and then the culture disintegrates.

Religion is introduced at this point. What is common to all classes and specializations of the culture is the religion. For example, religious art embraces all levels of the society: those who like it for the subject matter, those who like it for aesthetic reasons, and those who like it for both. The conclusion which Eliot draws from this is that without a religious basis in the society no culture is possible. Eliot here complicates the issue by equating religion with what people believe, consciously or unconsciously, asleep or awake, which is also shown in their culture: "Yet there is an aspect in which we can see a religion as the *whole way of life* of a people, from birth to the grave, from morning to night and even in sleep, and that way of life is also its culture" (*Notes Towards a Definition of Culture*, p. 31).

Under this aspect, then, all our actions and impulses reflect our almost unconsciously held beliefs and are cultural. This works against the argument which Eliot has previously put forward: that without religion there is no culture. For if it is impossible not to have a religion, consciously or unconsciously, then it is also impossible not to have a culture consciously or unconsciously. Eliot further complicates the issue by qualifying and refining his arguments to the point where they seem to vanish into thin air. For example whereas, on the one hand, he thinks that culture cannot be "preserved, extended and developed in the absence of religion," on the other hand he admits that "a culture may linger on, and indeed produce some of its most brilliant artistic and other successes after the religious faith has fallen into decay." He thinks it possible that Britain, consummating "its apostasy by reforming itself according to the prescriptions of some inferior or materialistic religion, might blossom into a culture more brilliant than we can show today." However, this would not prove that the new religion was true and Christianity false or even that there was really a culture. It would merely prove "that any religion, while it lasts, and on its own level, gives apparent meaning to life, provides the framework for a culture, and protects the mass of humanity from boredom and despair" (*Notes Towards a Definition of Culture*, pp. 31, 34). At which point one wonders what has happened to the argument that we can have no culture without Christianity. The great interest of this book is that Eliot is completely honest about the difficulties he sees. He admits that his way of looking at culture and religion seems so difficult to him himself that he can only grasp it in flashes. When he is writing about religion here he gives the impression of striving. And that is better than the impression sometimes given in *The Idea of a Christian Society* that he is fitting himself for the suit of an *éminence grise*. In the course of the argument he lets drop a remark which shows how far he has traveled from his early critical views:

Aesthetic sensibility must be extended into spiritual perception, and spiritual perception must be extended into aesthetic sensibility and disciplined taste before we are qualified to pass judgment upon decadence or nihilism in art. To judge a work of art by artistic or religious standards, to judge a religion by religious or artistic standards should come in the end to the same thing: though it is an end at which no individual can arrive.

This fusion or continual transition from the aesthetic to the religious is shown in *Four Quartets.*

After the *selva oscura* of the passages about religion and culture, we emerge into the light of a very interesting discussion (carried on from The Moot) between Eliot and Karl Mannheim. Eliot has taken the view that for transmission of the culture the persistence of social classes is necessary, and that without an "upper class" there can be no continuance of a high culture. This view may sound snobbish, but Eliot sets it forth in with a reasonableness which runs him the risk rather of being called a liberal. He sees the injustice of the class system; thinks the privileged existence of the upper class unjustified unless they benefit the whole society. He sees the advantages of an elitist society which would tend to select and train from early on the members of the society for the jobs to which they were best suited. Yet elitism is a threat to culture because it is a threat to those who are by heredity bound to traditions of which they are the guardians. In his "Introduction" he states the choice between an upper class and an elite with his usual bleakness. Addressing the equalitarian who wishes to abolish all class distinctions, he writes: "if . . . he finds it shocking that culture and equalitarianism should conflict, if it seems monstrous to him that anyone should have 'advantages of birth'—I do not ask him to change his faith, I merely ask him to stop paying lip-service to culture" (*Notes Towards a Definition of Culture,* pp. 31, 34). He draws faint comfort from the hope that the future society will offer a mixture of elitism and class distinctions, based on the continuity of interest of the family.

Rather surprisingly (though characteristically), George Orwell expressed sympathy in his review of Eliot's book in *The Observer* (November 28, 1948), for Eliot's misgivings about the effects on culture of the disappearance of the upper class. Sharing Eliot's distaste for Karl Mannheim's elites, Orwell writes: "The elites will plan, organise and administer: whether they can become the guardians and transmitters of culture, as certain social classes have been in the past, Mr. Eliot doubts, perhaps justifiably." Orwell even reproaches Eliot for not making a stronger attack on elites. Thinking no doubt of communism, Orwell points out that a society directed by its elites "may ossify very rapidly" because the members of the elites tend to choose as their successors people like themselves. Orwell sees it as against them that the directors of elites are not eccentrics. An eccentric aristocrat is a common enough figure: an eccentric political commissar scarcely occurs.

Orwell the Socialist with a high Tory side is sympathetic to the later Eliot, the high churchman and Tory. All the same Orwell puts his finger on Eliot's weakness in his writings about society: "One continues to have, throughout this book, the feeling that something is wrong, and that he himself is aware of it. The fact is that class privilege, like slavery, has somehow ceased to be defensible. It conflicts with certain moral assumptions which Mr Eliot appears to share, although intellectually he may be in disagreement with them."[5]

This insight would be even truer of *The Idea of a Christian Society*, and applies perhaps to some degree

[5] *The Collected Essays, Journalism and Letters of George Orwell*, Sonia Orwell and Ian Angus, eds. (New York, 1968), IV, 455–56.

to all Eliot's writings about culture, education, and society. They are self-undermining. Fundamentally, Eliot had no faith in modern civilization. In his early work he thought of it as barbarous compared with past civilizations, though he thought of the past as something still present within the heritage of tradition.

Orwell quotes from Eliot's *Notes Towards a Definition of Culture*: "We can assert with some confidence that our own period is one of decline; that the standards of culture are lower than they were fifty years ago; and that the evidence of this decline is visible in every department of human activity."

Eliot undertook improving social and cultural tasks in a spirit of cooperative cheerfulness: but the gloom keeps on breaking in, and when it does so one has the feeling that it was always there under the surface, though above the surface Eliot may have been considerably encouraged by conversation with the spiritually muscular and cooperative members of The Moot, forever plotting to set up cells and penetrate every branch of the community with their redemptive schemes; clergymen, dons, and intellectuals asking one another, anxiously sometimes indeed, whether they were not in danger of acting as a kind of spiritual Gestapo or Communist cell; the old polemical Eliot drawing up at one time a list of enemies of any given socially active Christian Fraternity. As he wrote in *Christian News-Letter*:

> But a Fraternity dedicated to action must be prepared for some all-in wrestling with no holds barred and no words minced: and I do not know of any revolution which has done without attack on particular institutions and particular people. If the Fraternity was at all militant whether *in* or *beyond* politics makes no difference—it would have to name the enemies.

Among the supposititious enemies were "popular demagogues and *philosophes* with quasi-Christian wild-cat schemes already antiquated and always superficial." "He suggested J. B. Priestley, Sir Richard Acland, Edward Hulton and Julian Huxley as having generous motives but no rigorous *examen de conscience.*"[6] It is rather as though Don Quixote were to have labeled his windmills with the names of several prominent contemporaries.

What makes for the interest of *The Idea of a Christian Society* and *Notes Towards a Definition of Culture* is not the practical use to which they might be put by government, but the spectacle they provide of a mind which moves between two worlds, one of supernatural eternal values, the other of that in which we live. Providing this involuntary self-portrait of Eliot, they do also throw light on the present state of our civilization dominated by power and vast accumulations of things, so that whether a government is called "Christian" or "pagan," whether it is capitalist or equalitarian it is inevitably "materialist" in being dominated by caluculations about wealth and production, private, national, international, or equalitarian. What is moving about Eliot's social writings is the way in which he sets the cat of the Holy Spirit among the pigeons of all existing politics:

> However bigoted the announcement may sound, the Christian can be satisfied with nothing less than a Christian organisation of society—which is not the same thing as a society consisting exclusively of devout Christians. It would be a society in which the natural end of man—virtue and well-being in community—is acknowledged for all, and the super-

6 Roger Kojecký, *T. S. Eliot's Social Criticism,* p. 182.

natural end—beatitude—for those who have the eyes to see it. (*The Idea of a Christian Society*, pp. 33–34)

As far as he himself is concerned, one may suppose that Eliot's Christian social thinking is a self-imposed task of discipline and humility: rejection of the view that came so easily to him, that the modern world can be dismissed as the decadence of the civilization, and acceptance of the role of the Christian, he is not just spiritually to be a citizen of the Eternal City who happens, for his lifetime, to be lodged in the temporal city, but he has to work for the redemption of the world. There is humility in a passage such as the following:

I have tried to restrict my ambition of a Christian society to a social minimum: to picture, not a society of saints, but of ordinary men, of men whose Christianity is communal before being individual. It is very easy for speculation on a possible Christian order in the future to tend to come to rest in a kind of apocalyptic vision of a golden age of virtue. But we have to remember that the Kingdom of Christ on earth will never be realised, and also that it is always being realized; we must remember that whatever reform or revolution we carry out, the result will always be a sordid travesty of what human society should be—though the world is never left wholly without glory (*Ibid.*, p. 59)

Epilogue: The Second and Third Voice

To write about Eliot's later plays and his social criticism after "Little Gidding" is to be reminded that the last of the *Four Quartets* did, in more than the obvious sense, "set a crown upon a lifetime's effort."

The poem is not only Eliot's masterpiece, but it is also the end of his poetic quest for the true ritual. It seems to open out beyond his own death, which is accepted in it. There is a deeply personal aspect to "Little Gidding" in which the the poet, meeting other poets who are now dead, returns through the poetry to the sources of his own life:

> *At the source of the longest river*
> *The voice of the hidden waterfall*
> *And the children in the apple-tree.*

This personal aspect corresponds in Eliot's development to that of D. H. Lawrence in "The Ship of Death."

Eliot did not, however, like Lawrence, die after preparing for his last imaginable journey. He lived for another twenty years. After "Little Gidding," though, we have the sense of Eliot's life and work going gently down an incline on the farther side of a mountain. This was accomplished with much grace and public acclaim. He wrote partly because the theater really was new territory for him and partly out of a sense of duty and benevolence. He did so without repeating himself and with some striking successes. *The Family Reunion* and *The Cocktail Party* are certainly achievements of a high order, signposts along a path which might be described as his descent into becoming a "celebrity"—a process which he regarded with some irony, not unmixed with pleasure and relief.

Two anecdotes may serve to indicate the contrast between Eliot's quiet enjoyment of his theatrical success (which, after all, appeared in the light of Poetry's conquest of Shaftesbury Avenue and Broadway) and his sardonic sense of living. The first was told me by Conrad Aiken, a friend of his youth. He said that in the early 1950s he visited Eliot in his office at Faber and Faber. As he came into the room to greet the friend whom he had not seen for many years, Eliot got up from his chair and pressed into his hands his latest volume, which he had been scrutinizing with evident satisfaction, and exclaimed, "I've done it again!" The volume was the published edition of *The Cocktail Party.*

The other anecdote, told me at about the same time, shows that despite all the acclaim, Eliot had not lost his Prufrockian self-irony. Auden told me how, visiting Eliot at the flat which he shared with John Hayward in Chelsea, he found him playing Patience. "Tell me," he asked, "why do you like playing Patience?" Eliot reflected gravely for a few moments and then replied,

"Well, I suppose it's because it's the nearest thing to being dead."

With "Little Gidding" the poet had found the true ritual. The word and the Word, the philosophical subject matter and the literally held belief, the mystery which was the religion, and the language which was rich and strange, had, as I have suggested above, become one. Eliot had gone as far as it was possible to go along the vein which produced his finest poetry, that is, in writing what he called the poetry of the "first voice." After this he could only write out of the "second" or the "third voice."

So he wrote poetry—and also prose—of these two latter voices. In the essay which I have discussed above, "The Three Voices of Poetry," he distinguished between these three voices as follows:

> The first is the voice of the poet talking to himself—or to nobody. The second is the voice of the poet addressing an audience, whether large or small. The third is the voice of the poet when he attempts to create dramatic character in verse: when he is saying, not what he would say in his own person, but only what he would say within the limits of one imaginary character addressing another imaginary character.

In developing this theme Eliot tends to break down the distinctions between the voices, pointing out that in the poetry of any one voice, that of the other two is also present. But one voice is always dominant. Thus, the dominating voice in "Little Gidding" is the first voice, that of the poet speaking himself, which becomes merged with that of the individual alone with God. Perhaps in that poem the first voice moves beyond poetry into prayer. The quest is finished and the grail defined.

All that was left for the poet to do were the poetically minor tasks of writing out of the other two voices: to become public and to address an audience, sometimes in poetry for the theater, sometimes in prose in essays and lectures. The first voice—that of the poet addressing himself—could, it is true, in the theater take over from the third voice: in fact, the best poetry in Eliot's plays is that in which this happens. It happens because Eliot's protagonists are in search of a vocation, which turns out to be religious, and they therefore enter into situations which speak out of his own inner life. The best poetry of Harry and Agatha in *The Family Reunion* is like this. It is the first voice poetry of the *Four Quartets*. When, to meet the demands of his West End audience Eliot diminished the "dosage" of poetry in his plays it was by suppressing his own "first voice."

Putting this another way, after "Little Gidding" Eliot stopped writing out of the center of his ritualistic sensibility and wrote out of the periphery of conscience. Conscience told him that it was his duty to apply Christian principles to social problems and to write and lecture about politics, education, and culture. A friend of Eliot, Herbert Read, expressed the view of many when he condemned the later work by saying that Eliot had ceased to be a poet and had become a moralizer.[1] But such judgments are open to the objection that they themselves are moralistic. It would be truer to say that Eliot's real poetry was that of what he called the "first voice," but that he could not go further in this voice than he had done in the last of the *Four Quartets*, and that he had therefore turned to something different in which a diminution of the poetry had to be borne. In doing this, he showed that critical self-awareness which prevented him from ever repeating himself, ever writ-

[1] *T. S. Eliot: The Man and His Work*, Allen Tate, ed., p. 34.

ing a new poem that was not really new. The truth, surely, is that, having finished his high poetic task with "Little Gidding," he then discovered in the theater a means of summarizing his attitude toward his double vocation, that of poetry and religion, and of making use of some material which was still available from the *Four Quartets*.

The rest of his work was an epilogue, which was not without some interesting developments for the history of poetic drama, some authoritative lessons drawn from a lifetime of combining poetry with criticism, some revealing wisdom in remarks about society and culture, and something of the grace and urbanity of a "distinguished guest" who rises at the end of the banquet of his life and answers with gratitude, humor, and a few amusing, revealing, partly mysterious and ironic reminiscences, the toast which has been made to him by his hosts. Such an example of politeness is, of course, suspect in days when, for many of those present, it would seem that the guarantee of the integrity of the poet at such a feast is that he strip off his clothes, throw his glass in his host's face, and scream. If Eliot had no great last period in his poetry to correspond to that of Yeats, he at any rate knew when his greatest work was achieved, and did nothing in his later writing to spoil or debase it.

SHORT BIBLIOGRAPHY

Books by Eliot

VERSE

Four Quartets. New York: Harcourt Brace Jovanovich, 1943; new ed., 1968.
Collected Poems, 1909–1962. New York: Harcourt Brace Jovanovich, 1963.
The Waste Land: A Facsimile and Transcript. Valerie Eliot, ed. New York: Harcourt Brace Jovanovich, 1971.
Poems Written in Early Youth. New York: Farrar, Straus & Giroux, 1967.

CHILDREN'S VERSE

Old Possum's Book of Practical Cats. New York: Harcourt Brace Jovanovich, 1939; new ed., 1968.

PLAYS

The Rock. New York: Harcourt Brace Jovanovich, 1934.

Murder in the Cathedral. New York: Harcourt Brace Jovanovich, 1935.
The Family Reunion. New York: Harcourt Brace Jovanovich, 1939.
The Cocktail Party. New York: Harcourt Brace Jovanovich, 1950.
The Confidential Clerk. New York: Harcourt Brace Jovanovich, 1954.
The Elder Statesman. New York: Farrar, Straus & Giroux, 1959.
Complete Plays. New York: Harcourt Brace Jovanovich, 1967.

LITERARY CRITICISM

Selected Essays. First ed., London: Faber & Faber, 1932; rev. ed., New York: Harcourt Brace Jovanovich, 1950.
The Use of Poetry and the Use of Criticism: Studies in the Relation of Criticism to Poetry in England. First ed., London: Faber & Faber, 1933; 2d ed., New York: Barnes and Noble, 1968.
On Poetry and Poets. New York: Farrar, Straus & Giroux, 1957.
To Criticize the Critic and Other Writings. Farrar, Straus & Giroux, 1965.
Introducing James Joyce. London: Faber & Faber, 1942.
After Strange Gods: A Primer of Modern Heresy. New York: Harcourt Brace Jovanovich, 1934.

SOCIAL CRITICISM

The Idea of a Christian Society. New York: Harcourt Brace Jovanovich, 1940.
Notes Towards the Definition of Culture. New York: Harcourt Brace Jovanovich, 1949.

PHILOSOPHY

Knowledge and Experience in the Philosophy of F. H. Bradley. New York: Farrar, Straus & Giroux, 1964.

TRANSLATION

Anabasis, a poem by St.-John Perse. First ed., London: Faber & Faber, 1930; 2d ed., New York: Harcourt Brace Jovanovich, 1959.

EDITED BY ELIOT

The Criterion 1922–1939. 18 Vols. New York: Barnes & Noble, 1967.

BIBLIOGRAPHY

Gallup, Donald. *T. S. Eliot: A Bibliography.* Rev. ed.: New York: Harcourt Brace Jovanovich, 1969.

Books on Eliot

BIOGRAPHICAL

Howarth, Herbert. *Notes on Some Figures Behind T. S. Eliot.* London: Chatto & Windus, 1965.
Sencourt, Robert. *T. S. Eliot: A Memoir.* Adamson, Donald, ed. New York: Dodd, 1971.

CRITICAL WORKS

Auden, W. H. *The Dyer's Hand.* New York: Random House, 1962.
Bergonzi, Bernard. *T. S. Eliot.* New York: Macmillan, 1972.
Browne, E. Martin. *The Making of T. S. Eliot's Plays.* New York: Cambridge University Press, 1969.
Drew, Elizabeth. *T. S. Eliot: The Design of His Poetry.* New York: Scribner, 1961.
Frye, Northrop. *T. S. Eliot.* New York: Grove, 1963.
Gardner, Helen. *The Art of T. S. Eliot.* New York: Dutton, 1959.
Kenner, Hugh. *The Invisible Poet.* New York: Harcourt Brace Jovanovich, paperback, 1969.

Kojecký, Roger. *T. S. Eliot's Social Criticism.* New York: Farrar, Straus & Giroux, 1972.

Leavis, F. R. *New Bearings in English Poetry.* 2d ed., Ann Arbor: University of Michigan Press, 1960.

Lucy, Sean. *T. S. Eliot and the Idea of Tradition.* New York: Routledge & Kegan, 1960.

March, Richard and Tambimuttu, eds. *T. S. Eliot: A Symposium.* London: Editions Poetry, 1948.

Margolis, John D. *T. S. Eliot's Intellectual Development.* Chicago, Ill.: University of Chicago Press, 1972.

Martin, Graham, ed. *Eliot in Perspective: A Symposium.* New York: Humanities, 1970.

Matthiessen, F. O. *The Achievement of T. S. Eliot: An Essay on the Nature of Poetry.* 3d ed., New York: Oxford University Press, 1958.

Preston, Raymond. *Four Quartets Rehearsed.* New York: Haskell, 1970.

Richards, I. A. *Poetries & Sciences.* New York: Norton, 1970.

Smith, Grover. *T. S. Eliot's Poetry and Plays: A Study in Sources and Meaning.* Chicago, Ill.: University of Chicago Press, 1956.

Stead, C. K. *New Poetics.* New York: Hutchinson, 1964.

Tate, Allen, ed. *T. S. Eliot: The Man and His Work.* London: Chatto & Windus, 1967.

Unger, Leonard. *T. S. Eliot: Moments and Patterns.* Minneapolis: University of Minnesota Press, 1967.

Williamson, George. *A Reader's Guide to T. S. Eliot.* New York: Farrar, Straus & Giroux, 1953.

Wilson, Edmund. *Axel's Castle.* New York: Scribner, 1931.

INDEX